LAW OF CONTEMPT OF COURT IN INDIA

LAW OF CONTEMPT OF COURT IN INDIA

K. BALASANKARAN NAIR

ATLANTIC
PUBLISHERS & DISTRIBUTORS

Published by
ATLANTIC PUBLISHERS AND DISTRIBUTORS
B-2, Vishal Enclave, Opp. Rajouri Garden, New Delhi-110027
Phones : 25413460, 25429987, 25466842

Sales Office
7/22, Ansari Road, Darya Ganj, New Delhi-110002
Phones : 23273880, 23275880, 23280451
Fax : 91-11-23285873
web : www.atlanticbooks.com
e-mail : info@atlanticbooks.com

ISBN 81-269-0359-7

Printed in India at
Nice Printing Press, Delhi

Preface

"Be you ever so high, law is above you." Any kind of action which injures the majesty of law is being sternly dealt with by the judiciary in the name of contempt of court, as a guardian of the rule of law. Contempt jurisprudence, because of its uniqueness and controversial character, has led to contradictory opinions among jurists and scholars. Born and brought up in the common law jurisprudence, migrated into Indian jurisprudence by the creation of different Courts of Record through various charters, Indian Constitution has also recognized and accepted this extraordinary jurisdiction to punish a person, for contempt, by recognizing the Supreme Court and High Courts as Courts of Record. Indian Parliament, through Contempt of Courts Act, 1971, tried in vain to regulate this power of the judiciary. The Supreme Court, in Vinay Chandra Mishra's Case, had categorically laid down that the Parliament's power to legislate in relation to law of contempt relating to Supreme Court is limited and, therefore, the Act does not impinge upon this Court's power with regard to the contempt of subordinate courts under Article 129 of the Constitution.

Our Constitution, through Articles 129 and 215, has made the Supreme Court and High Courts as Courts of Record and hence the contempt power is a necessary adjunct of Court of Record. The Constitution itself, through Article 19, has conferred the invaluable rights of freedom of speech and expression to the citizens as well as to the Press. This freedom is not absolute and can be restricted on the ground of contempt of court under Article 19(2) of the Constitution. So, possible contradiction and compromise is unavoidable. Sincere attempt has been made in this book to ascertain and identify the contours of this branch of law in relation to the freedom of the individual and also that of the Press.

Any disobedience to the orders of the court will result in degradation of the Institution and will be a blow to the majesty of law. No one should be allowed to disobey the orders of the court with impunity. The study further tries to ascertain the extent to which this power is being utilised to control the other organs of the state and also the individuals.

No indepth study of this branch of law has so far been undertaken in relation to these aspects. The present study is a humble attempt to ascertain the various nuances of this branch of law and to see as to how this jurisprudence is being applied by the judiciary to control the individuals and other organs of the state. The concept of criminal contempt which includes prejudicing fair trial or interference with the administration of justice or scandalising the court has been analysed in relation to the rights of individuals and also that of the Press. The concept of civil contempt which includes disobedience to the orders of the court or breach of an undertaking has been analysed in relation to administrative authorities and corporations, individuals and subordinate judiciary.

The existing political and social scenario requires a comprehensive understanding of this branch of law so as to check possible misinterpretation.

It is my bounden duty to express my sense of gratitude to those who helped me in pursuing and completing this study. The first and foremost among such luminaries is my esteemed Professor Dr. N.K. Jayakumar, Professor and Head, Department of Law, University of Kerala, Thiruvananthapuram, who has been a constant source of inspiration from the beginning to the end. His scholarship, courtesy and humane approach have made my task much easier. His zealous and untiring guidance helped me in identifying and ascertaining the problem and finding a solution to it.

I am extremely grateful to Dr. N. Narayanan Nair, Director, Centre for Advanced Legal Studies and Research, Thiruvananthapuram for his guidance and permission to utilise his esteemed institution for completing this study. Further, I express my indebtedness to Prof. R. Sankaradasan Thampi, former Principal of Government Law College, Thiruvananthapuram, Dr. K. Parameswaran, Professor, National Law School of

India University, Bangalore and Dr. K.C. Sunny, Reader, Department of Law, University of Kerala, Thiruvananthapuram for their benign help at various stages during the course of this study.

Equally, I am beholden to Dr. S. Velayudha Perumal, former Professor, Department of Labour Studies and P.V. Ramachandran, former Professor, Department of English, Directorate of Distance Education, Madurai Kamaraj University for their timely help and ceaseless encouragement all through.

I shall be failing in my duty if I do not adequately record my thanks to M/s Atlantic Publishers and Distributors for their endeavour to publish this book with a majestic and impressive get up.

K. BALASANKARAN NAIR

CONTENTS

PART 3

PART 4

ABBREVIATIONS

A.I.R.	*All India Reporter*
Cri. L.J.	*Criminal Law Journal*
M.L.J.	*Madras Law Journal*
M.L.R.	*Madras Law Reporter*
I.L.R.	*Indian Law Reporter*
J.I.L.I.	*Journal of the Indian Law Institute*
K.L.T.	*Kerala Law Times*
L.Q.R.	*The Law Quarterly Review*
Harv. L.R.	*Harvard Law Review*
S.C.C.	*Supreme Court Cases*
S.C.W.R.	*Supreme Court Weekly Reporter*
E.P.W.	*Economic and Political Weekly*
A.M. Juri	*American Jurisprudence*
M.L.R.	*Modern Law Review*
All E.R.	*All England Law Reports*
E.R.	England Reports
S.C.	Supreme Court
P.C.	Privy Council
P.L.	Public Law
Q.B.D.	Queen's Bench Division
K.B.	King's Bench
Ch.D.	Chancery Division
Cr. P.C.	Criminal Procedure Code
I.P.C.	Indian Penal Code.

PART 1

1

INTRODUCTION

The term 'contempt of court' is a generic term descriptive of conduct in relation to particular proceedings in a court of law which tends to undermine that system or inhibit citizens from availing themselves of it for the settlement of their disputes.[1]

In exercising this extraordinary jurisdiction, in which the judge and the prosecutor are combined, the judiciary generally show a sense of self-restraint and apply the jurisdiction for maintaining the supremacy of law. Though judges as individuals and courts as institutions do not require more protection than an ordinary citizen or an institution, when the fundamental supremacy of law is brought into question they require special privilege for protecting it.

Free and fair administration of justice depends upon non-interference by any authority or organ in that great process. When there is interference by an individual, press or any other organ of the state in the administration of justice, judiciary intervenes as the protector of the rule of law through its contempt power. The basic purpose of the contempt jurisdiction is to provide sanction against any word or conduct which is likely to prejudice or interfere with fair trial.

Difficulty arises in ascertaining the kind of interference which justifies the judiciary in exercising this extraordinary jurisdiction. Should all kinds of interference be treated as contempt or only interference of a substantial nature? It becomes more problematic when we face indirect interference including contempt through publication. The press with a view to attract

1. *See* Lord Diplock in *Attorney General* v. *Times News Papers Ltd.* (1973) 3 All. E.R. 54, 71.

the public may give misleading headlines or distorted versions of proceedings and judgments. The press as well as the individual at times resort to uncharitable remarks or scurrilous abuse against the judges, leading to scandalising the judiciary. In such cases judiciary as the aggrieved party, judge and prosecutor, has to play a balanced role.

Impartial administration of justice and respect of judiciary depend not only on the non-interference in the judicial process but also on the due execution of the orders of the court. If the orders of the court can be disobeyed with impunity, the tendency to disobey will receive encouragement. In order to check such tendencies, special provisions have been made in the form of contempt jurisdiction.

The present study aims at ascertaining the approach and attitude of the judiciary when there is interference with the administration of justice and of any action affecting the dignity of the judges. It also aims at ascertaining the approach of the judiciary in case of disobedience of its orders either by individuals or by administrative authorities including public corporations and also by the subordinate judiciary.

Judicial Approach

Though there was no Contempt of Courts Act as such before 1926, the Indian judges had been following the common law concept in identifying contempt. Even today the common law concept as modified by the Contempt of Courts Act, 1971, is being followed. However, the judicial approach has registered a more liberal attitude towards criminal contempt after 1971. This marks a significant change in the judicial outlook, in tune with the emphasis on individual rights in a democracy. But in the case of civil contempt, the judges have not been so liberal.

In general, the Indian judiciary has been very tolerant in reacting to healthy criticism. But this does not mean that the judges are insensitive to criticism whatsoever.

Parameters of the Study

The study of the subject is of much practical value in a modern democratic society where freedom of speech and expression is guaranteed by the Constitution. It is possible that an abuse of the freedom may affect the impartiality and authority of the court, and hence become detrimental to the dignity of the court. Such abuse has to be checked by the judiciary by the use of its contempt jurisdiction. This seems to be the only way to check the increasing modern tendency to question the power of all duly appointed authorities.

Sources

The study has used various sources. Important among them are the verdicts and observations of courts in India and England as found in law reports, articles in law journals, law reviews, standard books on law, statutes, committee reports and Constituent Assembly Debates.

The study is limited to the proceedings of the courts in India. Hence no comparative study of contempt proceedings in other countries has been attempted. Because of the vastness of the subject, only a few aspects of the contempt problem could be analysed.

Chapterisation

The second chapter which follows the introduction deals with the concept and function of contempt jurisdiction.

The third chapter deals with the historical development of the concept of contempt, leading to the passing of the Contempt of Courts Act, 1971. It also discusses the development of the contempt law in England.

Certain principles which are commonly applicable to cases of indirect contempt by the press and the individual are dealt with in the fourth chapter. Emphasis is laid on pendency or imminence of proceedings and knowledge of such proceedings.

The fifth chapter deals with the principles which are applicable to the press alone, with special emphasis on the principle of true reporting.

In the sixth chapter prejudicing fair trial as a test of contempt as it relates to the individuals and the press is analysed.

Scandalising the judiciary as a test of criminal contempt is analysed in the seventh chapter. It analyses the application of the test as it relates to the individual and that of the press and also as it existed before and after the passing of the Contempt of Courts Act, 1971. Judicial approach is analysed critically, especially when public speeches and other publications which affect the dignity and authority of the court are made by persons in authority.

When there is disobedience of the orders of the court it amounts to civil contempt. The eighth chapter focuses attention on the problems faced by the administrative authorities and the corporations when the orders of the court are disobeyed.

The ninth chapter deals with the disobedience of orders of the court by the individuals and further discusses breach of undertaking given to the court by the individuals.

The tenth chapter deals with the disobedience of the orders of the higher judiciary by subordinate judiciary and its consequences.

The concluding chapter, presents a summary of findings and suggestions made at appropriate places in the study.

2

Concept and Function

The power to punish for contempt anyone who interferes with the administration of justice is an inherent power vested in the judiciary.[1] This may appear to be an arbitrary power, because the role of prosecutor and adjudicator is combined in one person or one body of persons. But it is a necessary power for the protection of the impartial administration of justice to maintain the majesty of law.

Contempt jurisdiction which is special[2] in its character

1. "The particular aspects of inherent power...concerns their incidental capacity to remove obstructions to the discharge of their work. The conventional description of such obstruction is contempt and the mode of dealing with it is characterised as the power of courts to punish for contempt. The fact of obstruction to courts is as old as English courts and so also the endeavour to remove them" Felix Frankfurter, "Power of Congress over Procedure in Criminal Contempts in Inferior Federal Courts—a Study in Separation of Powers" 37 *Harv. L. Rev.* 1010, 1023 (1923-24).
2. Two special features of contempt jurisdiction as given by Phillimore Committee Report (Report of the Committee on Contempt of Court), 1974 are:
   (i) Summary procedure: One of the outstanding features of contempt of court is the summary procedure which is unknown to any other branch of law. It is an inherent jurisdiction vested upon the superior courts. One consequence of the use of this summary procedure is that while proof of contempt must be established beyond reasonable doubt, the person alleged to be in contempt does not enjoy the benefit of some of the safeguards of the ordinary criminal law (at p. 8). *See* also John Charles Fox, "The Summary Process to Punish Contempt." 25 *L.Q.R.* 238 (1909). The Nature of Contempt of Court 37 *L.Q.R.* 191 (1921).

originated in England and developed over the centuries as a means of enforcing the orders of the court.

The use of the phrase "contempt of court" though criticised as misleading[3] till continues to be a good one. It is of ancient origin yet of fundamental contemporary importance.[4] It has always served as a continuing protector of the fundamental supremacy of law.

One of the basic principles of any civilised system of justice is that a person is entitled to fair trial free from prejudice. One purpose of the law of contempt is to provide sanctions against any word or conduct which is likely to prejudice fair trial. There is no unanimity of opinion as to the exact purpose of the law of contempt. Lord President Clyde,[5] Phillimore Committee,[6] and Justice Frankfurter[7] expressed the opinion that the contempt law exists for the maintenance of fundamental supremacy of law.

(ii) Mental element: The mental element required to create liability for contempt depends on the form the contempt takes. In some areas of the law, particularly as it affects the press, the liability does not for the most depend upon the proof of intent.... In these areas therefore liability in contempt is strict. This contrasts with the position in the ordinary criminal law (at p. 9).

3. Lord Cross in *Attorney General* v. *Times News Papers Ltd.* (1974) A.C. 273, 322. *See* also Report of the Committee on Contempt of Court, 6 (1974).

4. C.J. Miller, Contempt of Court 1 (1976).

5. The phrase "contempt of court" does not in the least describe the true nature of the class of offence with which we are here concerned.... The offence consists in interfering with the administration of the law, in impeding and perverting the course of justice.... It is not the dignity of the court which is offended a petty and misleading view of the issue involved—it is the fundamental supremacy of law which is challenged *Johnson* v. *Grant* (1923) S.C. 789, 790.

6. The term suggests in general that the law exists to protect the dignity of judges whereas in fact it exists to protect the administration of justice and in the words of Lord Clyde the fundamental supremacy of law. Report of the Committee on Contempt of Court, 6 (1974).

7. It is a mode of vindicating the majesty of law in its active manifestation against obstruction and outrage, *Frankfurter in Offut* v. *U.S.* (1954) 348, U.S. 11.

Justice Tek Chand,[8] V.G. Ramachandran[9] and the Allahabad High Court[10] are of the view that the purpose of contempt law is to maintain the supremacy of courts of justice and the stream of justice unsullied. Justice V.R. Krishna Iyer[11] K.J. Aiyar[12] and the Delhi High Court[13] emphasised that contempt jurisdiction exists for the protection of the rights of the public.

In a democratic society, the three organs of the government namely the executive, the legislature and the judiciary are expected to perform their functions within their limitations for the benefit of the public. No one organ is expected to interfere with the functioning of the other. Though judiciary is entrusted with the function of administration of justice, it cannot claim

---

8. Tek Chand stated two reasons for substantiating his view. In the first place decree of law courts on account of their inexorable nature could not be flouted without serious risk to the victim of judicial displeasure...the authority of the judges is supreme and they are therefore in a position to command dutiful and prompt obedience.... In the second place according to the time honoured legal fiction, the king who is ultimate source of all judicial authority is supposed to be present in person in all courts though he is visible only to the eye of law. Justice Tek Chand *Contempt of Court and Legislature*, 1, 2 (1949).
9. There can be no doubt that the purpose of contempt jurisdiction is to uphold the majesty and dignity of law courts and their image in the minds of the public and that this in no way is whittled down. V.G. Ramachandran, *Contempt of Court*, 6 (1983).
10. Allahabad High Court also expressed the same view in *State* v. *Rajeswari Prasad* AIR 1966 All. 588, 589 and in *Ramsurat Singh* v. *Shivakumar* AIR 1971 All. 170, 172.
11. Punishment is inflicted not for the purpose of protecting either the court as a whole or individual judges of the court, from a repetition of the attack but of protecting the public and especially those who either voluntarily or by compulsion are subject to the jurisdiction of the court from mischief that will incur if the authority of the tribunal is undermined or impaired. *Baradakanta Misra* v. *Registrar*, Orissa High Court AIR 1974 S.C. 710, 732.
12. The law of contempt is intended to be a protection to the public. Those interests would be very much affected if by the act or the conduct of any party, the authority of the court is lowered and the sense of confidence which people have in the administration of justice by it, is weakened. K.J. Aiyar, *Contempt of Court Legislatures and Public Servants*, 3 (1983).
13. Delhi High Court also expressed a similar view in *Omesh Saigal* v. *R.K. Dalmia* AIR 1969 Del. 214, 218.

superiority over other two organs and hence it has to be given all the requirements needed for upholding the majesty of law, particularly when it has neither the power of purse nor the power of the police. So, through contempt proceedings, the judiciary performs its function of proper administration of justice and safeguards the rule of law. But the contempt jurisdiction which is extraordinary in its character, should not be used for the personal protection of judges. This jurisdiction is applied against any authority or person whenever there is any kind of interference in the administration of justice. The judiciary uses the weapon of contempt jurisdiction to maintain the supremacy of law when interference is caused by the executive or the individual or the press.

1. DEFINITION AND MEANING

No satisfactory definition of the term contempt of court can be had,[14] because the offence is manifesting itself in a variety of ways. But the classical and celebrated explanation as given by Lord Hardwicke L.C. has obtained general acceptance.

> There are three different sorts of contempt. One kind of contempt is scandalising the court itself. There may be likewise a contempt of this court in abusing parties who are concerned in causes here. There may also be a contempt of this court in prejudicing mankind against persons before the cause is heard.[15]

---

14. *Report of the Committee on Contempt of Court*, 48 (1974). The same view was expressed by Shawcross Committee also "Not the least of the difficulties in this field (definition) is that contempt, being a growth of the common law, has no authoritative definition or limitation...it can be defined in the most general terms" *Shawcross Committee Report*, 4 (1959). *See* also Niyogi J. in *Telhara Cotton Ginning Co. Ltd.* v. *Kashinath* ILR 1940 Nag. 69. "It is indeed difficult and almost impossible to frame a comprehensive and complete definition of contempt of court. The law of contempt covers the whole field of litigation itself. The real end of a judicial proceedings civil or criminal, is to ascertain the true facts and dispense justice.... Anything that tends to curtail or impair the freedom of the judicial proceedings must of necessity result in hampering the due administration of law and in interfering with the course of justice" (at pp. 71, 72).
15. *Re Read and Hugginson* (*St. James Evening Post* Case) (1742) 2 Atk 469, 470-471.

This explanation includes different instances of contempt which later on are characterised as criminal contempt. Though it is silent about disobedience of the orders of the court, as a pioneer attempt to define the term, it deserves appreciation.

Lord Russel[16] and Oswald[17] also tried to define the term. Lord Russel's statement of contempt of court is not precise but an explanatory statement. Oswald's definition does not include all categories of contempt and silent on disobedience of the orders of the court. So also by using the term during the litigation, it excluded from the purview of contempt, scandalising the judiciary, probably with a view to give effect to the opinion of Lord Morris in *Mc Leod* v. *St. Abyn.*[18] The Contempt of Court Act, 1981 used the term

---

16. Any act done or writing published calculated to bring a court or a judge of the court into contempt or to lower his authority is contempt of court. That is one class of contempt. Further any act done or writing published calculated to obstruct or interfere with the due course of justice or the lawful process of the court is contempt of court. The former class belongs to the category which Lord Hardwicke L.C. characterised as scandalising a court or a judge. That description of that class of contempt is to be taken subject to one and an important qualification. Judges and courts are alike open to criticism, and if reasonable arguments or expostulation is offered against any judicial act as contrary to law or the public good, no court could or would treat that as contempt of court. The law ought not to be astute in such cases to criticise adversely what under such circumstances, and with such an object, is published, but it is to be remembered that in this matter the liberty of the press is no greater and no less than the liberty of every subject of the *Queen Reg* v. *Grey* (1900) 2 QB. 36, 40.
17. To speak generally, contempt of court may be said to be constituted by any conduct that tends to bring the authority and administration of law into disrespect or disregard or to interfere with or prejudice parties, litigants or their witnesses during the litigation. Oswald, *Contempt of Court,* 6 (1910). This definition was quoted with approval in India also. *See, e.g., Pratap Singh* v. *Gurbakhsh Singh* AIR 1962 S.C. 1172, *E.T. Sen* v. *Edatata Narayanan* AIR 1969 Del. 201, *Jugal Kishore* v. *Sitamarhi* AIR 1967 S.C. 1494.
18. (1899) A.C. 549, 561 Lord Morris observed that committal for contempt by scandalising the court itself has become obsolete in England. But this view was subsequently modified in *Reg* v. *Grey* (1900) 2 QBD. 36 followed in *Devi Prasad* v. *Emperor* 70 IA 216.

'strict liability rule,[19] instead of using the term contempt of court.

The 'strict liability rule' excluded application of contempt proceedings against criticism of the judiciary. Only interference is brought within the purview of the strict liability rule.

American Jurisprudence gave a better explanation for contempt of court. It states:

> Generally speaking he whose conduct which tends to bring the authority and the administration of the law into disrespect or disregard, interferes with or prejudices parties or their witnesses during a litigation or otherwise tends to impede, embarrass or obstruct the court in discharge of its duties is guilty of contempt.[20]

Sanyal Committee[21] which made an exhaustive study of the law of contempt of court in India, was reluctant to give a precise definition of the term. The committee observed:

> We would certainly not favour a definition which may have the effect of placing undue fetters on the courts thereby rendering them powerless to deal with great evils threatening or likely to threaten the administration of justice.[22]

But absence of a clear definition may debar persons from expressing opinion on matters requiring judicial or legislative reform.[23] At the same time contempt can be defined only by

---

19. Contempt of Court Act, 1981, S.1 reads: "Strict liability rule means the rule of law whereby conduct may be treated as contempt of court as tending to interfere with the course of justice in particular legal proceedings regardless of the intent to do so."
20. 17 Am. Jur 2d 3.
21. *The Committee on Contempt of Court, 1963.* The Committee inclined to make a definition of criminal contempt on the following lines:

    "Whoever by words, either spoken or written or by signs or by visible representation or otherwise—(a) interferes or attempts to interfere with or obstructs or attempts to obstruct the administration of justice, or (b) scandalises or attempts to scandalise or lowers or attempts to lower the authority of a court of justice or (c) publishes or makes false or misleading reports of or comments on pending proceedings or any stage thereof; is said to commit contempt of court." (at pp. 23, 24)
22. *Id.* at 24.
23. *Ibid.*

enumerating the different heads under which it may be classified. A definition merely incorporating such heads under which criminal contempt is classified, would be totally unnecessary. An inclusive definition would be wholly unsatisfactory. Section 2[24] of the Contempt of Courts Act, 1971 defined the term contempt of court, thus restricting the possibility of widening the scope of the contempt law.

As stated by Craies "the ingenuity of the judges and of those who are concerned to defeat or defy justice has rendered contempt almost protean in its character."[25]

2. CONTEMPT OF COURT DISTINGUISHED FROM LIBEL

Contempt of court differs from libel inasmuch as whether the attack is made on the official act of the judge or his personal act. A libel on a judge is contempt when it refers to his action in court or as to what he did judicially out of it.[26] But a libel is not contempt if it refers to the judge outside his judicial capacity.[27] When a libelous statement though justifiable, actually interferes with the course of justice, there is contempt.[28]

3. DISTINCTION BETWEEN CIVIL AND CRIMINAL CONTEMPTS OF COURT

Contempt of court has traditionally been divided into two main constituent parts, according to whether the contempt is

---

24. (a) Contempt of court means civil contempt or criminal contempt.
    (b) Civil contempt means wilful disobedience to any judgment, decree, direction, order, writ or other process of a court or wilful breach of an undertaking given to a court.
    (c) Criminal contempt means the publication (whether by words, spoken or written or by signs or by visible representations or otherwise) of any matter or the doing of any other act whatsoever which—
        (i) scandalises or tends to scandalise or lowers or tends to lower the authority of any court, or
        (ii) prejudices or interferes or tends to interfere with, the due course of any judicial proceeding; or
        (iii) interferes or tends to interfere with, or obstructs or tends to obstruct, the administration of justice in any other manner.
25. Cited by Goodhart, "News Paper and Contempt of Court in English law," 48 *Harv. L. Rev.* 885, 886 (1935).
26. In re Wallace (1866) L.R.I. P.C. 283.
27. In re Bahama Island 1893 A.C. 183 P.C.
28. *Coats* v. *Chadurck* (1894) I Ch. 347.

criminal or civil in nature. The distinction is time honoured and is of continuing importance, as it has immediate practical consequences in the interest of justice.[29]

The reason behind the classification is mainly that the person against whom the contempt proceedings are initiated should be informed as to which is the contempt he is charged with, whether civil or criminal, since it might result in significant differences in regard to the following matters: (1) rules of appeal; (2) privilege from arrest; (3) power to pardon; (4) punishment and execution; (5) rules of evidence and procedure; (6) settlement of the dispute; and (7) discharge or release on compliance.[30]

> Broadly speaking, civil contempts are contempts which involve a private injury occasioned by disobedience to the judgment, order or other process of the court. On the other hand, criminal contempts are right from their inception in the nature of offences.[31]
>
> A criminal contempt is conduct that is directed against the dignity and authority of the court. A civil contempt is failure to do something ordered to be done by a court in a civil action for the benefit of the opposite party therein.... It is conceivable that the dividing line between the acts constituting criminal and those constituting civil contempts may become indistinct in those cases where the two gradually merge into each other.[32]

---

29. C.J. Miller, *Contempt of Court*, 1 (1976).
30. Eliahu Harnon, "Civil and Criminal Contempts of Court" 25 *Mod. L.R.* 179 (1962). The author after distinguishing contempt on the above lines, concludes that the distinction is not purely academic.
31. *Report of the Committee on Contempt of Court*, 21 (1963). Contempt of Courts Act, 1971 also recognized the distinction in the definition providing special procedure for cognizance of criminal contempt, hearing of cases and in the matter of appeals.
32. Legal Remembrancer *vs.* Motilal Ghose ILR 41 Cal. 173, 252. The same view was expressed by Solmon L.J. in Jennison *vs.* Baker (1971) 2QB 52: "Contempts have some times been classified as criminal and civil contempts. I think that at any rate today this is an unhelpful and almost meaningless classification" (at p. 61). The Phillimore Committee recommended that the distinction between civil contempt and criminal contempt should be abolished, because there is diminution of distinction in recent years. Chapter 8, *Report of the Committee on Contempt of Court* (1974).

In *Dulal Chandra* v. *Sukumar*[33] it was held that the line between civil and criminal contempt can be broad as well as thin. Where the contempt consists in mere failure to comply with or carry out an order of a court made for the benefit of a private party, it is plainly civil contempt and it has been said that when the party in whose interest the order was made, moves the court for action to be taken in contempt against the contemner with a view to an enforcement of his right, the proceedings are only a form of execution. In such a case, there is no criminality in the disobedience, and the contempt, as it is, is not criminal. If however the contemner adds defiance of the court to disobedience of the order and conducts himself in a manner which amounts to obstruction or interference with the course of justice, the contempt committed by him is of a mixed character, partaking as between him and his opponent, of the nature of a civil contempt and as between him and the court of the state, of the nature of a criminal contempt. In cases of this type no clear distinction between civil and criminal contempt can be drawn and the contempt committed cannot be broadly classified as either civil or criminal contempt.[34]

Unless the disobedience is wilful, civil contempt is not involved.[35] But in case of criminal contempt, intention, motive, or even knowledge is not the criterion though they may be considered for the mitigation of a sentence. In a civil contempt the purpose is to force the contemner to do something for the benefit of the other party. In criminal contempt the proceedings are by way of punishment for a wrong not so much to a party or individual but to the public at large by interfering with the normal process of law or diminishing the majesty of the court.[36]

---

33. AIR 1958 Cal. 474.
34. *Id.* at 476, 477. The same view was expressed by Oswald, *Contempt of Court,* 8 (1910); *see* also American Jurisprudence. 17 Am. Jur. 2d p. 4.
35. *State* v. *Dasirathi Jha* AIR 1951 Pat. 443.
36. *Vijay Pratap Singh* v. *Ajit Prasad* AIR 1966 All. 305. *See* also Tek Chand, *The Law of Contempt of Court and Legislature* 65 (1949); Note "procedure for trying contempts in the Federal Courts" 73 *Harv. L. Rev.* 353 (1959-60).

4. LEGISLATIVE INTERVENTION

Though the court of record has the inherent jurisdiction to punish the contempt of itself, doubt arose as to its jurisdiction to punish contempt of subordinate courts. For removing that doubt, Contempt of Courts Act of 1926 was passed, which was amended in 1937 to make it clear that the limits of punishment provided in the Act related not only to contempt of subordinate courts but also to all other cases of contempt. But the 1926 Act did not contain any provision with regard to contempt of courts which were subordinate to Chief Courts and Judicial Commissioner's Court. This also did not cover the extra territorial jurisdiction of High Courts in matters of contempt. For removing these defects Contempt of Courts Act, 1952 was passed which in turn repealed the 1926 Act.

In exercise of the freedom of speech and expression guaranteed by Art. 19(1)(a) of the Constitution, the press as well as the individual may criticise the judiciary. The High Courts and Supreme Court used their inherent power to control any kind of criticism. This gave way to a new controversy. So, for studying the matter comprehensively a committee was constituted under the Chairmanship of Shri H.N. Sanyal.

The Committee was required:

(i) to examine the law relating to contempt of courts generally, and in particular, the law relating to the procedure for the punishment thereof;

(ii) to suggest amendments therein with a view to clarifying and reforming the law wherever necessary; and

(iii) to make recommendations for codification of the law in the light of the examination made.

The Committee first considered the opinion of Desai, J. in *State* v. *Padma Kant Malviya*[37] and held that the Parliament had the power to legislate in relation to the substantive law of contempt of Supreme Court and High Courts[38] subject to three limitations:

---

37. AIR 1954 All. 523. According to Desai J. legislature had no power to define contempt of court. The court of record has the exclusive power to define and determine what amounts to contempt. (*Id.* at 530)

38. *Report of the Committee on Contempt of Court*, 15 (1963).

(i) It (contempt power) cannot be abrogated, nullified or transferred to some other body, save by an amendment of the Constitution.

(ii) Parliament's power to legislate as to contempt ought not to be so exercised as to stultify the status and dignity of these courts.

(iii) Legislation in relation to contempt imposing unreasonable restrictions on the right of citizens to freedom of speech and expression will be, *protanto* unconstitutional.

Based on the report of the Sanyal Committee, the Contempt of Courts Act, 1971 was passed. This Act defines the term contempt of court and deals with the defences in case of criminal contempt and the procedure to be followed in exercising contempt jurisdiction.

But the Supreme Court in *In re Vinay Chandra Mishra*[39] expressed the view that inherent powers of a superior court of record have remained unaffected even after codification of contempt law.[40]

The court further observed:

> The Parliament's power to legislate in relation to law of contempt relating to Supreme Court is limited, therefore the Act does not impinge upon this court's power with regard to the contempt of subordinate courts under Art. 129 of the Constitution.[41]

Therefore the attempt of the legislature to intervene and regulate contempt jurisdiction of the higher judiciary has been restricted by the Supreme Court and this jurisdiction is kept as the exclusive domain of the judiciary.

It is worth mentioning the opinion of the Supreme Court in *Pallav Sheth* v. *Custodian.*[42] There can be no doubt that the Supreme Court and High Courts are Courts of Record and the constitution has given them the powers to punish for contempt. This power cannot be abrogated or stultified. But if the power

39. (1995) 2 S.C.C. 584.

40. *Id.* at 605.

41. *Ibid.*

42. AIR 2001 S.C. 2763.

under Art. 129 and Art. 215 is absoluie can there be any legislation indicating the manner and to the extent that the power can be exercised? If there is any provision of the law which stultifies or abrogates the power under Art. 129 and/or Art. 215 there can be little doubt that such law would not be regarded as having been validly enacted. It however appears to us that providing for quantum of punishment or what may or may not be regarded as acts of contempt or even providing for a period of limitation for initiating proceedings for contempt cannot be taken to be a provision which abrogates or stultifies the contempt jurisdiction under Art. 129 or Art. 215 of the constitution.[43]

43. *Id.* at 2773.

3

Historical Perspective

1. ORIGIN AND DEVELOPMENT OF THE LAW OF CONTEMPT OF COURT IN ENGLAND

The law of contempt of court is a branch of law which originated and developed in a manner quite different from other laws. Judges created the contempt jurisdiction and claimed it was a natural adjunct to their adjudicating work. A law which began as a convenient method to enforce their orders was subsequently used to extract respect from the challenges of the press. Phillimore Committee stated the samething in the following words:

> The law relating to contempt of court has developed over the centuries as a means whereby the courts may act to prevent or punish conduct which tends to obstruct, prejudice or abuse the administration of justice either in relation to a particular case or generally.[1]

In ancient period king as the fountain of justice used to hear the cases for himself. But due to burden of work he was forced to delegate the function to an organ created by him. Sir William Holdsworth recognised the same in the following words:

> The common law courts were royal courts and the judges of these courts were royal justices. From these facts three consequences followed: (1) the king had a large control over the business before the courts, we have seen that in early days the king actually decided the cases; and there

1. *Report of the Committee on Contempt of Court*, 2 (1974).

are instances of this practice in Henry-III, Edward-I and Edward-II's reigns.[2]

The phrase contempt of court (*Contemptus curiae*) has been in use in English law for eight centuries and the offence is as old as the law. The law conferred the power to enforce discipline within its precincts and punish those who fail to comply with its orders.[3]

The idea of contempt of the king is referred to as an offence in the laws set forth in the first half of the twelfth century. Contempt of the king's writ was mentioned in the laws of king Henry-I. In the same laws there was mention of pecuniary penalty for contempt or disregard of orders. Thus in England before the end of the twelfth century contempt of court was a recognized expression and applied to the defaults and wrongful acts of suitors.[4]

After making a study of cases in the thirteenth century John Charles Fox concluded that there was no indication of trial of a contempt out of court otherwise than in the ordinary course of the law and many cases of contempt in court were tried by indictment and not by a summary process.[5]

2. Sir William Holdsworth, *History of English Law*, Vol. I, 194 (1969). On this early origin of courts of law and administration of justice by Tek Chand states:

   Early kings used to hear the grievances of their subjects personally. Administration of justice was a paramount duty of the English Kings in early times.... The history of English law courts is the history of the delegation of judicial powers by the king to the council. The experiences of the times led to the emanation of its various offshoots *e.g.*, the courts of Exchequer, common pleas and later on of common law. The *Curia Regis* the mother of Royal courts still retained the residue of justice and gave birth to the Court of Chancery in the fifteenth century, and during the Tudor periods to the Court of Star Chamber, Courts of Requests and Admiralty. The establishment of the Judicial Committee of the Privy Council, necessitated by the growth of the British possessions overseas is a much later creation of the reserve power of the King's Council. *Law of Contempt of Court and Legislature*, 3 (1949).
3. *See* Oswald, *Contempt of Court, 1* (1910). This early origin of the contempt law has been acknowledged by Encyclopedia Britannica (Vol. 6—p. 414, 3rd edn.) and also by Joseph H. Beale in his article "Contempt of Court Criminal and Civil" 21 *Harv. L.R.* 161 (1908).
4. John Charles Fox "The Nature of Contempt of Court" 37 *L.Q.R.*, 191, 194 (1921).
5. *Id.* at 198.

If the contempt is confessed there was no need for trial by jury and such cases of contempt were disposed off by sentence upon confession.[6] The earlier form of procedure was attachment by bill, when trial by jury was followed, unless the accused confessed. Later the Star Chamber practice of attachment and examination without jury was substituted for the procedure by bill.[7]

From fourteenth century onwards the jurisdiction of the King's Justices to punish contempts of a criminal nature summarily was limited to offences not heinous, committed in court in the actual view of the justices. The summary jurisdiction was held to extend to all contempts whether committed in or out of court.[8]

Later, the law of contempt identified two types of contempt, civil and criminal. Civil contempt appears to have originated in the seventeenth century from the practice of the Court of Chancery.[9]

Civil contempt of court provides for punishment of a person who refused to comply with the orders of a court. Consequential sanction will be committal to prison or fine.

Criminal contempt includes any kind of interruption or interference in the administration of justice in or out of court. But contempt committed out of court was punished in the sixteenth century, by common law, only after trial in the ordinary courts and not by any summary process.[10] A distinction was made between contempt in court and out of court in the case of strangers. Contempt by strangers out of court were tried by information or by attachment and examination in the common law courts. This practice continued through the eighteenth century and the procedure by attachment and examination was confirmed by the opinion of Chief Justice

6. *Id.* at 199.
7. *Ibid.*
8. John Charles Fox, "The summary process to punish contempt" 25 *L.Q.R.* 238, 252 (1909).
9. *Report of the Committee on Contempt of Court*, 10 (1974).
10. *See* John Charles Fox *Supra* n. 4.

Wilmot in *Almon's*[11] case and finally established as law by Mr. Justice Holrayed in *The King* v. *Clements*.[12]

Contempt in the face of the court includes any act which interferes with the administration of justice such as throwing missiles at judges, insulting any person in court, impeding the passage into or out of court by those who have business there and the like. Summary power is used to punish such acts.

The art of printing and publishing brought into prominence another form of criminal contempt discussed as indirect criminal contempt or constructive contempt.

The origin of indirect contempt is traceable from the opinion expressed by Lord Hardwicke L.C. in *St. James Evening Post*[13] case.

Scandalising the court, abusing parties and prejudicing mankind against persons before the cause is heard[14] are instances of indirect criminal contempt.

Further extension of the law of constructive contempt could be seen in the opinion of Wilmot J. in *Almon's*[15] case. In this case a pamphlet was published accusing Lord Mansfield of officiously, arbitrarily and illegally making an out of court order. The opinion states as follows:

> The power, which the courts in West Minster Hall have of vindicating their own authority is coeval with their first foundation and institution, it is a necessary incident to every court of justice, whether of record or not to fine and imprison for a contempt to the court, acted in the face of it and the issuing of attachments by the Supreme Courts of Justice in West Minster Hall, for contempts out of court, stands upon the same immemorial usage as supports the whole fabric of the common law.... But when the nature

11. King *vs.* Almon 97 E.R. 94.
12. 106 E.R. 918.
13. (1742) 2 Atk. 469. There are three different sorts of contempt. One kind of contempt is scandalising the court itself. There may likewise be a contempt of this court in abusing the parties who are concerned in causes here. There may also be contempt of court in prejudicing mankind against persons before the cause is heard.
14. *Id.* at 470, 471.
15. *Supra* n. 11.

> of the offence of libelling judges for what they do in their judicial capacities, either in court or out of court, comes to be considered, it does, in my opinion become more proper for an attachment than any other case whatsoever.[16]

This opinion has been referred to in a later case[17] as the most valuable exposition of law on the subject. Criminal contempt may also be tried by indictment or information but these procedures were rarely adopted.[18] As stated by the Committee on Contempt of Court, though the historical reasoning of the judgment has been criticised by the learned authorities, the opinion expressed by Wilmot in *King* v. *Almon*[19] has long been accepted and applied by the courts as the firmly established basis of the modern law on the subject.[20] Had this important transformation not taken place, the nature of contempt jurisdiction in relation to the press might have been different.[21] The necessity to have this summary jurisdiction has been justified by subsequent verdicts.[22]

In the year 1888 Libel Act was passed and it permitted fair and accurate reports of judicial proceedings. But contempt proceedings were followed against erring publishers.[23]

Regarding jurisdiction of courts to deal with constructive contempt, there have been different judicial opinions.

---

16. *Id.* at 99

    Though John Charles Fox criticised Wilmot's view, he admitted that Wilmot's opinion was adopted by succeeding judges without question and without examination of earlier authorities.
17. As per Lord Esher M.R. in *Reg* v. *Johnson* (1887) 2 Q.B.D. 72.
18. *See* J.C. Fox. "The writ of Attachment" 40 *L.Q.R.*, 43, 59 (1924).
19. *Supra* n. 11.
20. *Report of the Committee on Contempt of Court*, 2 (1974).
21. R.L. Goldfarb, *The Contempt Power*, 25 (1963).
22. *Mc Leod* v. *St. Abyn* 1899 A.C. 549; *R.* v. *Tibbits and another* [1900-3] All. E.R. Rep. 896-901. In this case Lord Alverstone C.J. expressed: "Publications of that character have been punished over and over again as contempt of court, where the legal proceedings pending did not involve trial by jury and where no one would imagine the minds of the magistrates or judges charged with the case would or could be induced thereby to swerve from the straight course. (*Id.* at 901)
23. *R.* v. *Parke* (1900-3) All. E.R. 721.

In *R.* v. *Odham Press Ltd.*[24] and in *R.* v. *Griffiths Ex. P. Attn. Gen.*[25], it was held by the Queen's Bench Division that lack of knowledge regarding imminence of proceedings could not be cited as justification for contemptuous publications. But section 11[26] of the Administration of Justice Act, 1960[27] reversed this position. This provision had been reenacted in a modified form in section 3[28] of the Contempt of Court Act, 1981. The County Courts Act, 1959 provided for punishment to any person who wilfully insulted the judge of the County Courts, jurors, witnesses or any officer of the court including courts other than court of record.

---

24. (1956) 3 Q.B.D. 494.
25. (1957) 2 Q.B.D. 379.
26. Sec. 11 of the Administration of Justice Act, 1960 reads: Innocent publication and distribution:
    (i) A person shall not be guilty of contempt of court on the ground that he has published any matter calculated to interfere with the course of justice in connection with any proceedings pending or imminent at the time of publication if at that time (having taken all reasonable care) he did not know and had no reason to suspect that the proceedings were pending or that such proceedings were imminent, as the case may be.
    (ii) A person shall not be guilty of contempt of court on the ground that he has distributed a publication containing such matter as is mentioned in sub. sec. (1) of this section if at the time of distribution (having taken all reasonable care) he did not know that it contained any such matter as aforesaid and had no reason to suspect that it was likely to do so.
    (iii) The proof of any fact tending to establish a defence afforded by this section to any person in proceedings for contempt of court shall lie upon that person.
27. The report of the British section of the International Commission of Jurists presided over by Lord Shawcross, was published in April 1959 and it formed the basis of certain provisions relating to contempt of court embodied in the Administration of Justice Act, 1960.
28. Sec. 3: Defence of innocent publication or distribution:
    (i) A person is not guilty of contempt of court under the strict liability rule as the publisher of any matter to which that rule applies if at the time of publication having taken all reasonable care he does not know and has no reason to suspect that relevant proceedings are active.
    (ii) A person is not guilty of contempt of court under strict liability rule as the distributor of a publication containing any such matter if at

In England as well as in Scotland contempt came to be identified with summary procedure.[29]

Justice Buckley commenting on the right of the press to publish a pending case observed:

> The rights of the press to comment on any matter of general public interest, as long as the comment is fair comment; is a matter of very great public interest, but it is a right which is subject to certain restrictions, one of which is that the organs of the press must not be used in a way to prejudice the proper trial of actions in the courts of the country.[30]

Until the decision of the House of Lords in the *Sunday Times*[31] case, the test of constructive contempt formulated by the courts were all based on the concept of prejudice or improper interference with legal process. The Divisional Court[32] in the *Sunday Times* case granted an injunction restraining the publication on the ground that it would be contempt of court. But the Court of Appeal[33] decided that there was no contempt as the words complained of did not create a serious risk of interference with the course of justice, and discharged the injunction.[34] On appeal the House of Lords reversed the decision by applying the test of prejudging the issue. Lord Reid observed that trial by newspaper was wrong and should be prevented.[35]

Being aggrieved by the decision of the House of Lords, the *Sunday Times* and the journalists applied to the European

---

the time of distribution (having taken all reasonable care) he does not know that it contains such matter and has no reason to suspect that it is likely to do so.

(iii) The burden of proof of any fact tending to establish a defence afforded by this section to any person lies upon that person.

29. *Supra* n. 20, p. 3.
30. Justice Buckley in *Vine Products* v. *Meckenzie and Co.* (1965) All. E.R. 53.
31. *Attorney General* v. *Times News Papers Ltd.* (1973), 3, All. E.R. 54.
32. *Attorney General* v. *Times News Papers Ltd.* (1973), 3, All. E.R. 1136.
33. *Attorney General* v. *Times News Papers Ltd.* (1972), I All. E.R. 815.
34. *Id.* at 824.
35. *Supra* n. 31 p. 64.

Court of Human Rights[36] as the ban on publication violated Art. 10 of the European Convention. The majority ruled that the Court was faced not with a choice between two conflicting principles but with a principle of freedom of expression that is subject to a number of exceptions which must be narrowly interpreted.[37]

The Court was of the opinion that the "Thalidomide Disaster" published by *Sunday Times* against which the contempt case was pending, was a matter of public concern, and the public had a right to be properly informed. The article was moderate in tone and presented both sides of the case and it in no way impaired judicial authority. Hence, the Court concluded that interference complained of did not correspond to a social need sufficiently pressing to outweigh the public interest in freedom of expression.

In 1974, a Committee on Contempt of Court chaired by Justice Phillimore had laid down the basic test for deciding contempt by publication.

The test of contempt is whether the publication complained of creates a risk that the court of justice will be seriously impeded or prejudiced.[38] The Committee recommended that a defence on the line of general public discussion should be created by statute.[39] At the same time the Committee recommended that public benefit should not be made as a defence.[40] These recommendations of the Committee found a place in the Contempt of Court Act, 1981.[41]

On a reading of the Act it is clear that it mainly deals with the 'strict liability' rule and its application to publications which affect the judicial proceedings. However uncertain its definition and scope may be in some respects contempt of court is undoubtedly one of the great contributions the common

36. *The Sunday Times* v. *United Kingdom* (1979), 2, EHHR, 24.
37. *Id.* at 281.
38. *Supra* n. 20 p. 48, 49.
39. *Id.* at 61.
40. *Ibid.*
41. The Contempt of Court Act, 1981 is the result of the report filed by Phillimore Committee and also the decision of the European Court of Human Rights.

law has made to the civilised behaviour of a large part of the world beyond the continent of Europe where the institution was unknown.[42]

2. DEVELOPMENT OF THE LAW OF CONTEMPT OF COURT IN INDIA

The law of contempt of court in India is nothing but the off spring of the British administration of justice in India. Creation of different courts of record[43] in India necessarily meant the introduction of English Law of Contempt in some measure.[44]

Establishment of the Court of Mayor and Corporation of Madras under the East India Company's Charter of 1687[45] was the earliest court of record created in India. Admiralty Court established under the Royal Charter of 1683 had the right to hear appeals and hence Admiralty Court was also considered a court of record. Later Mayor's Court was created by the Charter of 1727,[46] which was reconstituted by the Charter of 1753.[47] These courts had power to punish for contempt.

---

42. F.A. Mann, "Contempt of Court in the House of Lords and European Court of Human Rights" 95 *L.Q.R.* 348-349 (1979).
43. A Court of Record has been defined as a court where the acts and judicial proceedings are enrolled in Parliament for a perpetual memorial and testimony and which has power to fine and imprison for contempt of its authority.... Courts not of record are those of inferior dignity which have no power to fine or imprison and in which proceedings are enrolled or recorded and all courts which do not come within the definition of a Court of Record are courts not of record (XV *The Corpus Juris* 720, 721). The proceedings of a Court of Record preserved in its archives are called records and are conclusive evidence of that which is recorded therein: II *Halsbury's Laws of England* 527 (3rd Edn.) I may briefly say that a court of record is a court the records of which are admitted to be of evidentiary value and they are not to be questioned when they are produced before any court. That is the meaning of the words "Court of Records"...the court shall have the power to punish for contempt of itself. Dr. B.R. Ambedkar VIII CAD 382.
44. *Report of the Committee on Contempt of Court*, 4 (1963).
45. Charter granted by the Governor and Company of Merchants Trading into the East Indies, to the Mayor Aldermen and Burgesses of Madras (at p. 88).
46. II Vestiges of Old Madras 1640 — 1800. 241, 242 (Charter of 1727, 249).
47. *Id.* at 439-440 (Charter of 1753, 253).

In pursuance of the Regulating Act, 1773 the Mayor's Court at Calcutta was succeeded by the Supreme Court established under a charter granted in 1774. The Mayor's Court at Bombay and Madras were superseded by the Recorder's Court at Madras. It was abolished by the Government of India Act, 1800 and the Supreme Court was established in its place by the Charter of 1801. A Supreme Court was established in the place of Recorder's Court at Bombay by a Charter granted under the Statute of 1823. The Recorder's Court and Supreme Court had the same powers for punishing for contempt as the superior courts of England. The Supreme Courts were in turn succeeded by the High Courts under the High Courts Act of 1861. The High Court of Calcutta was a court of record in all its jurisdictions and therefore possessed power to commit for contempt.[48] In 1886, the High Court of Allahabad was established under the High Courts Act, 1861 and was constituted a court of record.

The Division Bench of the Calcutta High Court considered this jurisdiction of the High Court in 1879 in *Martin* v. *Lawrence*.[49] Mr. Justice White observed:

> The jurisdiction of the court, under which this process (of contempt) issued is a jurisdiction that it has inherited from the old Supreme Court and was conferred upon that court by the Charters of the authority of the then court of King's Bench and the High Court of Chancery in Great Britain, and this jurisdiction has not been removed or affected by the Civil Procedure Code.[50]

By virtue of section 106 of the Government of India Act, 1915 the same jurisdiction, powers and authority, were allowed to be continued in all High Courts then in existence. Section 113 of the Act authorised the establishment of new High Courts by Letters Patent with the same authority, powers and jurisdiction. In 1919 the Lahore High Court was established by Letters Patent as a court of record. In 1925 that High Court punished a contempt of itself in a summary manner in *Habib, son of Sadullah Khan, in the matter of*.[51] In this case it was observed by Broadway, J.:

48. *In Re Abdool and Mehtaf* (1867) 8 W.R. (Cr.) 32.
49. I.L.R. 4 Cal. 444.
50. *Id.* at 445.
51. AIR 1926 Lah. 1 (Full Bench).

> The authorities on the subject have been carefully examined by me and I am satisfied that this court as a court of record has jurisdiction to deal summarily with contempts of this nature.[52]

The leading authority on the subject is the Privy Council and its decision in *Surendranath Banerjee* v. *The Chief Justice and Judges of the High Court at Fort William in Bengal.*[53] It was held by Justice Peacock that the High Court in the presidencies are superior courts of record and the offence of contempt and the powers of High Court for punishing it, are the same there as in the country, not by virtue of the Penal Code for British India, and the Code of Criminal Procedure 1882, but by virtue of the common law of England.[54]

The inherent summary powers of the High Courts to punish for contempt were later affirmed by Lahore[55] and Patna[56] High Courts. Privy Council also accepted the same view in *Ambard* v. *Attorney General, Trinidad and Tabago.*[57] These decisions show that the power to punish summarily for contempt is not created by statute but inherent in every court of record. The Government of India Act, 1935 continued the power, authority and special summary jurisdiction of various High Courts then existing.[58]

Arts. 129[59] and 215[60] of our Constitution made the Supreme Court and High Courts respectively as courts of record.

52. *Id.* at 2.
53. I.L.R. 10 Cal. 109.
54. *Id.* at 132.
55. *In the Matter of Muslim Outlook* AIR 1927 Lah. 610.
56. *Emperor* v. *Murali Manohar Prasad.* AIR 1929 Pat. 72.
57. AIR 1936 P.C. 141.
58. Section 220(1) of the Government of India Act, 1935 declared that every High Court shall be a court of record and by Section 223, the existing courts were allowed to continue, the summary jurisdiction and powers which they had immediately before the commencement of Part III of this Act.
59. Art. 129: The Supreme Court shall be a court of record and shall have all the powers of such a court including the power to punish for contempt of itself.
60. Art. 215: Every High Court shall be a court of record and shall have all the powers of such a court including the power to punish for contempt of itself.

Art. 225, permits the High Courts to continue the jurisdiction and powers which they possessed immediately before the commencement of the Constitution. Though the High Court as a court of record had the power to punish contempt of itself, doubt arose as to the power of the court of record to punish contempt of subordinate courts.

Prior to the passing of the Contempt of Courts Act, 1926, there was a conflict of opinion among the different High Courts as to their power to commit for contempt of subordinate courts. Madras[61] and Bombay[62] High Courts expressed the view that the High Courts could have jurisdiction to deal with contempts of the mofussil courts. But the Calcutta High Court[63] expressed the view that the High Courts in India did not possess identical powers in matters of contempt of their subordinate courts as possessed by the Court of King's Bench in England.

In 1926, the Full Bench of the Allahabad High Court dealt with contempt of subordinate court under its inherent powers as a court of record.[64]

There was no general law providing for punishment of contempt of these courts. The Indian Penal Code 1862[65] made certain acts constituting specific offences punishable as contempt.

For making the concept of contempt more specific and for providing punishment for contempt of subordinate courts, the Contempt of Courts Act, 1926 was passed. Section 2[66] of the Act empowered the High Courts of judicature to exercise the

61. *In the Matter of K. Venkat Rao*, 12 I.C. 293.
62. *In re Mohandas Karamchand Gandhi*, AIR 1920 Bom. 175.
63. *Legal Remembrancer* v. *Motilal Ghose*, 1913, ILR Cal.173.
64. *In re. Hadi Hussain* v. *Nassiruddin Haider* AIR 192 All. 623.
65. Sections 191 to 229 of the Indian Penal Code: Sec. 191 deals with giving false evidence; Sec. 192 fabricating false evidence; Ss. 201 to 204 Disappearance of evidence and false information; Ss. 206-210, Abuse of the process of court; Sec. 228 contempt of court; Ss. 217-223, 225A Unlawful acts of public servants.
66. Section 2 of the 1926 Act:
    (i) Subject to the provisions of sub-section (3), the High Courts of Judicature established by Letters Patent shall have and exercise the same jurisdiction powers and authority in accordance with

jurisdiction, power and authority to punish contempt of subordinate courts.

The Act was amended in 1937 to make it clear that the limits of punishment provided in the Act related not only to contempt of subordinate courts but also to all cases.

The 1926 Act did not contain any provision with regard to contempt of courts subordinate to Chief Courts and Judicial Commissioner's Court and also extra-territorial jurisdiction of High Courts in matters of contempt. So the Contempt of Courts Act, 1952 was passed to remove these doubts and this Act replaced the 1926 Act. Section 3[67] of the Contempt of Courts Act, 1952 conferred the power on the High Courts including that of the Judicial Commissioner's Court to punish contempt of subordinate courts. Section 4 of the Act limited the punishment to be awarded in case of contempt.

The Contempt of Courts Act, 1952 though sound so far as it goes, touches only the fringes of the subject. While its existing provisions should be continued there is need for widening considerably the scope of the Act.[68] The unsatisfactory

---

the same procedure and practice in respect of contempts of courts subordinate to them as they have and exercise in respect of contempt of themselves.

(ii) Subject to the provisions of sub-sec. 3 a Chief Court shall have and exercise the same jurisdiction and powers and authority in accordance with the same procedure and practice in respect of contempt of itself as a High Court referred to in sub-sec. (1).

(iii) No High Court shall take cognizance of a contempt alleged to have been committed in respect of a court subordinate to it where such contempt is an offence punishable under the Indian Penal Code.

67. Section 3 of the 1952 Act:

(i) Subject to the provisions of sub-sec. 2 every High Court shall have and exercise the same jurisdiction, powers and authority in accordance with the same procedure and practice, in respect of contempt of courts subordinate to it has and exercise in respect of contempt of itself.

(ii) No High Court shall take cognizance of a contempt alleged to have been committed in respect of a court subordinate to it where such contempt is an offence punishable under the Indian Penal Code.

68. *Supra* n. 44, p. 9.

nature of the Contempt of Courts Act, 1952 necessitated the government to constitute a Committee in 1961 with H.N. Sanyal as Chairman to study the matter and make recommendations for the proper functioning of the law of contempt, because the government felt that the law relating to contempt of court was uncertain, undefined and unsatisfactory. On the basis of the recommendations made by the Committee, Contempt of Courts Act, 1971 was passed which can be described as a comprehensive legislation.

Contempt by publication, though used to be punished by the court of record in exercise of its inherent jurisdiction had not been regulated either by the Contempt of Courts Act, 1926 or by the 1952 Act. Its development till the passing of the Contempt of Courts Act, 1971 was based on case law only. So the development of contempt by publications is traced in the succeeding pages.

Criminal contempt has been classified into two categories. They are direct criminal contempt or contempt in the face of the court and indirect criminal contempt or contempt through words spoken, written or through publication made outside the court.

Direct criminal contempt is treated as specific offence and it is dealt with in the Indian Penal Code.[69] Corresponding procedure is contained in the Criminal Procedure Code.[70]

Indirect criminal contempt or contempt through publication was first considered by the Calcutta High Court in *In the Matter of William Taylor*.[71]

The question for consideration was whether libel committed out of court was punishable by the court as contempt of court. Justice Peacock expressed the following view:

> All I claim is that there shall be no misrepresentation and no wilful or unfair concealment of facts and that those who deny infallibility to the judges shall not claim infallibility for themselves.[72]

---

69. Section 228.
70. Sections 480-487.
71. Reported years later in AIR 1918 Cal. 713.
72. *Id.* at 735, 736.

This principle was followed in *In the Matter of Banks and Fenwick*[73] in the year 1869. For the first time an editor was punished in the *Bengalee case*[74] for making an adverse comment on an English Judge. By punishing Surendranath Banerjee, the editor, the court clearly established its contempt jurisdiction on indirect contempt and made it clear that the court could impose punishment irrespective of the apology made to the court. The Privy Council also accepted the court's jurisdiction and refused to interfere on the question of punishment.

At the turn of the nineteenth century, the contempt jurisdiction was not really a thorn on the sides of the publishers. The press simply continued to make comments about the administration of justice. Very little notice was taken of these comments. The contempt jurisdiction of the court was sparingly invoked by litigants and the courts, as such comments had no tendency to prejudice the trial.[75]

In *Legal Remembrancer* v. *Motilal Ghose*[76] the Calcutta High Court refused to follow the summary process. So also, in *E.* v. *Balakrishna Govinda Kulkarni*,[77] Bombay High Court expressed doubts as to the use of summary procedure in constructive contempts. But the same High Court in *In the Matter of Tusharakanthi Ghose Editor of Amrit Bazar Patrika*[78] clearly laid down that the High Court had jurisdiction to deal with constructive contempt in a summary manner.

The jurisdiction of the Supreme Court as a court of record to punish for contempt of lower court was considered by the Supreme Court in *In re Vinaya Chandra Mishra*[79] and the court held:

> The English and the Indian authorities are based on the basic foundation of inherent power of Court of Record having jurisdiction to correct the judicial orders of

---

73. Reported later in AIR 1918 Cal. 752.
74. *Surendranath Banerjee* v. *The Chief Justice and Judges of the High Court at Fort William in Bengal.* ILR 10 Cal. 109.
75. Rajeev Dhavan, *Contempt of Court and the Press*, 45 (1982).
76. *Supra* n. 63.
77. AIR 1922 Bom. 52.
78. AIR 1935 Cal. 419.
79. (1995) 2, S.C.C. 584.

> subordinate courts.... Inherent powers of a superior Court of Record have remained unaffected even after codification of contempt law.[80]

Thus the application of Contempt of Courts Act, 1971, when the contempt proceedings are taken up by the High Courts and Supreme Court, is very much limited because those courts exercise jurisdiction as a court of record.

The question of constructive contempt was considered by Bombay,[81] Calcutta,[82] Lahore,[83] Madras[84] and Ludhiana[85] High Courts. Bombay High Court in *Mohandas Karamchand Gandhi's*[86] case, rejecting the argument that the press had a right to discuss questions of public importance and to indulge in public criticism laid down the principle that the contempt process was a summary process, affording practically no defences and truth was no defence and fair comment was not a permissible plea. In this case Gandhiji published certain documents during the pendency of the case. The court further stated that principles which were quite familiar in England were imperfectly known or understood in India and that the respondents had paid more attention to the liberty of the press than to the duties which accompany that and every other liberty.[87] The same principle was followed by the Calcutta High Court in *Bankin Chandra Paira* v. *Ananda Bazar Patrika*.[88] In this case Ananda Bazar Patrika during the pendency of a criminal case published a report in which it was stated:

---

80. *Id.* at 605.
81. *In re Mohandas Karamchand Gandhi* AIR 1920 Bom. 175 *E.* v. *Balakrishna Govinda Kulkarni*, AIR 1922 Bom. 52.
82. *Motilal Ghose and others In re* (1917) ILR 45 Cal. 169 *Ananta Lal Singh* v. *Alfred Hendry Watson* AIR 1931 Cal. 257; *In the matter of Tusharkanti Ghose, Editor Amrit Bazar Patrika* AIR 1935 Cal. 419; *Bankin Chandra Paira* v. *Ananda Bazar Patrika* AIR (37) 1950 Cal. 129.
83. *In re Subramanian, Editor, Tribune* AIR (30) 1943 Lah. 329; *Crown* v. *Amin-Ud-Din-Sahrait* AIR 1949 Lah. 266.
84. *P.S. Tuljaram Rao* v. *Sir James Taylor, Governor Reserve Bank of India* AIR (26) 1939 Mad. 257.
85. *Mohammed Ibrahim* v. *Bhopal Singh* AIR 1948 Ludh.131.
86. AIR 1920 Bom. 175.
87. *Id.* at 180.
88. AIR (37) 1950 Cal. 129.

> "It is desirable that either bail bonds of the accused should be cancelled till their trial is finished or arrangements made for providing police guards."

This passage was held to have the effect of interfering with the free exercise of judicial discretion by the trying magistrate.[89] Madras High Court further liberalised the principle of pendency of proceedings to cases which are about to come before the court in *P.S. Tuljaram Rao* v. *Sir James Taylor, Governor Reserve Bank of India.*[90] It was held that to comment on a case which was about to come before the court with his knowledge of the fact was just as much a contempt as comment on a case actually launched.[91]

So also the test of real prejudice or substantial interference was accepted by the Calcutta High Court in *Ananta Lal Singh* v. *Alfred Hendry Watson.*[92] In this case Rankin C.J. observed:

> The court's jurisdiction in contempt is not to be invoked unless there is a real prejudice which can be regarded as a substantial interference with the due course of justice. It is not very theoretical tendency that will attract the actions of court in its very special jurisdiction. The purpose of the court's action is a practical purpose and it is reasonably clear on the authorities that this court will not exercise its jurisdiction upon a mere question of propriety where the tendency of the article to do harm is slight and the character and circumstances of the comment is otherwise such that it can properly be ignored.[93]

---

89. *Id.* at 133.
90. AIR (26) 1939 Mad. 257.
91. *Id.* at 259. The same principle was followed by the Lahore High Court in *In Re Subramaniyan, Editor Tribune* AIR 1943 Lah. 329. It was held that the proceedings need not actually be pending and that it was sufficient that the proceedings were imminent to the knowledge of the person charged with contempt.
92. AIR 1931 Cal. 257. The test of real prejudice as laid down by Rankin C.J. in *Ananta Lal Singh* v. *Alfred Hendry Watson* was followed by the Ludhiana High Court in *Mohammed Ibrahim* v. *Bhopal Singh* AIR 1948 Ludh. 131.
93. *Id.* at 261. The same principle was followed by Lahore High Court in *In re Subramaniyan, Editor Tribune,* AIR 1943 Lah. 329; the publication of

It was further liberalised and accepted as tendency to poison the fountain of justice by the same High Court in *In the matter of Tusharakanthi Ghose, Editor Amrit Bazar Patrika.*[94] In this case it was held that it was immaterial whether the attack on the judge was with reference to a cause about to be tried or actually under trial or recently adjudged. In each instance the tendency was to poison the fountain of justice, to create distrust and to destroy the confidence of the people in the courts which were of prime importance to them in the protection of their rights and liberties.[95]

Scandalising the court, as a test of constructive contempt was also accepted by the Calcutta High Court in *In the matter of Tushar Kanti Ghosh, Editor Amrit Bazar Patrika.*[96] In this case it was held that the court had the right to punish scandalising the court by summary procedure as contempt. The same principle was followed by the Lahore High Court in *Crown* v. *Amin-ud-Din-Sahrait.*[97]

In this case it was held that the published article clearly amounted to contempt of the High Court as it scandalises, ridicules and creates disrespect and contempt for a distinguished member of the High Court, grossly misrepresents court proceedings and tends to interfere with the due course of justice by intimidating the judge and undermining public confidence in the administration of justice.[98]

> Judges loathe to take proceedings for their own contempt and do not mind any honest criticism of the judgments.... But if motives are attributed to a judge and it is alleged that he gave a wrong decision intending to favour a particular party or to oblige or to please or in fear of a

---

matter which tends to or is calculated to interfere with the due course of justice may amount to contempt, but before a court will take notice of such publication the court must be satisfied that the matter published tended substantially to interfere with the due course justice or was calculated substantially to create prejudice in the public mind.

94. AIR 1935 Cal. 419.
95. *Motilal Ghose and others In re* I.L.R. 45 Cal. 169, 234, 235.
96. *Supra* n. 94.
97. AIR 1949 Lah. 266.
98. *Id.* at 269.

> particular person or authority, the position is different because the suggestion then is that the very fountain of justice is tainted and consequently that judgment that stream out of that fountain is impure and contaminated. In such cases, it is the bounden duty of the court to step in to remove a potential menace to the confidence of the public in their judges.[99]

Interfering with the administration of justice, prejudicing fair trial and scandalising the court have been generally the tests of constructive contempt.

99. *Ibid.*

PART 2

4

Criminal Contempt—By the Individual and the Press—The Common Grounds

1. INTRODUCTION

Constitutional guarantee of freedom of speech and expression[1] does not permit either the individual or the press to commit contempt of court.[2] The purpose of the contempt jurisdiction is to safeguard the administration of justice from undue interference and verbal attacks from any agency. The judiciary though competent to use the contempt power, used it only sparingly.[3] It cannot as a rule be too sensitive. Free and fair criticism of the judicial act motivated by *bona fide* reasons has to be permitted, but scurrilous attack on the judiciary motivated by *mala fides* has to be viewed seriously and should be restricted.

---

1. Art. 19(1). All citizens shall have the right—(a) to freedom of speech and expression.
2. Art. 19(2). Nothing in sub-clause (a) of clause (1) shall affect the operation of any existing law or prevent the state from making any law in so far as such law imposes reasonable restriction on the exercise of the right conferred by the said sub-clause in the interest of sovereignty and integrity of India...in relation to contempt of court.
3. N.G. Shelat, "Contempt of Court," XII *Gujarat Law Reporter* (Jnl.) XIII (1972). The author further stated:

   It has to be used only for the vindication of its authority and prestige and also only when there is interference or an attempt at interference in the course of justice...while criticism passed by persons may well be tolerated, if that exceeds its legitimate bounds by imputing motives or extraneous considerations in deciding matters etc. or in other words where the good faith in the judges is sought to be shaken in the eyes of the public it becomes a part of the duty of the courts to take due notice thereof and punish such persons (*Ibid.*).

Before the passing of the Contempt of Courts Act, 1971, the law of contempt of court in India especially as it related to the press, was based on the common law principles as adopted by the Indian courts from time to time. Two enactments which preceded the 1971 Act, one in the year 1926[4] and another in the year 1952[5] have not made any mention about constructive contempt. Contempt of Courts Act, 1926 empowered the High Courts constituted under the Letters Patent to exercise contempt jurisdiction in case of contempt of subordinate courts so also that of the Chief Court.[6] It also restricted the punishment to be given to the contemner.[7] Contempt of Courts Act, 1952 also dealt with the power of the High Court to punish contempt of subordinate courts[8] and also restricted the punishment to be awarded.[9] Further the High Court was made to include Judicial Commissioner's Court also.

The necessity to restrict the freedom of speech of the individual on the ground of contempt of court had been recognized by Lord Hardwicke. L.C. in *St. James Evening Post Case*[10] in the year 1742. It was subsequently followed by Justice Wilmot in *The King* v. *Almon*[11] who expressed the view that

4. Contempt of Courts Act, 1926.
5. Contempt of Courts Act, 1952.
6. *Supra* n. 66 Ch. III.
7. Sec. 3 of the Contempt of Courts Act, 1926. Save as expressly provided by any law for the time being in force a contempt of court may be punished with simple imprisonment for a term which may extend to six months or with fine which may extend to Rs. Two thousand or with both....
8. *Supra* n. 67 Ch. III.
9. Sec. 4 of the Contempt of Courts Act, 1952: Save as otherwise expressly provided by any law for the time being in force a contempt of court may be punished with simple imprisonment for a term which may extend to six months or with fine which may extend to two thousand rupees or with both....
10. (1742) 2 Atk. 469.
11. 97 E.R. 94. "When the nature of the offence of libeling judges for what they do in their judicial capacities, either in court or out of court comes to be considered, it does in my opinion, become more proper for attachment than any other cause whatsoever (*Id.* at 99).

constructive contempt or indirect contempt[12] can be dealt with by summary procedure. The principle of law as laid down in *Almon's*[13] case has long been accepted by the courts as the firmly established basis of the modern law on the subject.[14] Indirect contempt or constructive contempt was subsequently followed in the case of *Clement*,[15] *Miller* v. *Knox*,[16] *Re Johnson*,[17] *Reg* v. *Grey*[18] and so on.

Indian judiciary which adopted the common law concept of contempt also applied the constructive contempt. Calcutta High Court first considered the scope of indirect contempt in *In the matter of William Taylor.*[19] Calcutta High Court though accepted the right to criticise the judiciary also recognized the limitation that, there shall be no misrepresentation and no wilful or unfair concealment of facts.[20] It was further followed in *In the matter of Banks and Fenwick*[21] and also in *Bengalee*

12. Contempt is traditionally classified into civil contempt and criminal contempt. Criminal contempt can be contempt in the face of the court which is sometimes designated as direct contempt; while other have been termed as constructive or indirect contempt. C.J. Miller, *Contempt of Court*, 2 (1976).
13. *Supra* n. 11.
14. *Report of the Committee on Contempt of Court*, 2 (1971). This committee has been constituted in England in the year 1971, under the Chairmanship of The Right Honourable Lord Justice Phillimore. It was constituted to study the law of contempt of court and to ascertain whether any change is required in the law relating to contempt of court. Other members of the committee are: The Honourable Lord Cameron; Robin Day Esq. The Right Hon'ble Lord Grant, General Sir John Hackett Derek Hodgson Esq; Q.C. David Hopkinson, Esq; I.G. Inglis Esq. The committee submitted its report with recommendations in the year 1974.
15. 106 E.R. 918.
16. 132 E.R. 915.
17. (1887) 2 Q.B.D. 68.
18. (1900) 2 Q.B. 36.
19. AIR 1918 Cal. 713.
20. The press is fair, it is not scurrilous, the public are not captious and public man do not object to have their public acts freely discussed and fairly criticised. Our courts therefore are generally free from all complaints against the press, either civil or criminal on the ground of defamation. (*Id.* at 736).
21. AIR 1918 Cal. 752.

case.[22] Renkin C.J. of Calcutta High Court also applied constructive contempt in *Ananta Lal Singh* v. *Alfred Henry Watson.*[23] The Privy Council accepted these principles in *Ambard* v. *Attorney General Trinidad and Tobago*[24] and in *Debi Prasad* v. *Emperor.*[25] The principles as enunciated by the Privy Council was followed by the Lahore High Court in *Emperor* v. *Khushal Chand*[26] and laid down the following tests to ascertain whether a publication amounted to contempt of court or not.

(a) That something has been published which either is clearly intended or atleast is calculated to prejudice a trial which is pending; (b) That the offending matter was published with the knowledge of the pending cause or with the knowledge that the cause was imminent; and (c) That the matter published tended substantially to interfere with the due course of justice or was calculated substantially to create prejudice in the public mind.[27]

These principles as laid down by the Lahore High Court havè been invariably applied in subsequent cases to ascertain whether there is contempt of court or not. So, they are dealt with in the subsequent chapters.

---

22. I.L.R. 10 Cal. 109.
23. AIR 1931 Cal. 257.
24. AIR 1936 P.C. 141. Lord Atkin observed: "The path of criticism is a public way the wrong headed are permitted to err therein provided that the members of the public abstain from imputing improper motives to those taking part in the administration of justice and are generally exercising a right of criticism and not acting in malice or attempting to impair the administration of justice, they are immune. Justice is not a cloistered virtue, she must be allowed to suffer the scrutiny and respectful, even though outspoken comments of ordinary men. (*Id.* at 145, 146)
25. AIR 1943 P.C. 202. "The test to be applied in such a case is to see whether the words complained of interfere with the course of justice and the due administration of the law. If the Judge is defamed in such a way as not to affect the administration of justice he has the ordinary remedies for defamation if he should feel impelled to use them." (*Id.* at 204, 205)
26. AIR 1945 Lah. 206.
27. *Id.* at 207.

Of the above principles, the grounds of pendency of proceedings, knowledge of pendency of proceedings and imminence of proceedings which are commonly applicable to contempt committed by the individuals and press are discussed in this chapter.

2. PENDENCY OF PROCEEDINGS

Publication of any matter which interferes or tends to interfere with the administration of justice, relating to pending judicial proceedings will amount to contempt of court.[28] So the first and foremost task is to ascertain whether the proceedings are pending.[29]

Under English law the difficulty in ascertaining whether the proceedings are pending or not was settled in *Clarke ex parte Crippen*[30] where the Divisional Court held that criminal proceedings were certainly pending from the time when a suspect was arrested under a warrant, since the issue of the warrant is an act of a magistrate not merely ministerial, but involving the exercise of a judicial discretion.[31]

Although there is little authority in point, it is clear in principle that civil proceedings will become pending once a writ is issued and as long as any proceedings can be taken.[32] Because of the wide scope of the term pending proceedings, Contempt of Court Act, 1981 used the phrase "proceedings in question are active."[33]

---

28. *Wasudeoraoji Sheorey* v. *A.D. Mani, Managing Editor, Hitavada* 52 Cri. L.J. 1951 (Nagpur High Court) 452. (Facts *see* n. 19 ch. v)
29. Traditionally the solution has been sought by asking whether the proceedings allegedly prejudiced were 'pending' or perhaps 'imminent' at the material time. Both these terms have proved to be extremely elastic and not susceptible of precise definition. *See* C.J. Miller, *Contempt of Court* 73 (1976).
30. (1910) 103 L.T. 636.
31. *Id.* at 641.

    Where a person is arrested without a warrant common sense would suggest that proceedings may again be regarded as pending forthwith. C.J. Miller, *Contempt of Court,* 75 (1976).
32. Oswald, *Contempt of Court,* 97 (3rd Edn.).
33. Sec. 2 (3) of the Contempt of Court Act, 1981. The strict liability rule applies to a publication only if the proceedings in question are active within the meaning of this section at the time of the publication.

In India, before passing the Contempt of Courts Act, 1971, there was no uniformity of views among the High Courts. Patna High Court[34] and Allahabad High Court[35] refused to take cognizance of a publication which is made after the matter is being taken up by the court or when it is in the course of investigation. So also Calcutta High Court[36] refused to take cognizance of a publication which was made before the arrest of a person in connection with an incident. Allahabad High Court modified its earlier view in its subsequent decision in *Rajendra Kumar Garg* v. *Shafiq Ahmed Azad*[37] and held:

> As far as mere arrest of a person is concerned, we are of the opinion that it might not mean pendency or imminence of legal proceedings. It would depend upon the circumstances of each particular case.[38]

But, Naik J. of Madhya Pradesh High Court in *Smt. Padmavati Devi Bhargava* v. *R.K. Karanjia*[39] refused to follow the view expressed by the Allahabad High Court in *Dwarka Prasad* v. *Krishna Chandra*[40] and held:

> As soon as a suitor has taken any effective steps in the prosecution of his case, the law extends its protection on him.[41]

In civil cases, the giving of a notice under section 80[42] of

34. *Superintendent of Legal affairs* v. *Murali Manohar Prasad* AIR 1941 Pat. 185.
35. *Dwarka Prasad Agarwal* v. *Krishna Chandra* AIR 1953 All. 600. In this case the learned Judge observed. We are of the opinion that contempt proceedings cannot be taken in connection with the publication of news or articles as along as a criminal case is during the course of investigation and has not actually come to the magistrate's court for enquiry or trial. (*Id.* at 604)
36. *Emperor* v. *J. Choudhary*, AIR 1947 Cal. 414.
37. AIR 1957 All. 37 (facts see *infra* n. 57).
38. *Id.* at 41.
39. AIR 1963 M.P. 61 (facts see *infra* n. 61).
40. *Supra* n. 35.
41. *Supra* n. 39, p. 66.
42. Sec. 80, Civil Procedure Code 1908: Save as otherwise provided in Sub-Sec. 2, no suit shall be instituted against the government including the government of the State of Jammu and Kashmir or against a public officer in respect of any act purporting to be done by such public officer in his official capacity until the expiration of two months next after notice in writing has been delivered to, or left at the office of....

the Code of Civil Procedure, 1908 or any other statutory notice required by law, and in suitable cases even the giving of a private notice where a server's intention to file a suit is clearly discernible, or the filing of a plaint in court would be such effective step. In criminal cases, such a step could have been taken in the case of non-cognizable offences by the filing of a criminal complaint in court, and in the case of cognizable offences by the making of a first information report. Subsequent arrest of the accused during investigation would, therefore, be during the pendency of the cause.[43]

This view as it relates to civil matters, cannot be correct because parties may give Sec. 80 notice or any other statutory notice but may not proceed with the matter.

Patna High Court in *Ram Parikchan Pandey* v. *M.S.M. Sharma*[44] however held that judicial proceedings cannot be deemed to have commenced against an accused unless and until the magistrate issues process for his attendance.[45]

The difficulty in ascertaining whether proceedings are pending or not is set at rest by the explanation[46] to section 3

---

43. *Supra* n. 39, p. 66

44. AIR 1961 Pat. 217. In this case Justice Tarkeshwar Nath referred to the meaning of pending as given in Stroud's *Judicial Dictionary* (3rd Edn. 3rd Vol.) 2141. A legal proceeding is pending as soon as commenced and until it is concluded, *i.e.* so long as the court have original cognizance of it can make an order on the matter in issue or to be dealt with therein.

    The respondents in this case, were the editor, printer and publisher. They published extracts from a petition under Sec. 110 Criminal Procedure Code 1898 containing serious allegations against the character and integrity of the petitioner.

45. *Id.* at 224.

46. Explanation: For the purpose of this section, a judicial proceeding.

    (a) is said to be pending—

    A. In the case of civil proceeding, when it is instituted by the filing of a plaint or otherwise:

    B. In the case of criminal proceeding under the Code of Criminal Procedure, 1898, or any other law—

    (i) Where it relates to the commission of an offence, when the charge sheet or challan is filed, or when the court issues summons or warrant, as the case may be, against the accused, and

of the Contempt of Courts Act, 1971. This explanation, to a limited extent, accepts the opinion expressed by Naik J. in *R.K. Karanjia's case*[47] which gives the correct meaning of the term pending.

The same was accepted by the Bombay High Court in *Prabhakar Laxman Mokashi* v. *Sadanand Trimbak Yard*.[48] The important, question considered in this case was, whether a judicial proceeding is pending or not. After considering the earlier case law the court accepted the explanation given in section 3 of the Act and stated:

> However, when a Legislature proceeds to define the concept of when a criminal proceeding shall be deemed to be pending, the statutory provision will have to prevail against the prior existing concept thereof based upon judicial pronouncements. From that point of view one has to look at the Explanation to section 3 which is quoted above.[49]

(ii) In any other case, when the court takes cognizance of the matter to which the proceeding relates, and in the case of a civil or criminal proceeding, shall be deemed to continue to be pending until it is heard and finally decided, that is to say, in a case where an appeal or revision is competent, until the appeal or revision is heard and finally decided or, where no appeal or revision is preferred until the period of limitation prescribed for such appeal or revision has expired.

(b) Which has been heard and finally decided shall not be deemed to be pending merely by reason of the fact that proceedings for the execution of the decree, order or sentence passed therein are pending.

47. *Supra* n. 39.

48. 1975 Cri. L.J. (Bombay High Court) 531. There was a rioting in Vikhroli. On suspicion several persons were arrested. Some of them were released on bail and some of them were detained in custody. While so a public meeting was convened and in that several speakers spoke about the incident and leaflets were published. That was the subject of the contempt petition.

49. *Id.* at 534. Same view was followed by the Madhya Pradesh High Court in *D.K. Paliwal* v. *Editor, Dainik Bhaskar News Paper* [1994 Cri. L.J. (Madhya Pradesh High Court) 2933] "when a case can be said to be pending in a court of law? Explanation appended to Sec. 3 of the Act provides the answer."

3. KNOWLEDGE OF PENDING PROCEEDINGS

Knowledge of pending proceedings as a precondition for contempt proceedings was put forth in the famous *St. James Evening Post*[50] case. Later it was followed in *Rex* v. *Evening Standard Co.*[51] In this case contention based on knowledge was negatived because knowledge relates to knowledge of the contents of the publication and not knowledge of the pending proceedings. Oswald in his treatise on contempt of court expressed the view that in order to constitute contempt of court, "...it must be proved that the comments were made with knowledge of the pending cause."[52]

In India, knowledge as a pre-requisite was accepted by the Lahore High Court in *Emperor* v. *Khushal Chand*[53] wherein it was laid down that the offending matter should be published with the knowledge of the pending cause or with the knowledge that the cause was imminent. After the adoption of the Constitution the question whether knowledge of pending proceedings at the time of publication of the offending matter was necessary or not, was considered by the Madhya Bharat High Court in *Sunnulal Badhavallabha* v. *Yeshwant Singh.*[54]

---

50. *Supra* n.10.
51. (1954) All. E.R. 1026.
52. Oswald, *Law of Contempt of Court,* 93 (third edn.).
    He quoted *Metropolitan Music Hall* v. *Lake* (1889) 58. L.J. Ch. 513 and *Foster* v. *Newnes* (1894) *Times* Feb. 5.
53. A.I.R. 1945 Lah. 206. Tests (a) that something has been published which either is clearly intended or atleast is calculated, to prejudice a trial which is pending or (b) that the offending matter was published with the knowledge of the pending cause, or with the knowledge that the cause was imminent (c) that the matter published tended substantially to interfere with the due course of justice or was calculated substantially to create prejudice in the public mind (*Id.* at 207).
54. 52 Cri. L.J. (1951) (Madhya Bharat High Court) 632. In this case an application was made by Sunnulal to commit the editor and the printer of the newspaper "Nav Prabhat" for contempt of court. The petition stated that while the criminal case was pending against the petitioner, the non applicant published a news item in the 'Nav Prabhat' (Publication in Hindi). The headlines suggested that a notorious gang of gamblers had been arrested. The news also suggested that Sunnulal had been keeping a gambling house for nearly ten years. The second paragraph of the news also suggested that some police officers were in league with the gamblers.

In this case the court reiterated the principle laid down by the Lahore High Court in *Emperor* v. *Khushal Chand*[55] and observed:

> Even if the opposite party did not have the knowledge that any case was pending they certainly had the knowledge that the cause was imminent and as they published the offending matter with the knowledge that the cause was imminent they are guilty of contempt.[56]

But the Allahabad High Court in *Rajendrakumar Garg* v. *Shafiq Ahamed Azad*[57] authoritatively laid down that the editor, printer or publisher is to be held liable for contempt only if the publication is made with the knowledge of imminence or pendency of legal proceedings.

After analysing English decisions and opinion expressed by Oswald, Tek Chand and V.G. Ramachandran, Beg J. expressed the view that the finding of complete want of knowledge whether direct or inferential on the part of the opposite parties in the present case was enough to entitle them to a rejection of the contempt application.[58] The court further observed:

> In our opinion, it is not possible to lay down in this regard a rigid, inflexible or invariable rule which should govern all cases of contempt of court in respect of

55. *Supra* n. 26.
56. *Supra* n. 54, p. 634.
57. *Supra* n. 37. The petitioner Sri Rajendra Kumar Garg is a pleader and the opposite parties Syed Shafiq Ahamed Azad and Rashid Ahamed Ghazi are managing editor and editor respectively of the Urdu weekly "Azad". The petitioner in the said application prayed for taking action against the opposite parties in respect of an article published in *Azad* under the Contempt of Courts Act, 1952. At a meeting in which the collector participated, there was a conflict between two groups and that gave way to two criminal cases one under Sec. 107/117 of Criminal Procedure Code and another under sections 88, 342 and 252 of the Indian Penal Code. During the pendency of these cases the offending article appeared in the weekly called *Azad*. The actual words are as follows: "These persons took the law into their own hands and raised their shoes towards the Collector. It is obvious that under these circumstances it was justifiable and necessary to have the arrest of such persons effected because no one can be allowed to take the law in his own hands." Other editorials also followed.
58. *Id.* at 44.

> knowledge. There might be cases in which actual knowledge of pending proceedings might be required before a court considers it desirable to fasten a person with liability for contempt. There might be second category of cases in which the court might consider presumptive knowledge of the alleged contemner enough to be the requirements of the case. There might also cases of third category in which the court might find a person guilty of contempt irrespective of the question of knowledge.[59]

The court elaborately discussed the practical difficulty in ascertaining the existence of pending proceedings. Further the court expressed the possibility of innocent persons being punished, if knowledge is made an irrelevant consideration for contempt proceedings.

The following principles could be deducted from this decision:

1. Incidental reference to the matter in dispute will not amount to contempt of court.
2. Reference should be made to the case which is imminent or pending or of any investigation connected therewith.
3. Knowledge of the case, whether imminent or pending should also be proved to make one guilty of contempt.

So far as knowledge is concerned, it can be knowledge of the contents of the publication or knowledge of the pendency of proceedings. So far as the contents of the publication is concerned, the editor and publisher cannot plead ignorance because of the principle of vicarious liability. But so far as knowledge of the pendency of proceedings is concerned want of knowledge is a good defence.

Justice Tek Chand in *Rao Harnarain Singh Sheoji Singh* v. *Gumani Ram Arya*[60] opined that lack of knowledge of publication is not a good defence in contempt proceedings.

---

59. *Id.* at 41.

60. AIR 1958 Punj. 273 (For facts *see* n. 37 Ch. 5).

Madhya Pradesh High Court in *Padmavathi Devi Bhargava* v. *R.K. Karanjia*[61] modified the law on this branch of contempt and held that knowledge of the pendency of a cause was not the *sine quo non* of the liability of the non-applicants for contempt.[62]

By laying down that knowledge is not a *sine qua non* for contempt proceedings, Naik J. who decided the matter created a new precedent. To hold a person guilty of contempt, who has no knowledge of pending proceedings may virtually amount to an unreasonable restriction on the freedom of the press.

This principle as laid down by Naik J. is in contradiction to the principle and reasoning given by Beg J. in *Rajendra Kumar Garg* v. *Shafiq Ahamed Azad.*[63] Also it is in contradiction to the principle laid down by Tarkeshwarnath J. in *Ram Parikchan Pandey* v. *M.S.M. Sharma.*[64]

It seems that Naik J. misconceived the idea of intention to commit contempt with knowledge of pending proceedings.[65] Though actual intention to commit contempt is immaterial, knowledge of the pendency of proceedings should be made relevant.

According to Naik J. if the matter is published, parties may discontinue the action or compromise it or deter witnesses

61. *Supra* n. 39.
The publication reads as follows: Atleast one of the boys arrested in connection with the rape case was not a stranger to the Bhargava family. He was a friend of Usha Bhargava's youngest sister. The two boys, Maksood, and Latif, were arrested by the police on the basis of a statement by a neighbour who had claimed to have seen the boys around the place of Feb. 3.
62. *Id.* at 67.
63. *Supra* n. 37.
64. *Supra* n. 44. In this case it was accepted that knowledge of pendency or imminence of proceedings is necessary to hold a person liable for contempt. From the facts court inferred that the respondent had knowledge.
65. If the publication of an article in Newspaper, howsoever objective, which the contemners undertook at their own risk while the criminal law had been set in motion, has these results, we do not see how it is an answer to say that they never intended these results or that they had no knowledge that the cause was pending *Supra* n. 39, p. 69.

from coming forward for giving evidence. These are not the considerations for ascertaining whether there is contempt of court or not. By laying down that a person can be held liable for contempt even if the publication is made without the knowledge of the pendency of proceedings, the rights of the press are being unreasonably restricted.

In *State* v. *Kamara Ram Nathiyal*,[66] Allahabad High Court considered the effect of knowledge of pending proceedings to the publication. It was argued that the editor and the publisher of "Jan Yug" could not be held guilty of contempt because they had no knowledge of the pending case. But,

> It is clear from the article published which referred to a case which had been registered and in which a prosecution could be imminent. If the editor and publisher allowed the publication of the impugned article in their paper they are equally guilty of contempt of court.[67]

With a view to protect the innocent editors and publishers it is being specifically provided in Sec. 3[68] of the Contempt of Courts Act, 1971 that innocent publications without knowing

---

66. 1970 Cri. L.J. (Allahabad High Court) 1283.
67. *Id.* at 1285. It is important to note that the Allahabad High Court had not made any finding on the issue of knowledge of pending proceedings.
68. Sec. 3 Innocent publication and distribution of matter is not contempt.
    1. A person shall not be guilty of contempt of court on the ground that he had published (whether by words spoken or written or by signs or by visible representations or otherwise) any matter which interferes or tends to interfere with or obstructs or tends to obstruct the course of justice in connection with any civil or criminal proceedings pending at the time of publication, if at that time he had no reasonable grounds for believing that the proceeding was pending.
    2. Notwithstanding anything to the contrary contained in this Act or any other law for the time being in force the publication of any such matter as is mentioned in sub-section (1) in connection with any civil or criminal proceeding which is not pending at the time of publication shall not be deemed to constitute contempt of court.
    3. A person shall not be guilty of contempt on the ground that he has distributed a publication containing any such matter as is mentioned in sub-section (1) if at the time of distribution he had no reasonable grounds for believing that it contained or was likely to contain any such matter as aforesaid. (Proviso and explanation not reproduced)

the pendency of proceedings will not amount to contempt of court.

This provision contained in Sec. 3 is the acceptance of the principle of law laid down by the Allahabad High Court in *Rajendra Kumar Garg* v. *Shafiq Ahamed Azad*[69] though it was modified by the Madhya Pradesh High Court in *Smt. Padmavati Devi Bhargav* v. *R.K. Karanjia.*[70] This provision should continue for the protection of the rights of the press. An advocate writing on criminal contempt[71] expressed the view that the impugned publication must be either with the knowledge or belief that the proceedings in respect of which the said publication is made is pending at the point of time or that the said publication must contain any such matter which has a tendency to interfere with the due course of justice. If knowledge or belief as aforesaid is absent, then the publication even if it contains such matters, will not amount to criminal contempt as defined in the statute.[72] He further observed that the court is not to punish any person for violation of its order unless it is proved that the person has got knowledge about the said order while violating the same.[73]

After the passing of the Act, the Bombay High Court considered the scope of exception coming in section 3 and accepted those provisions in *Prabhakar Laxman Mokashi* v. *Sadanand Trimbak Yardi*[74] and laid down the following principle:

> The immunity which has been incorporated in Sec. 3 is limited to a publication by words spoken or written or signs or by visible representations or otherwise. Such a publication can include any matter which interferes or tends to interfere with or obstructs the course of justice in connection with the criminal proceedings pending or not pending at the time of the publication. When they are actually pending a person who wants to take advantage of this exception must prove that he falls within the

69. *Supra* n. 37.
70. *Supra* n. 39.
71. Parthasarathi, "Concept of Criminal Contempt" XIII *Lawyer*, 82 (1981).
72. *Id.* at 83.
73. *Ibid.*
74. 1975 Cri. L.J. (Bombay High Court) 531.

> provisions of sub-section (1) of section 3 described as innocent publication. However, if the proceedings are not pending immunity can be attached only to a publication as laid down in sub-section (1) of section 3 of a matter, the nature of which is also described in sub-section (1).[75]

The same view was expressed by the Supreme Court in *Rachapudi Subba Rao* v. *The Advocate General Andhra Pradesh.*[76]

> Section 3 is in the nature of an exception to those categories of criminal contempt which fall under sub-clause (ii) and to certain categories of criminal contempt which come under sub-clause (iii) of Sec. 2(c), but to that category of contempt which falls under sub-clause (i) of Sec. 2 (c). This is clear from a comparison of the language of Sec. 3(1) with that of Sec. 2(c). The words "interferes or tends to interfere with the course of justice in connection with any proceeding pending" in section 3(1) substantially reiterate the language of sub-clause (ii) of section 2(c). Similarly, the words "interferes or tends to interfere with or obstruct or tends to obstruct" in Sec. 3(i) are a reproduction of the first limb of sub-clause (ii) of section 2(c). The phrase 'the administration of justice in any other manner' used in section 2(c)(iii) has been substituted in section 3(i) by the narrower phrase "the course of justice in connection with any civil or criminal proceeding pending at the time of publication." But there are no words in section 3 which may be referable to that species of criminal contempt which would fall within sub-

---

75. *Id.* at 536.
76. AIR 1981 S.C. 755.

    In this case the appellant filed original suit in the court of subordinate judge and the same was dismissed. When the execution proceedings and applicants stay order were pending, the appellant issued a notice to the additional subordinate judge who decided the suit. This notice was the subject matter of the present contempt proceedings. It contained the following statement: "your honour has intentionally and with bad faith and maliciously disordered the existing oral and documentary evidence with a view to help the plaintiff in O.S. No. 275/72 causing damage and injury to me. Your honour has maintained different standards in the same judgment. Your honour is liable in tort to pay damage for the heavy monetary loss incurred by me and for the injury."

clause (1) of the definition given in section 2(c). Sub-clause (2) of section (3) expressly confines its operation to those categories of contempt, which are referred to in sub-section (1). Section 3(2) therefore is not applicable to that category of contempt which falls under sub-clause (1) of section 2(c) or which is otherwise of a kind different from those mentioned in section 3(1).[77]

4. IMMINENCE OF PROCEEDINGS

Although there is no binding authority directly in point, there is now substantial support for the view that a contempt may be committed even though the proceedings which were prejudiced were not technically pending at the time of publication, provided only that they were imminent.[78] Wills J. *in Parke*[79] observed that the proceedings to be pending merely accentuates the fact, not that the case has begun, but that it is not at an end. Though it is followed in subsequent decisions it created further difficulty by including the term imminent in Sec. 11 of the Administration of Justice Act, 1960.

In India during the pre-independence period it was well settled that to comment on proceedings which were imminent but not yet launched[80] in court with the knowledge of the fact that it is imminent, is as much a contempt as comment on a case actually launched. This view was followed in subsequent decisions also. The Nagpur High Court in *Ratnakar Jha* v. *Krishna Sewak Agarwal*[81] followed the earlier principle and extended the contempt jurisdiction to proceedings which were imminent. The editor and the publisher were held liable for

---

77. *Id.* at 759.
78. C.J. Miller, *Contempt of Court,* 75 (1976).
79. (1903) 2KB. 432.
80. *P.S. Tulajaram Rao* v. *Governor of Reserve Bank of India,* The Madras Law Journal Reports II (1939) 847-848.
81. AIR 1954 Nag. 99. In this case there was a rivalry between the petitioner and K.S. Agarwal. Police registered a case under Sec. 325 of the Indian Penal Code on 3rd October, 1952 and arrested on 9th October and enlarged on bail. Thereafter different articles appeared in the *Zindgi.* Article appeared on 27th October, 1952 which referred to the notorious activities of the petitioner's son, was the subject matter of this petition. On 31st October, 1952 the case against the petitioner under Sec. 325 was challenged. Subsequent publications were also there.

contempt of court since they were fully and intimately appraised of the fact that proceedings under Sec. 325 were imminent against the petitioner.[82] But according to the Orissa High Court,[83] the question whether proceedings are imminent or not is a question of fact. There may be cases, where inspite of the fact that F.I.R has been lodged by the police, proceedings may not be said to be imminent, if the F.I.R. does not disclose the name of the accused person or the police does not find any evidence in support of the occurrence. Each case will depend upon its own facts. The court has not laid down any broad proposition that until a case actually comes before the court and the court takes cognizance either upon a complaint or upon a charge sheet or otherwise, proceedings in contempt cannot be started.[84]

The opinion of the Orissa High Court seems reasonable. Contempt proceedings are expected to protect the administration of justice from unnecessary interference. So before a matter is taken up by the court there is no scope for interference except that of scandalising the court which is a different instance of contempt.

Patna High Court in *Ram Parikchan Pandey* v. *M.S.M. Sharma*[85] though accepted the above proposition laid down the reasonable presumption test. It was held that allegations[86] made against Ram Parikchan Pandey were so serious that it would be reasonable to presume that the District Magistrate was likely to take action against Ram Parikchan Pandey.[87] Hence the proceedings are said to be imminent.

As stated by Chaturvedi J. of Allahabad High Court in *Dwarka Prasad Agarwal* v. *Krishna Chandra*.[88]

> Extending the rule for the punishment of contempt of court to cases which are imminent would unduly hamper with the freedom of speech of the citizen. In many cases

82. *Id.* at 102.
83. *State* v. *Editor Printer and Publisher Matrubhumi* 1955 Cri. L.J. (Orissa High Court) 547.
84. *Id.* at 555.
85. *Supra* n. 44.
86. The allegations made included cheating, extortion and kidnapping.
87. *Supra* n. 44, p. 224.
88. *Supra* n. 35.

> the citizen will have to take the risk of the court coming to the conclusion that the case had become imminent, when he himself thought that it was not so imminent.[89]

Though Allahabad High Court has thus correctly applied the law, it goes against that of Nagpur High Court.[90] Nagpur High Court held the contemner liable because he is being informed of the imminence of the proceeding. But according to Patna High Court, as expressed in *Ram Parikchan Pandey's*[91] case though the contemner was not actually informed of the allegation, the allegation was so serious that the contemner would have presumed that the matter would be taken up by the judiciary. In these two cases the facts were such that the court viewed them as if they were pending.

It is worth mentioning that the Contempt of Courts Act, 1971 does not make any mention of imminent proceedings. So a publication, in order to constitute contempt of court should be made during the pendency of proceedings. Actual pendency of proceedings should be established. Imminence of proceedings should not be a justification for punishing a person for contempt of court.

5. CONCLUSION

Contempt jurisdiction of the judiciary has to be used for the maintenance of the dignity of the judiciary and also for safeguarding the proceedings of the court from outside interference. So any kind of interference with the administration of justice has to be strictly dealt with.

For applying the contempt jurisdiction on the basis of interference the proceedings should be pending. There is no uniformity of opinion among the different High Courts as to when a proceeding be said to be pending. The problem was settled by the explanation to Sec. 3 of the Contempt of Courts Act, 1971 which, more or less has given statutory recognition to the opinion given by the Madhya Pradesh High Court in *Smt. Padmavathi Devi Bhargava* v. *R.K. Karanjia*.[92]

89. *Id.* at 605.
90. *Ratnakar Jha* v. *Sewak Agarwal*, AIR 1954 Nag. 99.
91. *Supra* n. 44.
92. *Supra* n. 39.

Notwithstanding an earlier decision to the contrary[93] the judicial opinion has been settled in favour of the principle that the knowledge of pending proceedings is not a *sine qua non* for contempt by interference with the course of justice.[94]

But with a view to protect innocent editors and publishers, it is provided in Sec. 3 of the Act that innocent publication and distribution of matters is not contempt. This provision should continue for the better protection of the freedom of the press.

It has been clearly laid down that publication of proceedings which were imminent but not yet launched in court is as much a contempt as comment on a case actually launched. But the Allahabad High Court in *Dwarka Prasad Agarwal* v. *Krishna Chandra*[95] held that extending the rule for the punishment of contempt of court to cases which are imminent would unduly hamper the freedom of speech of the citizen. In this case and also in *Ram Parikchan Pandey's*[96] case the court viewed that the proceedings were pending and therefore held the respondents guilty of contempt.

The Act does not make any mention of the imminence of the proceedings. It is also difficult to ascertain when a proceeding can be said to be imminent. So liability for contempt should depend upon the actual pendency of proceedings and not on the imminence of proceedings.

---

93. *Supra* n. 37.
94. *Supra* n. 60, *Supra* n. 39.
95. *Supra* n. 35.
96. *Supra* n. 44.

5

Freedom of the Press and Contempt of Court: General Principles

1. INTRODUCTION

Free press[1] is the hallmark of a democratic society. It has to play a vital role in safeguarding the rights and liberties of people. This freedom is based on thinking, writing, printing and publishing with free access to information. The press has the same right as an ordinary citizen of the country. Though freedom of speech and expression include freedom of the press also,[2] it has no special privileges, which are enjoyed by the legislature[3] or the head of the state.[4]

In a democracy every citizen has the right to criticise the government as most of its actions are subject to public scrutiny. The press has a right to publish such criticism and its interests and privileges are protected within certain limits by various laws[5] passed by the legislature.

1. According to R.C.S. Sarkar, freedom of the press has three important elements. They are, freedom of publication, freedom of circulation and freedom of access to all sources of information. R.C.S. Sarkar, *The Press in India,* 35 (1984).
2. *Romesh Thappar* v. *State of Madras*—AIR 1950 S.C. 124; *Brij Bhushan* v. *State of Delhi,* AIR 1950 S.C. 129.
3. Art. 105 of the Constitution guarantees special privileges to Parliament and its Members, which include freedom of speech, immunity from legal proceedings for anything said in Parliament and also for the publication made under the authority of Parliament. Corresponding provision with regard to State Legislature is contained in Art. 194.
4. Art. 59, Art. 158, and second schedule of the Constitution guarantee certain privileges to the President of India and the Governor of a State.
5. For *e.g.* The Press and Registration of Books Act, 1867 deals with the procedural formalities and regulatory conditions to be complied with

But the press, as a powerful medium with tremendous influence over the public has the moral responsibility to abide by rules and regulations and also by its own ethical considerations. Though newspapers are the mirrors of the times, they can also foster and feed emotions and create complacent fictions and blind spots. The vital role of the press in the administration of justice has been emphasised by Lord Denning in the following words:

> It (press) is the watch dog to see that every trial is conducted fairly, openly and above board. Any misconduct in trial is sure to receive notice in the press and subsequent condemnation by public opinion. The press itself is liable to make mistakes. The watch dog may sometimes break loose and have to be punished for misbehaviour.[6]

The Press Council[7] is the competent authority to deal with the professional misconduct of the press. But the Press Council

---

by the press. It provides for the regulation of newspapers, for the preservation of copies of books and newspapers in India and for the registration of such books and newspapers. Violation of procedural formalities is made punishable.

The Copyright Act, 1957 provides certain safeguards to the author, to print, publish and sell copies of an original work. Anyone violating the provision is made punishable. This Act creates further statutory right of property in respect of a man's original literary, dramatic musical and other artistic works.

The Indian Telegraph Act, 1885 empowers the authorities to intercept, detain or withhold any telegraphic message which is harmful to the society.

The Indian Post Office Act, 1898 authorises the authorities to detain any newspaper or postal article if they find that the article contained any seditious matter. The Working Journalists and other Newspaper Employees (Conditions of Service and Miscellaneous Provisions) Act, 1955 provide for the payment of minimum wage to the workers. The Press Council Act, 1978 provides for the composition and functions of the Press Council. The main object of the Council is to preserve the freedom of the press and to maintain and improve the standards of newspapers and news agencies in India. One of the important tasks of the Council is to build up a code of conduct for newspapers, news agencies and journalists in accordance with high professional standards.

6. Lord Denning, *Road to Justice*, 78 (1955).
7. Press Council is constituted under the provisions of the Press Council Act, 1978, which is based on the report filed by the Press Laws Enquiry Committee, 1948.

Act, 1978 itself provided that in case such misconduct is under the consideration of the judiciary, the Council shall not express any opinion until such proceedings have terminated.[8] But the possibility of a publication coming in conflict with the judicial act cannot be avoided. So in case of conflict between journalistic ethics and legal obligations judiciary is expected to maintain a proper balance between the rights and the privileges of the press and the rights of the judiciary.

Articles or news published cannot be impugned as offending the law of contempt as long as the publication does not attack the integrity, honesty, good faith or the competency of a judge. The editors and reporters should not use the press as a sort of tribunal for trial by newspaper of a pending case. They should not report matters in such a way as to create sympathy in favour of one party.

Though justice is subject to public scrutiny, there should be some limits. Once it exceeds the limit of fair criticism, it may affect the dignity of the judiciary and weaken the judicial system itself. So for protecting the dignity of the judiciary, immunity has to be given to the judges.[9] Because independence of the country is always measured by the strength of its judiciary.

For protecting the dignity of the judiciary, Supreme Court and High Courts are made as courts of record by virtue of Art. 129[10] and 215[11] of the Constitution respectively. Though such wide power is vested in the Supreme Court and the High Courts, such power has to be sparingly used.

---

8. Sec. 14 (3) of the Press Council Act reads: "Nothing in Sub-section (1) shall be deemed to empower the council to hold an enquiry into any matter in respect of which any proceeding is pending in a court of law."
9. V.G. Ramachandran, 'Judicial Immunity' AIR 1951 (Jnl.) 70. *See* also, 'Contempt by the Press' AIR 1950 (Jnl.), 36, where the learned author lists out certain do's and don'ts for the press.
10. Art. 129. The Supreme Court shall be a court of record and shall have all the powers of such court including the power to punish for contempt of itself.
11. Art. 215. Every High Court shall be a court of record and shall have all the powers of such a court including the power to punish for contempt of itself.

The necessity to maintain a free press and an independent judiciary side by side without affecting either, has been emphasized by the Sanyal Committee[12] in the following words:

> A free press and an independent judiciary are absolutely necessary in a free society. Freedom of the press, however, is not an end in itself but a means to an end and the scope and nature of the constitutional protection of freedom of speech should be viewed in this light. The independence of the judiciary is no less a means to an end in a free society and the proper functioning of an independent judiciary puts the freedom of the press in its proper perspective. A judiciary cannot function properly, if what the press does is calculated to disturb the judicial judgment in its duty and capacity to act solely on the basis of what is put before.[13]

Free press, though at liberty to publish a true matter, in case such publication interferes with the administration of justice, judiciary used to resort to the weapon of contempt jurisdiction. To what extent judiciary has permitted the claim of true reporting and also the claim of public interest are discussed in this chapter.

2. TRUE REPORTING

(a) True report of judicial proceedings

There is undoubtedly a great responsibility cast upon the journalists to put in black and white only truth which they

---

12. *Committee on Contempt of Courts* (1963). This committee was constituted in the year 1961 under the Chairmanship of Shri H.N. Sanyal the Additional Solicitor General of India. The other members were Dr. W.S. Barlingay, Member of Parliament, Sri R. Rajagopal, Special Secretary and Member, Law Commission, Legislature Department, Ministry of Law; Sri H.O. Dega, Joint Secretary and Legal Advisor, Department of Legal Affairs, Ministry of Law.

    This committee was required : (i) to examine the law relating to contempt of court generally and in particular the law relating to the procedure for the punishment thereof; (ii) to suggest amendments therein with a view, to clarifying and reforming the law wherever necessary; and (iii) to make recommendations for the codification of the law in the light of the examination made. The committee submitted its report in 1963.

13. *Report of the Committee on Contempt of Court*, 34 (1963).

gather from even closed and hidden corners because it creates public opinion.[14] In *Shri Wasudeoraoji Sheorey* v. *A.D. Mani, Managing Editor Hitavada*[15] Madholkar J. traced the origin of this branch of law starting from *Stockdale* v. *Hansard*[16] followed by *Davison* v. *Duncan*[17] and held publication of a true and accurate report without malice is not contempt.[18]

In *Wasudeoraoji Sheorey* v. *A.D. Mani, Managing Editor Hitavada*[19] the publication was alleged to be contempt of court because, (i) it is not a complete report and it omits to reproduce all that happened, (ii) it tends to create an impression that the accused has no case for grant of exemption as claimed, and (iii) it gives emphatic publicity to libelous statements about the accused and thereby tends to create prejudice in the minds of the public as well. It was argued on behalf of the alleged

14. *State of U.P.* v. *Narendra Pal Singh* 1990 Cri. L.J. (Allahabad High Court) 1637, 1640. Narendra Pal Singh Chauhan, proprietor, editor and publisher of local weekly newspaper 'Ham Raj Express' published an editorial which was the subject matter of the contempt petition. Translated version of the editorial was as follows: The Additional District and Sessions Judge is sliding on the path of corruption (1) Law is sold there, (2) Law is torn into pieces there, (3) Law is always shelved there. The Additional District and Sessions Judge Sri X had taken lakhs of rupees as bribe and has thereby undermined the prestige of law....
15. 52 Cri. L.J. 1951 (Nagpur High Court) 452.
16. 3 States trials (N.S.) 723.
17. (1857) L.J.Q.B., 104.
18. *Supra* n. 15, p. 455.
19. *Supra* n. 15. Contempt petition arose in this case because of the publication made in "Hitavada" on 21-02-1950 during the pendency of a case. Shri G.D. Karkare the editor of a weekly newspaper called 'News Leader' presented a complaint before the First Class Magistrate, Nagpur against the applicant Shri W.G. Sheorey who is the Managing Editor of a daily newspaper called 'Nagpur Times'. In that complaint Shri Karkare has accused Sheorey of the commission of offences under sections 500 and 504 of the Indian Penal Code by publishing in the *Nagpur Times* of an article which according to him besides being defamatory was insulting and likely to cause breach of the public peace. In the issue of 'Hitavada' dated 22-02-1950 a column appeared concerning the complaint instituted by Shri Karkare. It mentioned the names of the accused, provisions of Indian Penal Code and also made a reference to the article which was under consideration, and certain statements made by Karkare in the complaint and those made in the court.

contemner that the courts are public institutions and it is the duty and responsibility of the press to keep the public truly, accurately and fairly informed of the proceedings before the courts. The court accepted the contention partially and held:

> ...that publication in newspapers of reports of proceedings before a court of law must be true and accurate and that it must be without malice.... The privilege quite obviously does not extend to the publication of false opinion on the facts of the case which may operate prejudicially to a party to the proceedings before the court. It would, therefore, seem that the right of a newspaper even to publish a faithful account of the proceedings before a court of law is subject to the condition that the publication does not tend to prejudice materially the fair trial of a case before a court of law.[20]

It was laid down by the Punjab High Court in *Express Newspapers* v. *M/s. Raisina Publications Pvt. Ltd.*[21] that, publication of a correct summary of the plaint did not tend to create such prejudice in the public mind against the defendants as to cause substantial interference with the course of justice.[22] The court further stated that the proceedings for contempt are not intended to satisfy the grudge of a private party but to ensure fair trial and to preserve the dignity of the court.

In *Brig. E.T. Sen (Retd.)* v. *Edatata Narayanan*[23] a question

---

20. *Id.* at 455.
21. AIR 1964 Punj. 428. In this case, the English daily 'Patriot' for which the respondents were editors and publishers published a report by its staff reporter under the heading "Cartoonist sues city daily." The report not only mentioned that the petitioner had been served with a notice issued by the subordinate judge but also gave a summary of the plaint in which Mr. Envar Ahmed a well-known cartoonist claimed Rs. 2,50,000/- as damages for breach of contract. This publication of the plaint was the subject matter of the contempt petition as it claimed that it interfered with the fair trial of the suit pending before the court of subordinate judge.
22. *Id.* at 432.
23. AIR 1969 Del. 201. E.T. Sen was a retired Brigadier in the Indian Army and was serving as Resident Manager of Messers Ceat Tyres. He filed an original complaint under Ss. 500, 501 and 502 of the Indian Penal Code against D.P. Sinha for publishing certain pamphlet. It was alleged

arose as to whether publication of a letter presented in connection with the case will amount to contempt of court or whether it will be protected on the principle of publication of true report of judicial proceedings. The court observed that the reporter and publisher might well have thought that the letter had been duly admitted in evidence though in fact it was only marked for identification and not admitted in evidence or proved.[24] In this case the court gave only a warning, giving the respondents the benefit of doubt. Nevertheless the court made it clear that in future it would take a more serious view of such publications and the ignorance of the law or inability of the legal advisers to properly advise their clients, would not be considered a mitigating circumstance.[25]

Though the Contempt of Courts Act, 1971 provided for certain defences,[26] it had not accepted true reporting but fair and accurate report of judicial proceedings.[27] So even if the person making the comment honestly believes it to be true still it is a contempt of court if he prejudices the truth before it is ascertained in the proceedings.[28] Kerala High Court in *Advocate General* v. *Abraham George*[29] expressed the view that the court is not concerned with the defence if any as to the truth of the allegations made though, the Advocate General asserted that it is well settled that if a publication about the court or the judges would scandalise the court and is for that reason objectionable, it is not sufficient to say that the

---

that there was a persistent one-sided press campaign by the patriot against the cause of the petitioner with a view to poison the minds of the public and thereby hamper the course of justice. He referred to the different issues of the patriot and to certain letters presented in the court.

24. *Id.* at 212.
25. *Id.* at 213.
26. Sections 3 to 8 of the Contempt of Courts Act, 1971 deal with the defences.
27. Sec. 4: Fair and accurate report of judicial proceedings not contempt. Subject to the provisions contained in section 7 a person shall not be guilty of contempt of court for publishing a fair and accurate report of a judicial proceeding or any stage thereof.
28. *Y.V. Hanumantha* v. *K.R. Pattabhiraman*, AIR 1975 A.P. 30, 31.
29. 1976, Cri. L.J. (Kerala High Court) 158.

alleged contemner honestly believed in the truth of his statements.[30]

Delhi High Court in *Subhash Chand* v. *S.M. Aggarwal*[31] considered the defence of fair and accurate report of judicial proceedings and held that the words judicial proceeding appearing in the section means day to day proceedings of the court. Assuming though not granting that it is capable of wider construction it only permits publication of fair and accurate report of a judicial proceeding.[32]

But the Madhya Pradesh High Court in *D.K. Paliwal* v. *Editor Dainik Bhaskar News Paper*[33] accepted true reporting as a defence. The question considered was the report published by the *Dainik Bhaskar* News Paper regarding a warrant issued by the Railway Magistrate. The court observed:

> The publication in a newspaper of report of proceedings before a court of law must be true and accurate and that it must be without malice.... It would therefore seem that the right of a newspaper even to publish a faithful account of the proceedings before the court of law is subject to the condition that the publication does not tend to prejudice materially the fair trial of a case before a court of law.[34]

(b) True report of matters during the pendency of judicial proceedings

Some High Courts[35] and the Supreme Court[36] made a distinction between true report of judicial proceedings and

30. *Id.* at 159.
31. 1984 Cri. L.J. (Delhi High Court) 481. In this case, the judge after giving a death sentence held press interview and in that he substantiated his decision.
32. *Id.* at 488.
33. 1994 Cri. L.J. (Madhya Pradesh High Court) 2933.
34. *Id.* at 2946.
35. Punjab High Court in *Rao Harnarain Singh Sheoji Singh* v. *Gumani Ram Arya* AIR 1958 Punj. 273; *Leo Roy Frey* v. *R. Prasad* AIR 1958 Punj. 377; Allahabad High Court in *G.N. Verma* v. *Har Govind Dayal* AIR 1975 All. 52; Bombay High Court in *V.M. Kanade* v. *Madhav Gadkari*. 1990 Cri. L.J. (Bombay High Court, 190; Patna High Court in *Kedar Prasad Sinha* v. *State of Bihar* AIR 1969 Pat. 140.
36. Supreme Court in *Sambu Nath Jha* v. *Kedar Prasad Sinha* AIR 1972 S.C. 1515.

true report of matters during the pendency of judicial proceedings. Justice Tek Chand who heard, *Rao Harnarain Singh Sheoji Singh* v. *Gumani Ram Arya*[37] held that truth or falsity of the facts or comments published was immaterial and that good faith or malice of the author was an equally irrelevant consideration.[38] The court observed:

> Any publication, which has a tendency to foil or thwart a fair and impartial trial, or any conduct, which in any manner prejudices or prevents judicial investigation, whether by intimidation of or by reflection on the court, counsel, parties or witnesses, in respect of a pending cause, constitute contempt of court.[39]

So also in *Leo Roy Frey* v. *R. Prasad*[40] it was held that true and impartial statements of news and acts were not available as a defence to the respondent. But the court observed:

> Although a technical contempt may be said to have been committed by the newspapers the articles themselves read as a whole justify me in holding that the respondents did not intend to prejudice the fair trial of the case. They merely published certain extracts from the order of the collector and gave certain facts which could enable the public to understand the conclusion at which the collector

---

37. AIR 1958 Punj. 273. In this case during the pendency of proceedings under Sections 302, 201 and 376 of the Indian Penal Code, the respondents the editor, printer and publisher of a newspaper 'Mewat' published an article commenting on the incident. The publications which were the subject matter of contempt included different statements including that of an eyewitness under Section 164 of Criminal Procedure Code. This statement contained the detailed account of what took place at the house of Rao Har Narain Singh on the night of occurrence.
38. *Id.* at 282.
39. *Id.* at 278.
40. AIR 1958 Punj. 377. The petitioners in this case were charged under the Sea Customs Act and Foreign Exchange Regulation Act for trying to smuggle Indian currency out of the country. The Additional District Magistrate before whom the petitioner were produced, released them on bail and the case was pending. But in the meantime the collector of customs under his powers, imposed a penalty of Rs. 25 Lakhs and the copy of the order was released to the press. 'Stateman' published the news and the same was the subject of contempt proceedings.

> had arrived. If the respondents were at liberty to publish what the collector had said, namely that the offence was the result of a most deliberate and calculated conspiracy to smuggle a huge sum of money out of the country, anything else that was stated by them of their own accord pales into insignificance.[41]

Here the opinion expressed by the court indicates that the court was prepared to accept the defence of true reporting, though the court justified the publication on the ground of lack of intention.

The Patna High Court in *Kedar Prasad Sinha* v. *State of Bihar*[42] held that publication of a true matter will amount to contempt of court if it prejudiced mankind against the petitioners in a pending case.[43] It was observed:

> The mere fact that it was published in the official gazette is no justification for the publication made by respondents 21 and 22 in their newspaper. These two respondents cannot be heard to say that because some wrongful act was committed by the officers responsible for the publication in the official gazette, they were also free to commit similar wrongful act.[44]

---

41. *Id.* at 383.
42. AIR 1969 Pat.140: Petitioner along with others was prosecuted for rioting. But subsequently the Assistant Public Prosecutor filed a petition for withdrawal. The court declined to grant revision application, filed before the High Court. It was pending before the court. During the pendency of the aforesaid criminal revisions certain matter was published in the official gazette known as the Bihar Gazette in its extra-ordinary issue dated 12th March, 1968 and the same was published in the daily newspaper of Patna known as the 'Search Light' in its issue dated 14th March, 1968. That was the subject matter of the contempt petition. The publication was as follows withdrawal of case against K.P. Sinha, Sri Kedar Prasad Sinha and Sri Arjun Pandey.... Law Secretary recommended against withdrawal of prosecution.... Sri Habibur Rahman however ignored the advice of District Magistrate as well as the Law Secretary and ordered the withdrawal of the case. Sri Habibur Rahman thus by misuse of his official position and power unnecessarily interfered with the administration of justice in a serious case of rioting and murder.
43. *Id.* at 142.
44. *Id.* at 147.

If the principle laid down by the Punjab High Court in *Leo Roy Frey* v. *R. Prasad*[45] is followed, 'Search Light' cannot be held guilty of contempt because it published only the official statement (that which was published in the official gazette). But the Patna High Court was reluctant to admit truth as a defence for contempt proceedings. But when the matter was taken in appeal to the Supreme Court in *Sambhu Nath Jah* v. *Kedar Prasad Sinha*[46] the Supreme Court set aside the judgment of the High Court and held that performance of a statutory requirement should not attract the liability under the Contempt of Courts Act. Sec. 3(1)[47] of the Commissions of Inquiry Act, 1952 makes it mandatory that the notification appointing commission of inquiry should be published in the official gazette.

---

45. *Supra* n. 40.
46. AIR 1972 S.C. 1515.
47. Sec. 3 of the Commissions of Inquiry Act, 1952 reads:
    (1) The appropriate government may if it is of opinion that it is necessary so to do and shall if a resolution in that behalf is passed by the House of the People as the case may be, the Legislative Assembly of the State, by notification in the Official Gazette appoint a Commission of Inquiry for the purpose of making an inquiry into any definite matter of public importance and performing such functions and within such time as may be specified in the notification and the commission so appointed shall make the inquiry and perform the functions accordingly.
    Provided that where any such commission has been appointed to inquire into any matter:
    (a) by the Central Government, no State Government shall except with the approval of the Central Government appoint another commission to inquire into the same matter for so long as the commission appointed by the Central Government is functioning;
    (b) by the State Government, the Central Government shall not appoint another commission to inquire into the same matter for so long as the commission appointed by the State Government is functioning unless the Central Government is of opinion that the scope of the inquiry should be extended to two or more States.
    (2) The commission may consist of one or more members appointed by the appropriate Government and where the commission consists of more than one member one of them may be appointed as the Chairman thereof.

Though the Supreme Court indirectly admitted that publication of true report will not amount to contempt of court, it has not made any finding as to whether true reporting of matter will amount to contempt of court or not.

Allahabad High Court in *G.N. Verma* v. *Hargovind Dayal*[48] held the alleged contemner guilty of contempt of court, though there was only true reporting. In this case accusation against the printer and publisher of 'Northern India Patrika' was that he printed and published a portion of the resolution passed by the Action Committee of the Avadh Bar which contained disparaging remarks about the honourable Chief Justice.[49] This news item was nothing but a news item supplied by the news agency namely the Press Trust of India. Though it is a true report, court has not made any finding on this issue, but held that:

> The person who gives publicity to a scandalising attack on a judge or court is as much guilty of criminal contempt as the person who makes the attack.[50]

The matter was taken in appeal to the Supreme Court in *Hargovind Dayal Srivastava* v. *G.N. Verma*.[51] But the Supreme Court also has not made any finding on true reporting.

The latest attempt to import true reporting as a defence for contempt proceedings was made in *V.M. Kanade* v. *Madhav Gadkari*.[52] It was argued on behalf of the alleged contemner

48. AIR 1975 All. 52. The subject matter for consideration was the resolution passed by the Avadh Bar Association. It made certain remarks about the Chief Justice of Allahabad High Court.
49. One portion of the news published in *National Herald* was as follows: "It also said that the Chief Justice had acted in a partisan manner while exercising his powers under Cl. 14 of the U.P. High Courts (Amalgamation) Order, 1948, presumably influenced by or under the pressure of the Allahabad Bar."
50. *Id.* at 65.
51. AIR 1977, S.C., 1334.
52. 1990, Cri. L.J. (Bombay High Court) 190. Contemners one and two were the editor and owner of the Marathi Newspaper called 'Lok Satta.' It published an article with the heading 'who will stop the downfall of the High Court.' A portion of the article reads as follows:

    Good judges and advocates are immensely bothered by the chaos that has been created by a lady advocate in the High Court by her

that if the law of contempt seeks to punish the utterance of truth because it points out a case of judicial aberration then that law will have to be declared void as being unreasonable restriction on the fundamental right of freedom of expression guaranteed by the Constitution. But the argument was negatived by the Bombay High Court[53] and held:

> Looking to the nature of the proceedings for contempt of court and the underlying idea of the contempt power and also the mischief which this power is supposed to prevent, we are of the opinion that the truth of the allegations, which the contemner says he can prove cannot be put up as a defence in a charge for contempt of court.[54]

The learned Judge further observed:

> ...effective functioning of the judiciary rests upon the public acceptance of its independence and integrity. It is this that will be seriously damaged if truth is allowed to be pleaded and examined as a defence to a charge of contempt of court.[55]

So the court refused to accept truth as a defence for contempt proceedings.[56]

---

seductive weapon. One advocate was conducting a case. The judge gave the judgment in his favour as it was justified. The opposite party decided to rectify their mistake. The party approached the lady advocate. Surprisingly they managed to bring the case for revision before the same judge. The judge who gave the first judgment passed just the opposite judgment....

53. True reporting is not mentioned as a defence in any provision of the Contempt of Courts Act, 1971. But Section 8 safeguards other defences not mentioned in the Act. Sec. 8, reads:

    Nothing contained in this Act shall be constructed as implying that any other defence which would have been a valid defence in any proceedings for contempt of court has ceased to be available merely by reason of the provisions of this Act.
54. *Supra* n. 52, p. 199.
55. *Id.* at 200.
56. According to Rajeev Dhavan an invisible fiction is maintained that judges are incorruptible. A public examination of the truth of any allegation may give rise to a public spectacle which will only further perpetrate the damage caused by the initial publication even if the allegations are ultimately proved to be false. Rajeev Dhavan, *Contempt of Court and the Press* 166, 167 (1982).

A well-known Indian Lawyer is of the view that truth should be accepted as a good defence. He stated:

> The doctrine that truth is no defence clearly inhibits press freedom and journalistic activity. The press would hesitate when it ought to make comments in the public interest. A freedom as cherished as the freedom of the press cannot be made dependent upon the over sensitivities of judges.[57]

It has been suggested that by an amendment in the Contempt of Courts Act, 1971 truth may be allowed to be pleaded as a defence.[58]

It is an unwarranted and unnecessary fear that if truth is permitted as a defence it will degrade the prestige and the dignity of the court. But on the other hand it will help the public to know the truth of the matter and justify the court in punishing a person who made unwanted allegations. If corrupt judicial officers are protected under the veil of contempt proceedings where truth of the matter is not permitted to be alleged and proved, that will amount to harbouring an offender which in course of time would degrade the institution itself.

On an analogy of reporting of fair and accurate judicial proceedings *bona fide* and faithful reporting of true matters should also be permitted and truth of the matter should be made as a good defence.

3. PUBLIC INTEREST

Contentions based on public interest and public welfare have not also been recognised by the judiciary.

In *Sunnulal Badha Vallabha* v. *Yeshwant Singh*[59] Madhya

---

57. Soli, J. Sorabjee, "Truth and Law of Contempt" 1985, *Supreme Court Weekly Reporter II* (Jnl.) 17.

58. "Now with the passing of the time the judicial office has lost its sense of royalty. It is now considered to be merely a post for earning bread and butter. Should we expect the same old standard from these earthly men with feet of clay as well ? Cannot the society be given a right to criticise the judicial functionary of today who departs from the path of truth ? If a criticism is based upon the basis of true facts, why the critic be penalised ?" 1983 *Allahabad Law Journal* (Jnl.) 45.

59. 52 Cri. L.J. (1951) (Madhya Bharat High Court) 632 (for facts *see* n. 54 Ch. 4).

Bharat High Court clearly laid down that public interest, public welfare and good intention need not be looked into for ascertaining whether a publication amount to contempt of court or not. But what is to be looked into is whether the publication interferes with the due and proper course of administration of justice.

Orissa High Court also considered the contention based on public interest in *State* v. *Editors Printers and Publishers of the Newspapers, Matrubhumi and Krushak*[60] and held that public interest and public welfare cannot be a good defence for contempt petitions.

Subsequent attempt to induct public interest as a defence to contempt of court proceedings was made in *Asgharali* v. *Motilal Dave.*[61] The argument based on public interest has not been accepted by the court because under the pretext of public interest or public welfare no one can interfere with the due course of justice.

So also in *Brig. E.T. Sen (Retd.)* v. *Edatata Narayanan*[62] the contention based on public interest and public welfare has been negatived by the Delhi High Court:

---

60. AIR 1954 Ori. 149. In this case during the pendency of two criminal cases a series of articles were published in the newspapers "Matrubhumi" and "Krushak" which were alleged to have tendency to interfere with the fair trial of those cases. Material portion of one article was as follows: It is a matter of great surprise that Bijayananda Patnaik and others are not yet arrested. These are the charges against them that they have opened false fraudulent company, arranged permits for flour, cycle, yarn, iron and other articles of daily use worth many lakhs and received a huge amount through black-marketing. It is however understood that no scent of the matter named Bijayananda Patnaik and Co. is ever known to the Income Tax Department. All their fraudulent attempts are thoroughly known to the government of India....
61. 1966 Cri. L.J. (Madhya Pradesh High Court) 214. In this case one Radha was alleged to have been kidnapped by Ramsingh Chowkidar and Asgharali. Charges were framed against the persons under sections 363, 366 and 368 of the Indian Penal Code. During the pendency of the investigation different articles were published in Gajan Ghosh for which the non-applicants Motilal Dave and Ishwarlal Paliwal were the printer and the editor. The article ended by an appeal to the police Superintendent to arrest immediately Asgharali and thus save himself and police department from condemnation.
62. *Supra* n. 23.

> The submission that the public has a right to be appraised of all that happens in the open court and that the respondents having merely answered to the rightful demand of the public by publishing the material in question, contempt of court cannot, as a matter of law, be held to be committed, has merely to be stated to be rejected. No such alleged right of the public and no such alleged obligation on the part of the respondents can override the law of contempt of court without which effective and pure administration of justice seems to us to be inconceivable in a set up like ours.[63]

Though the judiciary as well as the press exist for the benefit of the public, the press should not be permitted to put up the plea of public interest or public welfare when a publication interferes with the administration of justice. More so because we cannot, precisely state what constitutes public interest or public welfare. The Contempt of Courts Act, 1971, has also not recognized any defence as public interest or public welfare.

4. CONCLUSION

Press though competent to publish any matter subject to the ethics of journalism, should not use it for degrading others especially the judiciary. So restrictions have been imposed when reporting judicial matters. Press has the right to publish true matters. But when it relates to judicial proceedings and reporting of matters during the pendency of judicial proceedings, judiciary in general has accepted the right to make fair report of judicial proceedings provided it is a faithful account and made without any malice. In the case of reporting of matters during the pendency of judicial proceedings, judiciary has adopted the view that even truthfulness of the report is not a defence, if the statement had the tendency to prejudice fair trial. The courts refuse to accept truth as a defence for contempt proceedings because, if truth is allowed to be pleaded and examined as a defence it will seriously affect the independence and integrity of the judiciary.

But in certain contexts the truth of the matter can be permitted as a defence. On the analogy of reporting fair and

63. *Id.* at 211.

accurate judicial proceedings, *bona fide* and faithful reporting of true matters, though the matter is pending in the court, should be permitted and truth of the matter can be allowed as a good defence.

Judiciary is very strict in the case of defence of public interest also. Repeated attempts to induct public interest have not succeeded. It has been clearly laid down by courts that public interest, public welfare and good intention are not good defences for contempt proceedings. The Contempt of Courts Act, 1971 has also not introduced any such defence. The same position may be allowed to continue for the maintenance of dignity of the judiciary.

6

PREJUDICING FAIR TRIAL

1. INTRODUCTION

The purpose of the contempt jurisdiction is to safeguard the administration of justice from undue interference and verbal attacks from any external agency and thus to ensure free and fair administration of justice. A fair criticism of a judicial act motivated by *bona fide* reasons has always been permitted. But scurrilous attacks on the judge and the judicial act motivated by *mala fides* have always been viewed seriously.

The term prejudice denotes a sort of interference with the course of justice.[1] To prejudice or attempt to prejudice the course of justice is covered by the expression to interfere or tend to interfere with the course of justice.

Prejudicing fair trial as an instance of contempt of court was first recognized by Lord Hardwicke L.C. in *St. James Evening Post*[2] case and was subsequently followed by the English courts[3] and also by the Privy Council.[4]

---

1. B.R. Varma, *The Law of Contempt of Court*, 171 (1986). *See* also *Prabhakar Laxman Mokashi* v. *Sadanand Trimbak* 1975 Cri. L.J. (Bombay High Court) 531, 537.
2. (1742) 2 Atk, 469.

   There are three different sorts of contempt. One kind of contempt is scandalising the court itself. There may likewise be a contempt of this court in abusing the parties who are concerned in causes here. There may also be contempt of court in prejudicing mankind before the cause is heard (*Id.* at 471). It was applied in case of contempt by publication by Wilmot C.J. in *King* v. *Almon* 97 E.R. 94.
3. *In the case of Clement* 106 E.R. 918; *Miller* v. *Knox* 132 E.R. 915; *Re Johnson* (1887) 2 Q.B.D. 68; *Reg.* v. *Grey* (1900) 2 Q.B. 36.
4. *Andre Paul Terence Ambard* v. *Attorney General Trinidad and Tobago* AIR 1936, P.C. 141; *Debi Prasad* v. *Emperor* AIR 1943, P.C. 202.

In India, prejudicing fair trial as an instance of contempt of court, was followed in various decisions.[5] Renkin C.J. in *Anant Lal Singh* v. *Alfred Henry Watson*[6] categorically stated:

> A court's jurisdiction in contempt is not to be invoked unless there is real prejudice which can be regarded as substantial interference with the due course of justice.... This court will not exercise its jurisdiction upon a mere question of propriety where the tendency of the article to do harm is slight and the character and circumstances of the comment is otherwise such that it can properly be ignored.[7]

Lahore High Court also followed the same view in *Emperor* v. *Khushal Chand*:[8]

> That something has been published which either is clearly intended, or at least is calculated to prejudice a trial which is pending...that the matter published tended substantially to interfere with the due course of justice or was calculated substantially to create prejudice in the public mind.[9]

An attempt is made to ascertain how the test of real prejudice or substantial interference has been applied by the judiciary to control the freedom of speech of the individual and that of the press, after the adoption of the Constitution.

2. PREJUDICING FAIR TRIAL—BY THE INDIVIDUAL

(i) Before the Contempt of Courts Act, 1971

Real prejudice or substantial interference is the test laid down by the English courts and followed by the Indian High Courts. In view of the strict attitude maintained by the judiciary in India after the adoption of the Constitution, contempt jurisdiction has been resorted to even where the statement

5. *In the matter of William Taylor* AIR 1918 Cal. 713. *In the matter of Banks and Fenwick* AIR 1918 Cal. 752; *Bengalee case* I.L.R. 10 Cal. 109; *Ananta Lal Singh* v. *Alfred Henry Watson* AIR 1931 Cal. 257; *Emperor* v. *Khushal Chand* AIR 1945 Lah. 206.
6. AIR 1931 Cal. 257.
7. *Id.* at 261.
8. AIR 1945 Lah. 206.
9. *Id.* at 207.

had the tendency to prejudice fair trial. So prejudicing fair trial is analysed under the following heading; *viz.* tendency to prejudice, real prejudice and substantial interference.

(a) *Tendency to prejudice*

The test of tendency to prejudice fair trial has been applied by Calcutta, Allahabad, Orissa, Delhi, Madras, Andhra Pradesh and Bombay High Courts and also by the Supreme Court. The subject matter of the contempt included a letter written by an advocate to the judge, demi-official letters, notice issued by the party and also public speeches. Calcutta High Court considered a letter written by the advocate appearing for one of the parties, to the judge in *In the matter of Sudhir Chandra Ray Choudhuri.*[10] Chakravarthy C.J. who delivered the majority judgment is of the view that private letter written by an advocate to the judge may tend to interfere with the due course of justice in that the communication is calculated to bring the court or particular judge into contempt or lower his authority, which is an indirect interference with the due course of justice.

But Harries C.J. is of the view that the letter could not possibly be said to tend to interfere with the decision of the learned judge because no reference is made in the letter regarding the merits or demerits of the defence.[11] The opinion of Harries C.J. can be said to be correct because no mention is made in the letter about the pending case or the merits of the case. Without such mention it could not be said to interfere with the administration of justice. Even in such cases the court is of the view that the letter has the tendency to interfere with fair trial and would amount to contempt.

Allahabad High Court had occasion to consider the principle of tendency to prejudice fair trial in *Dwarka Prasad Agarwal* v.

10. AIR 1952 Cal. 258. In this case advocate Sudhir Chandra Ray Choudhuri was appearing for the defendant in a rent suit. Mitter, J. who was hearing the matter severely criticised and deprecated the advocate for filing an affidavit supported by a lot of rent receipt. One week later the advocate wrote a letter to the judge which mentioned the family affiliations and friendly relation between the advocate and the judge among other things. This letter was the subject matter of the contempt proceedings.

11. *Id.* at 263.

Krishna Chandra[12] and in *Rex* v. *Mohd. Etizad Rasul Khan*.[13] In the first case though the petition was dismissed on the ground of lack of knowledge of pending proceedings, Chaturvedi J. was of the view that exaggerated version of allegation contained in the police report may amount to contempt of court.[14]

The anxiety of the judge to protect the freedom of speech without interfering with the matters which are *subjudice* could be seen in the following statement:

> It is certainly desirable that people do not publish or resort to any other propaganda concerning matters which are likely to be subjudice; at the same time, regard must be had for the liberty of speech of the citizen. Our Constitution guarantees to the citizen liberty of speech with certain safeguards including safeguard against committing contempt of court. On the one hand, as stated above, it is desirable that the parties or their friends do not indulge in any propaganda, but the difficulty is to what length a court of law should go in stopping this type of propaganda, should all speeches concerning a particular incident be prohibited as soon as the incident has occurred or the prohibition should be imposed at some later stage but before the matter has come to court.[15]

In *Rex* v. *Mohd. Etizad Rasul Khan*[16] the court extended the rule to any conduct which tends to inculcate a belief in the public or any section of it that a particular state of affairs prejudicial to the other party to the litigation in fact exists

12. AIR 1953 All. 600. In this case there was a quarrel at the shop of one Jagadish Prasad and he was arrested and released on bail. Subsequent to the arrest, a resolution was passed in the District Congress Committee and the same was sent to District Magistrate and Superintendent of Police. Moreover, public meetings were organised in which the same matter was the subject matter of speeches.
13. AIR 1953 All. 266. The right of inheritance to late Maharaja of Jahangirabad Ejaz Rasul Khan was the matter in dispute. While the title deed of the plaintiff (will deed) was in dispute the plaintiff personally and through his agent published his title and denied the title of the defendant. He on the basis of the title deed collected rent from the tenants. This action was the subject matter of the contempt proceedings.
14. *Supra* n. 12, p. 605.
15. *Id.* at 601.
16. *Supra* n. 13.

which affairs are in issue between the parties to the cause. Further, it was held that it is contempt to publish any matter which has a tendency to prejudice the public for or against a party before the cause is finally determined.[17] Thus the court held that the act amounted to contempt of court by applying the test of tendency to prejudice fair trial.

When a magistrate is simply forwarding a letter without making comments, the act is said to have no tendency to interfere with the judicial proceedings and will not amount to contempt of court.[18] But a demi-official letter written by a person in authority expressing his opinion on a matter pending before the court of law may have the tendency to interfere in the administration of justice. Thus in *State* v. *Radha Gobinda Das*,[19] the opinion expressed by the Deputy Secretary in the demi-official letter was held to constitute contempt of court, because:

> The letter expressing the opinion of a superior officer of the position of the Deputy Secretary to the Government (enforcement) of Orissa that it is a spectacular case in which a large quantity of clothes was hoarded by the accused by fabricating false account of sale, with the endorsement of the District Magistrate, show this to S.D.M. Sadar for needful; and further containing similar endorsement of the Sub-Divisional Magistrate, when it

---

17. *Id.* at 269.

18. *Rizwan-Ul-Hasan* v. *State of Uttar Pradesh*, AIR 1953 S.C. 185. In this case during the pendency of criminal proceedings under Sec. 145 Criminal Procedure Code an application was moved by one of the parties and the same was supported by a recommendation letter from the Secretary, District Congress Committee. This letter was received by appellant No. 2, the District Magistrate and sent the same to the Sub-Divisional Magistrate in whose court the matter was pending. The Sub-Divisional Magistrate returned it with the remark that a proper complaint should be made in his court. The Magistrate in turn returned the same with the same advice to the party.

19. AIR 1954 Ori. 1. In this case the Deputy Secretary Government of Orissa wrote a demi-official letter to Radha Gobinda Das, District Magistrate. The District Magistrate made an endorsement on the letter to show this to S.D.M. Sadar for necessary action. S.D.M. made further endorsement "To trying magistrate for needful" the letter with the above endorsement was the subject matter of the contempt petition.

reaches the trying magistrate, is bound to embarrass him and has definite tendency of seriously affecting the fair trial of the case.[20]

A contrary view was adopted by the Delhi High Court in *A.N. Jindal* v. *P.L. Chhabra*[21] which also involved a demi-official letter. What the letter written by Shri Chhabra to the learned Sessions Judge purports, broadly speaking, to do is to request the superior court to see and verify as to what is the real situation on the facts and circumstances as disclosed in the letter.[22] Accordingly there is no contumacious conduct on the part of Shri Chhabra, nor could it be said that he tried unduly to interfere with the normal course of judicial process which called for invoking the drastic machinery of proceedings for contempt of court.[23] Though in both the cases, the court applied the test of tendency to interfere with the course of justice, in the former case a demi-official letter was said to constitute contempt because there was suggestion as to the guilt of the accused and in the latter there was no such suggestion.

The Madras High Court, in *E.V. Ramaswami* v. *Jawaharlal Nehru*[24] considered the effect of public speech made by Jawaharlal

20. *Id.* at 4.
21. AIR 1969 Del. 291. In this case certain charges under the Motor Vehicles Act were pending against certain drivers. While so, Chhabra, provincial Transport Controller, Haryana wrote a demi-official letter to the District and Sessions Judge Delhi referring to the pending charges. So the First Class Magistrate Delhi referred the letter to the High Court for taking action under Contempt of Courts Act.
22. *Id.* at 294.
23. *Ibid.*
24. AIR 1958 Mad. 558. In this case E.V. Ramaswamy was facing charges under Sec. 117 of the Indian Penal Code in the court of sessions at Thiruchirappalli. During the pendency of the proceedings Jawaharlal Nehru in his public speech at Thiruchirappalli made certain references to the action of E.V. Ramaswamy for which charges under Sec. 117 was pending. Nehru stated: "but one of the most remarkable and one of the most foolish agitation that I have experienced in India has recently been started in your own state of Madras. This I believe is known as Dravida Kazhagam agitation and the leader of the movement had said something which cannot be forgiven and which cannot be tolerated.... The speech meant an insult to the National flag and Constitution."

Nehru during the pendency of proceedings and dismissed the contempt petition on the ground of lack of knowledge. Further it was held that legitimate criticism on a matter of grave public concern cannot be said to interfere or tend to interfere with the course of justice.[25]

Statements contained in affidavits, petitions and notices have also been considered by the court.

In *Swarnamayi Panigrahi* v. *B. Nayak*[26] the offending passage, contained in a transfer application was held to have the tendency to undermine or impair the integrity and honesty of not only the lower court but also of the High Court. Such tendency or likelihood was sufficient for holding it as contempt.[27]

The Madras High Court in *C. Hari Prasad* v. *Vasantha Pai*[28] held that a threat against the advocate of the opposite party contained in an interlocutory application will not amount to contempt of court because it will not substantially interfere with the course of justice. But a contrary view was expressed by the Andhra Pradesh High Court in *Advocate General Andhra Pradesh* v. *Venkadaru Laxminarayana, Tobacco Merchant,*

---

25. *Id* at 561.
26. AIR 1959 Ori. 89. The present contempt petition arose from an ordinary rent suit between the landlord and the tenant. The alleged contemner made certain allegations in the transfer application about the lower court wherein he stated that he cannot get impartial justice. The offending passage is as follows:

    The lower court openly identified himself with the plaintiff Shrimati Swarnamayi Panigrahi and was so partial to her that no justice or impartial decision can be expected from him.... That the opposite party wields extraordinary influence in the state as she is the wife of Shri Lingaraj Panigrahi, Chief Justice of Orissa High Court. It is being openly talked about that the conclusions are foregone.
27. *Id.* at 93.
28. AIR 1966 Mad. 136. An application was made by a private party for taking action against the respondent an advocate for making certain allegations in the interlocutory application, under Contempt of Courts Act, 1952. It stated: I intend to proceed against you in a court of law in a suit for defamation and also to bring this to the notice of the Madras State Bar Council, unless you unconditionally apologise to me and take steps to have the said paragraph deleted from your client's affidavit within three days from today.

Eluru.[29] In this case the statement was contained in a notice issued by the party to the presiding officer. The notice was said to have the tendency to interfere with the course of justice. The court observed:

> Lawyers cannot claim privilege even when acting on behalf of their clients if the contents of their notices amount to making aspersions of the nature set out above.[30]

The test of tendency to prejudice fair trial had invariably been applied by the judiciary to ascertain the contumacious nature of the statement made by persons.

(b) *Real prejudice*

Though generally the courts applied the test of tendency to prejudice fair trial in exceptional cases certain High Courts[31] and the Supreme Court insisted upon the existence of real prejudice for vesting the liability for contempt.

Before the Himachal Pradesh High Court in *State of Himachal Pradesh* v. *Sri Raghunandan Lal Gupta*[32] it was argued that real prejudice should be established for constituting contempt. But the court held the respondent guilty of contempt because the statement was likely to prejudice fair trial.

So also when comments are made on the truth or falsity of a pending case it will amount to contempt of court, because

---

29. AIR 1968 A.P. 370. The respondent against whom criminal complaint was pending not only impolitely replied to the questions put by the magistrate but also issued Sec. 80 notice. The contents of the notice was the subject matter of the contempt petition. It was stated in the notice: "You are the presiding magistrate of the said court. You did not attend court till 12.40 hrs. That day when our client was saying what he had to say in answer to the question put by the court, you suddenly grew wild...please take notice: that our client is taking appropriate civil action for damages for Rs. 25,000/- against you and also taking criminal action against you for the offence committed by you."
30. *Id.* at 374.
31. Himachal Pradesh, Orissa, Bombay etc.
32. AIR 1954 H.P. 70. In this case during the pendency of cases under sections 302, 194 and 201 of the Indian Penal Code, the respondent made a public speech which was the cause of the contempt petition. The speech was made in Hindi. It was alleged that the utterances made by the respondent have the effect of prejudicing the mind of the court and also that of the general public.

the statement creates an atmosphere of prejudice in which the case has to be heard.[33] When the District Superintendent of Police expressed his personal opinion in his report in pursuance of the direction of the District Magistrate it would prejudice fair trial and would amount to contempt of court,[34] because the opinion in the report will be considered by the court before taking any decision. The general tenor of the report given by the Superintendent of Police was undoubtedly to demonstrate that the orders of the two civil courts are not real. Thus the District Superintendent of Police had overstepped the limits which had the effect of prejudicing fair trial. But a fair reading of the report shows that the District Superintendent of Police had expressed impartial opinion which has no effect of prejudicing fair trial.

To what extent public discussion and public speeches on a matter which is *subjudice* will really prejudice fair trial was considered by the Delhi High Court in *A.K. Sen*[35] and by the Supreme Court in *P.C. Sen.*[36] In *A.K. Sen,*[37] the Delhi High Court expressed the opinion that if the matter was *ex facie* of a judicial nature any expression of opinion about the matter

---

33. *Supra* n. 19, p. 4.
34. *District Magistrate, Bidar* v. *R. Madhava Rao, Bidar,* AIR 1961 Mys.12. In this case there was a property dispute which resulted in a clash between two sections. Proceedings under sections 144, 107 and 117 of Criminal Procedure Code were pending. While so, on the basis of another complaint made by Rama Reddy, the District Magistrate under Sec. 202 of the Criminal Procedure Code directed the District Superintendent of Police to investigate and report. The report, among other things, contained personal opinion of the District Superintendent of police. It stated that as it was impossible for the police to take action against any party for an offence under Sec. 447 of the Indian Penal Code impartial action under Sec. 107 of the Criminal Procedure Code was taken against both the parties to maintain public tranquility. It further stated that Rama Reddy was a habitual instigator of land disputes and was involved in two murder cases.
35. *Digvijaya Narain Singh* v. *A.K. Sen* (1971) ILR Del. 14. In this case A.K. Sen and others were cited for contempt because they discussed the legal and other pros and cons of the famous Congress Party split in 1969, while it was being considered by the Delhi High Court.
36. AIR 1970 S.C. 1821.
37. *Supra* n. 35.

which had to be decided by the court of law would be actionable.[38] But the speech of the respondent in this case was not calculated to obstruct or interfere with the course of justice and the due administration of law.[39] The court further opined that in matters of great public concern, general discussion of the subject should not be stifled by filing a suit. Madras High Court also adopted a similar view in *Jawaharlal Nehru.*[40]

But the Supreme Court adopted a contrary view in *P.C. Sen.*[41] According to the Supreme Court, justifying an ordinance by radio broadcast, the validity of which is under consideration, will interfere with the course of justice and amount to contempt of court.

Justice Shah observed:

> The statements in a broadcast speech by an important dignitary of the state that persons who prepare sweets out of milk in the course of their business are, on the version set up by him, criminals, and the suggestion that the order was issued in the interest of the public, whereas it was the contention of the petitioners that it was done "recklessly, arbitrarily and vindictively and without carring for the consequences, and without considering their duty to the public", are *prima facie* calculated to obstruct the administration of justice, since they are likely to create an atmosphere of prejudice against the petitioners and also to deter other persons having similar claims from approaching the court.[42] But public discussion of a matter of general importance has to be permitted.

---

38. *Supra* n. 35, p. 24.
39. *Id.* at 24.
40. *Supra* n. 24.
41. *In Re P.C. Sen* AIR 1970 S.C. 1821. In this case P.C. Sen, then Chief Minister of West Bengal broadcast a speech in the All India Radio Calcutta Station which justified West Bengal Milk Product Order, 1965 which was under challenge. In his speech he mentioned the object and scope of the ordinance and also stated that the producers of milk would be benefited by the ordinance. He concluded: "This new order will not only be beneficial to the buyers and sellers of milk alone, it will also be of help in solving the milk problem in the whole of West Bengal in the near future."
42. *Id.* at 1827.

(c) *Substantial interference*

The test of substantial interference as laid down by the Privy Council and followed by the Lahore High Court[43] was rarely applied in subsequent cases. *In the matter of Sudhir Chandra Ray Choudhuri an Attorney,*[44] the Calcutta High Court viewed that a private letter of an advocate deprecating something which happened in the court would amount to substantial interference with the course of justice and would amount to contempt of court. But from the facts it was clear that the letter could not have the effect of substantial interference. Harries C.J. expressed the view that the letter could not possibly be said to tend to interfere with the course of justice because no reference was made to the merits or demerits of the defence and nothing in the letter can be suggested as putting forward anything which could only be done in the open court.[45]

So the approach of the judiciary during the pre-Contempt of Courts Act, 1971 has been very strict. Though the common law principle insisted on proof of real prejudice or substantial interference with the course of justice for constituting contempt of court, the Indian judiciary in majority of cases held the alleged contemners guilty of contempt on the ground of tendency to interfere with the administration of justice.

(ii) After the Contempt of Courts Act, 1971

These tests, namely tendency to interfere, real prejudice and substantial interference as laid down by the judiciary are incorporated in section 2(c)[46] of the Contempt of Courts Act, 1971, which defines criminal contempt. This wide definition

43. *Supra* n. 8.
44. *Supra* n. 10.
45. *Id.* at 263.
46. Sec. 2(c): "Criminal contempt" means the publication (whether by words spoken or written, or by signs or by visible representations or otherwise) of any matter or the doing of any other act whatsoever which:
    (i) scandalises or tends to scandalise, or lowers or tends to lower the authority of any court; or
    (ii) prejudices, or interferes or tends to interfere with the due course of any judicial proceeding; or
    (iii) interferes or tends to interfere with, obstructs or tends to obstruct, the administration of justice in any other manner.

makes it possible to curtail the freedom of expression of the citizen on the ground of contempt of court. But a study of judicial decisions after the passing of the Contempt of Courts Act, 1971 shows that the courts have not been using the wide definition of criminal contempt to place unnecessary restraints on freedom of speech.

Delhi High Court considered the effect of publication of an article during the pendency of a case in the *Supersession*[47] case. The Court in this case rather restricted the scope of prejudicing fair trial and thus adopted a liberal view. Chief Justice Andley held:

> The fact that the cases were pending in court could not prevent discussion of matter of public importance. Nor were the public obliged to go on an exploratory expedition to discover whether the matter was pending in any court.[48]

The reason why any comment upon a pending case is considered to be contempt of court is that it is likely to prejudice the minds of the jury or the witnesses or prevent the witnesses or parties from coming before the court.

Certainly opinion by a person none other than the former Chief Justice on the merits of the case will prejudice a fair trial. But the Delhi High Court adopted a very liberal attitude in this case.

Such a liberal view was followed by the Andhra Pradesh High Court in *Y.V. Hanumantha Rao* v. *K. Pattabhiraman*,[49]

---

47. *Anil Kumar Gupta* v. *K. Subba Rao* (1974) I.L.R. Delhi. In this case former Chief Justice of India, K. Subba Rao was cited for contempt for publishing an article in 'The Statesman' discussing the matter of supersession of judges and the appointment of A.N. Ray as the Chief Justice.
48. *Id* at 4. This decision of the Delhi High Court is commended by the editorial of the Calcutta weekly Notes. "We think, this judgment of Chief Justice Andley will go down as an outstanding contribution to the law of contempt, taking as it does a liberal and sensible attitude in keeping with the modern tendencies as opposed to the rigid and illiberal attitude taken in some of the cases of the Indian High Courts." 8 *Calcutta Weekly Notes* No. 36, p. 134, 135 (1973).
49. AIR 1975 A.P. 30. In this case following the agitation for separate Andhra State a curfew was imposed in the town of Vijayawada. Questioning the legality of the curfew order, a writ petition was filed in the High Court and it was pending, while so, Sri P. Seethapathy,

wherein an article published in the *Deccan Chronicle* was in question. Since it did not refer either to the parties to the litigation, or the matter referred in the writ petition, the article could not be characterised in anyway as interfering with the course of justice. But the court laid down the following principle:

> When litigation is pending before a court, no one shall comment on it in such a way there is a real and substantial danger of prejudice to the trial of the action, as for instance by influence on the judge, the witnesses or by prejudicing mankind in general against a party to the cause. Even if the person making the comment honestly believes it to be true, still it is a contempt of court if it prejudices the truth before it is ascertained in the proceedings...there must appear to be a real and substantial danger of prejudice.[50]

Since the article contained only the academic discussion of the meaning of "curfew" and the provisions of law under which it is imposed and has no reference to the matter pending before the court of law, the article could not be said to constitute contempt.

But when allegations are contained in a notice issued to the additional subordinate judge who decided the suit, it was said to have the tendency to interfere with the course of justice and amounted to contempt of court:[51]

Secretary, Board of Revenue published an article entitled "The Law of Curfew" in the daily "Deccan Chronicle". In the article the author discussed the meaning, history, provisions of the law relating to curfew etc. It was alleged that this article amounted to contempt of court.

50. *Id.* at 31.

51. *Rachapudi Subba Rao* v. *The Advocate General, Andhra Pradesh* AIR 1981 S.C. 755, 758. In this case the appellant filed original suit in the court of subordinate judge and the same was dismissed. When the execution proceedings and appellant's stay order were pending, the appellant issued a notice to the additional subordinate judge who decided the suit. This notice was the subject matter of the present contempt proceedings. It contained the following statement "Your honour has intentionally with bad faith and maliciously disordered the existing oral and documentary evidence with a view to help the plaintiff in O.S. No. 275/72 causing damage and injury to me. Your honour has maintained different standards in the same judgment. Your honour is liable in tort to pay damage, the heavy monetary loss incurred by me and for the injury."

> The tone, temper and content of the notice, particularly of the passages extracted earlier, which impute malice, partiality and dishonesty to the subordinate judge in the judicial adjudication of the aforesaid suit against the appellant, constitute a deliberate attempt to scandalise the judge, to terribly embarrass him and to lower the authority of his office and the court. The act and the conduct of the appellant in issuing this notice, therefore fell squarely within sub-clauses (i) and (ii) of the definition of criminal contempt.[52]

The issue of notice itself may not be contempt, but if the language used imputes motive or lowers the authority of the judicial officer, that may amount to contempt of court.

Delhi High Court had occasion to consider the effect of press interview in *Subhash Chand* v. *S.M. Aggarwal.*[53] In this case a judge after giving death sentence to the accused and sending the record to the High Court for concurrence conducted press interview and doordarshan interview in which he substantiated his stand. It was held that the answers to some

52. *Id.* at 758.

53. 1984 Cri. L.J. (Delhi High Court) 481. One Subhash Chand, petitioner along with his brother Lakshman and mother Sakuntala were found guilty of having killed one Sudha, wife of the accused Lakshman by burning her and was given death sentence. After handing down the death sentence he submitted the record to the High Court for confirmation of the death sentence. Thus while the matter was *subjudice*, S.M. Aggarwal, Additional Sessions Judge, who decided the matter held a press interview and an interview to doordarshan where he was stated to have discussed the merits of the case. Different questions were put by the interviewer. *Q.* What was special in this case which forced you to award the death sentence? *Ans.* There are several reasons for this.... One of the reasons was that this murder was committed in a well planned manner. It was planned several days before it was committed. The second reason was the greed of money which turned into motive and ended in a murder. The third reason was the choosing of the barbarian weapon of murder which made the girl suffer agony for nine hours to die. Yet another most important reason according to me was having nine months old pregnancy. In my opinion it was not one murder but it was a double murder which compelled me to think that if sentence of death is not awarded in this case it would not go in the interest of society." Then he spoke about the role played by witnesses.

questions in the interview definitely had the capacity to generate an atmosphere of prejudice against the accused and to make it difficult for the higher court to deal with the case.[54]

Malik Shariff Ud-Din J. further held that expressing opinion on a matter of public importance or national importance was different from propagating views in respect of a pending case which has been pronounced by the same judge. Further, every citizen had a right to get a fair and impartial trial, free from the atmosphere of prejudice. Hence, the conclusion was that the contention of the respondent that after pronouncing the judgment he had a right as a free citizen of India to propagate his views in respect of topics of national importance cannot and will not sustain.[55]

In this case, the matter was pending before the High Court for confirmation. But a question may arise that in case the matter has been finally decided, whether a judge can conduct a press interview to substantiate his views? It is submitted that a judge can substantiate his decision in the judgment itself and he may also be permitted to air his views through public media, because it may not prejudice a fair trial. In such cases the judge is not performing any judicial function. Anything that is said by him is personal. So any criticism of his views cannot be held as contempt.

In *A. Haleem* v. *M.S. Tajudeen*[56] a District Judge was held guilty of contempt for having interfered with the administration of justice, by allowing a petition for reconstruction of the board of trustees, which was under the consideration of the Supreme Court in a special leave petition. The reason is:

54. *Id.* at 486.

55. *Id.* at 487.

56. AIR 1995 S.C. 260. In this case dispute arose in the selection of trustees for Madrasa thul salalhi Fir Adra Bail kilhai. The matter went upto Supreme Court by special leave. Supreme Court directed that the present trustees should continue till 31st May, 1992. Thereafter the trustees were to be selected by advertisement. After that date District Judge of Tanjavur selected certain persons as trustees after due advertisement. The matter was taken to the High Court on revision and from there to the Supreme Court on special leave. While it was under consideration of the Supreme Court, District Judge reconstituted the Board of Trustees on request by one of the trustees.

> The District Judge has been callous in entertaining the application in spite of the knowledge that this court was seized of the matter. Secondly there is remiss on his part in directing notice in a cavalier fashion to Mr. Justice V. Khalid without even looking at the array of the parties or going through the contents of the application.[57]

By following the principle laid down by the Supreme Court in *P.C. Sen's*[58] case Madras High Court in Video Movies by propr. *Haji Rasheed Mohammed* v. *D. Ramanujam, Madras*[59] held that the television interview of the respondent was likely to interfere with the fair hearing of the pending case which would amount to contempt of court. But the same Court, in *Jawaharlal Nehru's*[60] case held that public discussion of a matter of general importance will not amount to contempt of court. So such stifling of public discussion by simply filing a suit should not be justified. Everyone is free to discuss matters of general importance. As such the approach of the Madras High Court in *Ramanujam's*[61] case cannot be said to be correct.

Mr. A.G. Noorani[62] expressed the view that the Madras High Court erred badly because discussion of the legislation proper, during the contemporaneous legal proceedings is no bar.

As stated by Rajeev Dhavan:

> There is a strange myth that as soon as matters become *sub-judice* people lose their freedom of action in respect

57. *Id.* at 264.
58. *Supra* n. 41.
59. AIR 1986 Mad. 119. In this case during the pendency of a writ petition, questioning the validity of the Tamil Nadu Ordinance No. 2 of 1984, later replaced by Tamil Nadu Exhibition of films on Television screen through Video Cassette Recorders (Regulation) Act, 1984, a programme was broadcast from the T.V. Centre of Madras. The first respondent had explained the nature of legislation and had spoken in favour of it while he was fully aware of the fact that the legislation was under challenge before the court. The second respondent (Minister) in his speech had referred to certain facts leading to the necessity for making the Video legislation.
60. *Supra* n. 24.
61. *Supra* n. 59.
62. A.G. Noorani, "Public discussion and Contempt of Court," (1984) 19 *EPW*, 2070.

> of that cause or matter. It has been established that people have the freedom to exercise such rights which do not adversely affect or obstruct the course of a trial or the administration of justice.[63]

Of late verbal and non-verbal methods of interference are used by people which also may amount to contempt of court. Among such interference may be cited a demonstration before the residence of the Chief Justice with a view to influence the decision in a pending matter before a court.[64] Such a conduct lowers or tends to lower the authority as well as the personal dignity of the judge. It also has the effect of interfering with the due course of judicial proceedings. On appeal[65] the Supreme Court refused to accept the apology and admonished the advocate and directed that the money ordered by the High Court to be paid by the appellant to the Kerala Legal Aid Board has to be paid.

Another instance of non-verbal interference was considered by the same High Court in *High Court of Kerala* v. *Fazulludin.*[66] A peon of the High Court who went to serve the notice was attacked by the respondents, who claimed that they were unaware of the identity of the peon. But the court held that attacking without identifying a person is highly objectionable. Court further observed:

> It is clear that respondents tried to interfere with the administration of justice and wanted to lower the authority

---

63. Rajeev Dhavan, *Contempt of Court and The Press*, 160 (1982).
64. *Shri C.N. Presannan, Judicial Second Class Magistrate Cochin* v. *Shri K.A. Mohammed Ali, Advocate, Cochin.* 1991 Cri. L.J. (Kerala High Court) 2194, 2196. In this case the respondent, an advocate had used derogatory language against the magistrate and raised the pitch of his voice unusually high, and organised and caused the staging of a demonstration before the residence of the Hon'ble Chief Justice of Kerala to protest against judicial acts of a Judicial Second Class Magistrate. He caused to publish poster in and near the court premises containing contemptuous remarks against the judiciary and threats against Judicial Second Class Magistrate, Cochin.
65. *K.A. Mohammed Ali* v. *C.N. Prasannan* AIR 1995 S.C. 454.
66. 1994 Cri. L.J. (Kerala High Court) 2982. A peon of the court who was entrusted with the task of serving notice to the respondent in a *habeas corpus* petition was manhandled and locked up in a room. High Court on the statement of the peon took *suo motu* contempt action.

of this court. This is a case where there is proof of due interference with the administration of justice.[67]

Further it is the primary concern of the court to protect the peons. Or else, these peons may not be willing to go on such errands or they may fail to perform their duties. It is also likely that more people may be emboldened to manhandle or resort to violence or wilful obstruction of these peons.[68]

So also when the fabricated orders of the court have been obtained by the contemners, employees of the High Court in connivance with the Secretary Physical Education and used the orders to get favourable orders from the government, the contemners are guilty of criminal contempt.[69]

The court observed: When a person is found to have utilised an order of a court which he or she knows to be incorrect for conferring benefit on persons who are not entitled for the same, the very utilisation of the fabricated order by the person concerned would be sufficient to hold him/her guilty of contempt irrespective of the fact whether he or she himself or herself is the author of the fabrication.[70]

So also attacking the members of the commission sent by the Supreme Court to assess and report on a matter can be treated as constituting a gross interference with the course of justice.[71]

Another instance of verbal attack on the judge in the open court, was sternly dealt with by the Supreme Court in *In re*

67. *Id.* at 2985.
68. *Ibid.*
69. *In Re: Bineet Kumar Singh* (AIR 2001 S.C. 2018).
70. *Id.* at 2022.
71. *Tarun Bharat Sangh, Alwar* v. *Union of India.* AIR 1993 S.C. 293, 294. In this case, Tarun Bharat Sangh an Environmental Protection Organisation, moved the Supreme Court against large scale mining near Sariska Tiger National Park which would affect the environment there. So the Supreme Court sent a Commission including a High Court Judge to visit the place and report on the matter. The members were manhandled by the people of the mining licence holder. Hence the contempt petition.

Vinay Chandra Mishra[72] wherein an advocate, none other than the Chairman of the Bar Council of India, was punished for contempt of court. The contemner even threatened the judge with transfer and impeachment. Though he first justified his stand as an outspoken lawyer later he apologised, but the court refused to accept the apology.

> To resent the question asked by a judge to be disrespectful to him, to question his authority to ask questions, to shout at him, to threaten him with transfer and impeachment, to use insulting language and abuse him, to dictate the order that he should pass, to create scenes in the court, to address him by losing temper are all acts calculated to interfere with and obstruct the course of justice. Such acts tend to overawe the court and to prevent it from performing its duty to administer justice. Such conduct brings the authority of the court and the administration of justice into disrespect and disrepute and undermines and erodes the very foundation of the judiciary by shaking the confidence of the people in the ability of the court to deliver free and fair justice.[73]

Supreme Court in this case considered four important questions. First one is the jurisdiction of the Supreme Court to deal with contempt *facie curiae* of High Court and answered it in the affirmative because, though both are courts of record as per the Constitution, the judicial superintendence and control of all courts in India lies with the Supreme Court, which confers a duty to safeguard and protect the subordinate

---

72. (1995) 2 SCC 584. In connection with a money suit, the trial court directed to furnish security. Against the said order, appeal had been filed in the High Court. It was contended that the trial court had no jurisdiction to pass such orders. So Justice S.K. Keshote who was hearing the matter with Justice Anshuman Singh put the question to Shri Mishra, the contemner, "under which provision this order has been passed." On this the contemner started shouting and used abusive words at the court. Aggrieved by this Justice S.K. Keshote informed the matter in writing to the "Acting Chief Justice of the Allahabad High Court and he in turn referred the matter to the Supreme Court. Supreme Court being satisfied that there is a *prima facie* case of contempt issued notice.

73. *Id.* at 616.

judiciary.[74] Secondly the court considered the need to summon and examine the applicant judge and held that in contempt cases it was not necessary because of the provisions contained in Sec. 14[75] of the Contempt of Courts Act, 1971. Regarding the question as to compliance of natural justice the court held that it was not necessary because contempt proceedings are meant for protection of administration of justice. Finally the court considered whether there is contempt by interference with the administration of justice and court satisfied that the allegations amounted to criminal contempt.

The court further observed:

> It is not the heat generated in the arguments but the language used, the tone and the manner in which it is expressed and the intention behind using it which determine whether it was calculated to insult, show disrespect, to overbear and overawe the court and to threaten and obstruct the course of justice.[76]

Though the punishment is little harsh and unprecedented the conclusion of the court has to be appreciated as free and fair administration of justice depends upon the independence of the judiciary. If persons holding authority and political power try to secure favourable orders by threatening and intimidating the judge, the free and fair administration of justice which is the back bone of democracy will get eroded. People will lose faith in the independence and impartiality of judiciary. The Court further stated:

> Brazenness is not outspokenness and arrogance is not fearlessness. Use of intemperate language is not assertion of right nor is a threat or an argument. Humility is not

74. *Id.* at 607.
75. Sec. 14(3): Notwithstanding anything contained in any other law in any trial of a person charged with contempt under sub-section (1) which is held in pursuance of the direction given under sub-section (2) by a judge other than the judge or judges in whose presence or hearing the offence is alleged to have been committed, it shall not be necessary for the judge or judges in whose presence or hearing the offence is alleged to have been committed to appear as a witness and the statement placed before the Chief Justice urder sub-section (2) shall be treated as evidence in the case.
76. *Supra* n. 72, p. 613.

servility and courtesy and politeness are not lack of dignity. Self-restraint and respectful attitude towards the court, presentation of correct facts and law with a balanced mind and without over statement, suppression, distortion or embellishment are requisites of good advocacy.[77]

In *Red light on the cars of Hon'ble Judges of the High Court* v. *State of U.P.*,[78] the action of the constable in stopping the vehicle of the judges going to attend the Lucknow Bench was treated as contempt. The judges had the privilege of having a red light on the top of the vehicle to indicate the status. The constable followed the general traffic rules and stopped the judge's vehicle and interrogated them. As this was construed as a non-verbal interference with the dignity and status, the judges treated the incident as contempt of court.

But the High Court is exercising its contempt jurisdiction which is inherent in a court of record. So the power is to be exercised when the judges are exercising the judicial function and not when moving from one place to another. Extending the extraordinary jurisdiction to punish a constable who was only discharging his duty does not appear to be correct.

During the pre-Contempt of Courts Act period, judiciary adopted a stringent attitude and even where the statement or the act has the tendency to interfere with the administration of justice the courts used to punish the contemner. But after the Act though the judiciary is particular to maintain its authority and dignity used to exercise its contempt jurisdiction only when there is interference of a substantial nature whether verbal or non-verbal.

3. PREJUDICING FAIR TRIAL—BY THE PRESS

(i) Before the Contempt of Courts Act, 1971

A perusal of the cases decided after adoption of the Constitution and before the enactment of the Contempt of Courts Act, 1971 shows that the test of prejudicing fair trial has not been uniformly applied by the various High Courts and by

77. *Ibid.*

78. AIR 1993 All. 211. In this case the car of High Court Judges which used red light on the top of the car was stopped by the police for interrogation as per Motor Vehicles Rules, 1989.

the Supreme Court. The editors, printers and publishers have been found guilty of contempt either because the publication had reasonable tendency to prejudice,[79] or because of real prejudice[80] and in exceptional cases because of substantial interference.[81] In majority of the cases editors and publishers were found guilty of contempt by applying the principle of reasonable tendency to interfere with the administration of justice.

(a) *Tendency to prejudice*

Tendency to prejudice fair trial is not a correct test to ascertain whether a publication amounts to contempt of court or not.[82] Real prejudice or substantial interference should be established for vesting the liability. The principle was correctly applied in *Wasudeoraoji Sheorey* v. *A.D. Mani, Managing Editor Hitavada*[83] and also in *Sunnulal Badhavallabha* v. *Yeswant Singh.*[84]

---

79. *State* v. *Ram Briksh Benipuri* AIR 1953 Pat. 364; *State* v. *Editor, printer and publisher, Matrubhumi*; AIR. 1954 Ori. 149 etc.
80. *Wasudeoraoji Sheorey* v. *A.D. Mani, Managing Editor Hitavada.* 52 Cri. L.J. (Nagpur High Court) 452; *State* v. *Bhavani Prasad* A.I.R. 1954 Nag. 36 etc.
81. *Harekrishna Mahtab* v. *Balakrishnakar* AIR 1954 Ori. 57; *State* v. *Faquirchand* AIR 1957 All. 657 etc.
82. Earlier decisions insisted on the test of substantial interference. For *e.g.*: *R.* v. *Balakrishna Kulkarni* AIR 1922 Bomb. 52: A Court's jurisdiction in contempt is not to be invoked unless there is real prejudice which can be regarded as substantial interference with the due course of justice. *In re Subramanyam Editor Tribune* AIR (30) 1943 Lah. 329. Publication of a matter which tends or is calculated to interfere with the due course of justice may amount to contempt, but before taking notice of such a publication the court must be satisfied that the matter published tended substantially to interfere with the due course of justice. *Mohamed Ibrahim* v. *Bhopal Singh* AIR 1948 Oudh 131. The publication should be calculated to create an atmosphere of prejudice against a party. *Emperor* v. *Khushal Chand* AIR (35) 1945 Lah. 206. "...that the matter published tended substantially to interfere with the due course of justice or was calculated substantially to create prejudice in the public mind."
83. 52 Cri. L.J. (1951) (Nagpur High Court) 452 (For facts *see* n. 19 Ch. 5).
84. 52 Cri. L.J. (1951) (Madhya Bharat High Court) 632 (For facts *see* n. 54 Ch. 4).

In *Wasudeoraoji Sheorey* v. *A.D. Mani, Managing Editor Hitavada,*[85] it was held that the right of a newspaper even to publish a fair account of the proceedings before a court of law is subject to the condition that the publication does not tend to prejudice materially the fair trial of a case before a court of law.[86]

So also in *Sunnulal Badhavallabha* v. *Yeshwant Singh,*[87] Madhya Bharath High Court applied the test as laid down by the Lahore High Court in *Emperor* v. *Khushal Chand*[88] and held the editor liable for contempt but accepted his apology.

In these cases the court held that the tendency to prejudice fair trial is not a correct test and insisted upon the existence of substantial interference. But subsequent decisions show a slow process of dilution of the principle.

The Patna High Court in *State* v. *Ram Briksh Benipuri*[89] applied the test of tendency to prejudice a fair trial. In this case

---

85. *Supra* n. 83.
86. *Id.* at 455.
87. *Supra* n. 84.
88. AIR (35) 1945 Lah. 206. The tests to be satisfied are : (a) that something has been published which either is clearly intended or atleast is calculated to prejudice a trial which is pending; (b) that the offending matter was published with the knowledge that the cause was imminent or (c) that the matter published tended substantially to interfere with the due course of justice or was calculated substantially to create prejudice in the public mind. (*Id.* at 207)
89. AIR 1953 Pat. 364. In this case there had been an ill feeling and trouble between tenants and landlords in Paparia Diara which culminated in a clash between two groups. After the preliminary enquiry the case was committed to the court of sessions for trial. While so, the news items appeared. Allahabad High Court in *Lakhan Singh* v. *Balbir Singh*; (AIR 1953 All. 343) also applied the test of tendency to interfere. In this case the question for consideration was whether the statement "liquor is diluted with water is proved by the fact that the liquor which was seized by the Collector on the preceding day contained diluted liquor of the strength of 46 per cent, will prejudice fair trial while the same question is being considered by the court. In this case the court applied the test, likely to prejudice fair trial and held the statement amounted to contempt of court. So also Orissa High Court in *Harekrishna Mahatab* v. *Balakrishnakar* (AIR 1954 Ori. 57) expressed the view that assertion by a party that their stand is correct while that matter is pending before a court of law will amount to contempt of court, because

the question for consideration was whether the statement "the Zamindars with the help of the congressmen and local officers are oppressing the tenants," while that is being considered by the court, will amount to contempt of court. The statement is said to constitute contempt of court because it has the tendency to prejudice fair trial. But the same High Court in *Panchanand Jha* v. *Surendra Misra*[90] though applied the test of tendency to interfere with the fair trial, gave a negative decision since no reference was made to the petitioner. A publication could be said to interfere with fair trial only if reference was made of the pending proceedings. Such a view protects the interest of the publisher.

But the Allahabad High Court in *Rahmat Ali* v. *Beni Madho Baijpal*[91] held that the nature and import of the news item[92] was calculated to produce an atmosphere of prejudice in the midst of which the proceedings under Sec. 110, Criminal Procedure Code were going on and it was likely to embarrass and impede the petitioner's case and hence clearly amounted to contempt of court.[93]

---

it will tend to prejudice fair trial. In this case Balakrishnakar editor of 'Matrubhumi', criticised Sri Mahtab and a defamation suit filed by him was pending. While so the editor published an article mobilising public opinion in his favour. This publication was the subject matter of contempt petition as it interfered with the fair trial of the case.

90. AIR 1955, Pat. 141.

91. AIR 1957 All. 457. In this case, the petitioner Rahmat Ali obtained a rule upon the opposite parties Pandit Beni Madho Baijpal, the editor, printer and publisher of a newspaper known as *Vir Bharat* in Kanpur and Lakshmi Narain, the proprietor of the Mahesh Press where the paper was printed, to show cause why they should not be convicted or otherwise dealt with for contempt of court in as much as during the pendency of proceedings under Sec. 110, Criminal Procedure Code against Rahmat Ali in the court of the City Magistrate, Kanpur, a news item was printed in the *Vir Bharat* on 19th October, 1956 which was calculated to produce so to speak an atmosphere of prejudice.

92. The news item reads as follows: "Members of the Congress *ad hoc* committee appear in defence of Rahmat Ali, a history sheeter and a criminal. The local kotwali police had arrested Mian Rahmat Ali of Patkapur, a confirmed Criminal and a notorious history sheeter under Sec. 110, Criminal Procedure Code and his case is pending in the court of the city Magistrate."

93. *Supra* n. 91, p. 459.

The reason stated by the judge was that the publication might have an effect on the minds of witnesses who were to be examined before the magistrate. But such cases, which are likely to embarrass the petitioner's case should not be taken as a ground of prejudicing fair trial.

According to Justice Tek Chand, taking sides in criminal cases, suggesting innocence or guilt of accused persons can cause grave prejudice, by either influencing the minds of judges, jurors, witnesses, or by creating a sympathy for or prejudice against the accused.[94] The learned Judge observed:

> Any publication, which has a tendency to foil or thwart a fair and impartial trial, or any conduct which in any manner prejudices or prevents judicial investigations, whether by intimidation of or by reflection on the court, counsel, parties or witnesses, in respect of a pending cause, constitute contempt of court.[95]

The Judge further observed:

> Reasonable tendency to influence or interfere with a pending proceeding has been a long established standard, and still is the only accepted criterion, recognised by courts in India and in the countries, which have adopted their legal system on the pattern of common law.[96]

But this is not the only test to be looked into. Though the judge gave authentic recognition to the test of tendency to interfere, it cannot be correct because of the opinion given in the earlier cases.[97]

In *Express Newspapers Limited* v. *M/s. Raisina Publications Private Limited*[98] also it was held that the publication of a plaint, before the defendant had opportunity to appear before

---

94. *Rao Harnarain Singh Sheoji Singh* v. *Gumani Ram Arya* AIR 1958 Punj. 273, 278 (For facts *see* n. 37 Ch. 5).
95. *Id.* at 278.
96. *Id.* at 282. The same view was followed by the Punjab High Court in *State* v. *Pt. Ram Chander Sharma* AIR 1959 Punj. 41.
97. *Emperor* v. *Khushal Chand* AIR 1945 Lah. 206; *Wasudeoraoji Sheorey* v. *A.D. Mani, Managing Editor Hitavada* 52 Cri. L.J. (1951) (Nagpur High Court) 452; *Sunnulal Badha Vallabha* v. *Yeshwant Singh* 52 Cri. L.J. (1951) (Madhya Bharat High Court) 632.
98. AIR 1964 Punj. 428. (For facts *see* n. 21 Ch. 5).

the court, will tend to prejudice public mind and will amount to contempt of court. Because there can be no doubt that the publication of one-sided version of a party to a civil or criminal dispute pending in court or where proceedings between them are imminent may do incalculable harm to a party's case by prejudicing public mind against him or by deterring witnesses from coming forward to depose at the trial.[99]

So also the suggestion in a newspaper article that evidence intended to be used in a prosecution, which is either proceeding or is plainly contemplated has been obtained by improper means and is unreliable,[100] a statement in clear terms that public have lost confidence in the court in the administration of justice and the litigant against the state cannot get his legitimate grievance redressed,"[101] are said to have the tendency to bring the administration of justice into disrepute.

Though tendency to prejudice fair trial is not the correct test to ascertain the contemptuous nature of a publication, the courts used to apply that test, with the result that the freedom of the press had been to some extent restrained.

(b) *Real prejudice*

The jurisdiction in contempt is not to be invoked unless there is real prejudice which can be regarded as 'substantial interference'. But the application of the test of real prejudice was subsequently restricted by the Indian judiciary.

In certain exceptional cases the Supreme Court and the High Courts, insisted on the proof of real prejudice for testing the effect of publication.

99. *Id.* at 430.

100. *Asgharali* v. *Motilal Dave* 1966 Cri. L.J. (Madhya Pradesh High Court) 214. (For facts *see* n. 61 Ch. 5).

101. *Sarat Chandra Biswal* v. *Surendra Mohanty, Editor Kalinga* AIR 1969 Ori. 117, 134. During the pendency of a writ petition against the Chief Minister of Orissa, questioning certain deeds, on the flag hoisting ceremony the Chief Justice appreciated the co-operation of the Chief Minister in getting the tower of the High Court erected. These and other things were reported by Kalinga on Jan. 28, 1968. It stated that though the Governor had been officially invited, the presence of the Chief Minister Sri Singh Deo and the Jana Congress leader Sri Mahtab among the special invitees, invited strong criticism among the visitors. It was followed by editorials of 31st Jan. and 1st Feb. These statements were the subject matter of the contempt petition.

In The *State* v. *Editors, Printers and Publishers of the Newspapers Matrubhumi and Krushak,*[102] the Orissa High Court while holding that the publications tended to prejudice fair trial and amounted to contempt, observed:

> Hence though any attempt of trial by the press of a pending case should be sternly put down by enforcing the law of contempt, in appropriate cases, the said law should not be so strained as to materially affect the freedom of speech of newspapers. A line has to be drawn between the law of contempt on the one hand and the freedom of speech of the newspapers on the other. Where an article is published with the 'intention' of prejudicing the fair trial of a pending case, there can be no hesitation in applying the law of contempt against the offending newspaper. But where such intention is absent and the court is asked to infer fair trial of pending case, many other considerations should also be carefully weighed.[103]

Allahabad High Court in *Rahmat Ali* v. *Beni Madho Baijpal*[104] also expressed the view that in cases of contempt by publication, actual prejudice would be an important consideration. Use of words "confirmed criminal" and a notorious "history sheeter" in the publication had the effect of positive assertion of a matter which was yet to be decided by the court.

The court accepted the principle as laid down by Beasely C.J. of Madras High Court, in *Sathappa Chettiar* v. *Ramachandra Naidu,*[105] and held the statement in the present case was also calculated to produce an atmosphere of prejudice and hence amounted to contempt of court.[106]

---

102. AIR 1954 Ori. 149. (For facts *see* n. 60, Ch. 5).
103. *Id.* at 159.
104. *Supra* n. 91.
105. AIR 1932 Mad. 26. The essence of the offence of contempt of court is conduct calculated to produce an atmosphere of prejudice in the midst of which the proceedings must go on (*Id.* at 27).
106. *Supra* n. 91, p. 458. In *Prahlad Prasad Mahrotra* v. *Chandra Bhusan* AIR 1958 Pat. 144 and *Chunnilalken* v. *Shyamlal* AIR 1959 M.P. 50, the respective High Courts applied the real prejudice test. *Prahlad Prasad Mahrotra* v. *Chandra Bhushan* AIR 1958 Pat. 144. In this case during the election campaign for the Bihar Legislative Assembly, the petitioner came across a letter bearing the signature of one Ramavatar Shastri

Thus before the passing of the Contempt of Courts Act, 1971 Madhya Pradesh, Patna, Orissa and Allahabad High Courts applied the test of real prejudice as laid down in *R.V. Balakrishnakulkarni*[107] and *Emperor* v. *Khushal Chand.*[108]

(c) *Substantial interference*

The test of substantial interference was rarely applied by the judiciary in the post-independent period. Orissa High Court in *Sarat Chandra Biswal* v. *Surendra Mohanty, Editor Kalinga*[109] applied the test of substantial interference. In this case the Orissa High Court insisted that substantial exhibition of such conduct towards law courts should be brought out for establishing contempt of court. But impartial reporting of a petition and expression of fair comment will not amount to contempt of court. The publication in this case was unfair mischievous and motivated, and had been deliberately published with a view to tarnish the reputation of the Orissa High

---

addressed to one P. Ghosh of Calcutta, which disclosed that there was a plan to attack a candidate who had been set up by the Indian National Congress. The letter had been forwarded for further action. On 22-02-57 Ramavatar Shastri filed a petition under Sections 500, 456 and 471 of the Indian Penal Code and denied the authorship of the letter on 01-03-1957. The opposite party Shri Chandra Bhushan, the editor, printer and publisher of the paper called 'Shola', caused it to be published. The petitioner accordingly submitted that the opposite party had branded him a forger and a person out to concoct a defence with full knowledge that the matter is *subjudice.* It was alleged that the publication was bound to create prejudice in the minds of the public and as such tended effectively to divert the course of justice.

Chunnilalken v. *Shyamlal* AIR 1959 M.P. 50. The petitioner was a defeated candidate for the Lok Sabha. He filed an election petition before the Election Commissioner. It was alleged that the non-petitioners (Printer and proprietor of Maharashtra Press) printed and published certain pamphlet to the prejudice of the petitioner during the pendency of the election petition and thus committed contempt of the Election Tribunal. The translated English version is as follows: "There is no substance in the election petition. The idea behind it is to raise money in order to open a big shop in Bhopal.

107. AIR 1922 Bomb. 52.
108. *Supra* n. 8.
109. *Supra* n. 101.

Court. Madhya Bharat,[110] Allahabad,[111] Punjab[112] and Kerala[113] High Courts also adopted the test of substantial interference as laid down in *Emperor* v. *Khushal Chand.*[114] Madhya Bharat, Allahabad and Kerala High Courts by applying the test of substantial interference held the respondents guilty of contempt. But the Punjab High Court in *Express News Papers Ltd.* v. *M/s. Raisina Publications (Pvt.) Ltd.*[115] expressed the view that publication of the correct summary of a plaint will not amount to contempt of court.

The court observed:

> But it is a well settled rule in dealing with cases of this type that before a court will take notice of such publication, it must be satisfied that the matter published tended substantially to interfere with due course of justice or was calculated substantially to create prejudice in the public mind, and the courts will not take action where the

---

110. *Sunnulal Badhavallabha* v. *Yeswant Singh* 52 Cri. L.J. (1951) (Madhya Bharat High Court) 632.
111. *State* v. *Faquir Chand* AIR 1957 All. 657. During the pendency of a complaint under Sections 323 and 307 of the Indian Penal Code and under Sections 325 and 342 of the Indian Penal Code before the court of Sub-Divisional Magistrate, Shahabad a local weekly paper called 'Sathi' published a news item. Respondent No. 1 is the publisher of the weekly. This news item was published under the banner headline : "The realistic police of Tehsil, Shahabad, beat a person and made the Thana a bloody scene. When the walls of the Thana depicted a picture of the bloody scene the police got his clothes changed."
112. *Express News Papers Limited* v. *M/s. Raisina Publications (Pvt.) Ltd.* AIR 1964 Punj. 428.
113. *Rev. Father Sebastian Onamkulam* v. *K. Karunakaran* AIR 1967 Ker. 177. The petitioner in the original petition was the brother of Father Benedict Onamkulam. The first respondent Karunakaran was the Chief Editor and the second respondent Balakrishnan the printer and publisher of 'Janayugam' daily. The petitioner was the accused person and an enquiry was pending against him. During the pendency of the case 'Janayugam' published an article which gave the impression that Rev. Father Benedict Onamkulam committed the crime. It contained certain photographs and also alleged that the Pathanamthitta Magistrate who was trying the case was trying to help the accused.
114. *Supra* n. 8.
115. *Supra* n. 112.

offending matter amounts to what is sometimes referred to as a technical contempt.[116]

So even before the enactment of the Contempt of Courts Act, 1971 the test of substantial interference was followed by some High Courts.

(ii) After the Contempt of Courts Act, 1971

Prejudicing fair trial through publication as a test of contempt of court which the Indian judiciary adopted from common law of England, has got its horizons widened by the strict attitude of the judiciary in India. Thus prejudicing fair trial came to be understood as likely to prejudice,[117] tendency to prejudice,[118] tend to prejudice,[119] calculated to produce an atmosphere of prejudice[120] tendency to influence or tendency to interfere,[121] real prejudice or actual prejudice[122] and substantial interference.[123] Some of these judicially recognised principles obtained legislative authority through the Contempt of Courts Act, 1971. Sec. 2(c)[124] which defines criminal contempt incorporates most of the basic principles except substantial interference. By widening the scope of contempt jurisdiction, the legislature narrowed the freedom of the individual and of the press. Legislature, instead of protecting the freedom of the press in the light of the written Constitution, restricted the right of the press by giving a wide meaning to the term contempt of court.

But the right of the press is protected by providing certain statutory defences in Sections 3 to 8 of the Contempt of Courts Act, 1971. Though wide scope is given in the 1971 Act, the

116. *Id.* at 432.
117. *Lakhan Singh* v. *Balbir Singh* AIR 1953 All. 343.
118. *State* v. *A. Ram Briksh Benipuri* AIR 1953 Pat. 364.
119. *Express News Papers Limited* v. *M/s. Raisina Publications (Pvt.) Ltd.* AIR 1964, Punj. 428.
120. *Asgharali* v. *Motilal Dave* 1966 Cri. L.J. (Madhya Pradesh High Court) 214.
121. *Rao Harnarain Singh Sheoji Singh* v. *Gumani Ram Arya* AIR 1958 Punj. 273.
122. *Rahmat Ali* v. *Beni Madho Baijpal* AIR 1957 All. 457.
123. *State* v. *Faquir Chand* AIR 1957 All. 657; Rev. *Father Sebastian Onamkulam* v. *K. Karunakaran* AIR 1967 Ker. 177.
124. *Supra* n. 46.

Supreme Court restricted its content and scope in *Naraindas* v. *Government of Madhya Pradesh.*[125] In this case the question for consideration was whether the publication of a press note issued by the Government of Madhya Pradesh during the pendency of a revision application and a writ petition will prejudice against the party and interfere with the course of justice. The court after carefully considering the press note answered the matter in the negative.

Though it was argued that some of the statements were incorrect, the court opined that incorrect statement was different from statement prejudicing fair trial. The court observed:

> What we have to consider for the purpose of determining whether any of these statements constitutes contempt of court is whether these statements interfere or have a tendency to interfere with the due course of the appeal or the writ petition by creating prejudice against the appellant which would affect the fair hearing and disposal of the appeal or the writ petition. The effect, we are afraid, the statements in the press note complained of by the appellant do not have. It is not possible to hold that any of these statements constitutes contempt of court.[126]

Thus though it is possible to further widen the contempt jurisdiction because of the use of the phrase 'tends to interfere,'

---

125. 1974 Cri. L.J. (Supreme Court) 924. The subject matter of contempt proceedings in this case was the press note issued by the State of Madhya Pradesh and published by the English daily called 'Hitavada'. The press note was issued during the pendency of a civil suit and writ petition in relation to the printing and publication of textbooks for the primary and middle schools in Madhya Pradesh.

    The press note reads as follows: "The Primary, Middle and Higher Secondary Schools in the State are scheduled to open after summer vacation on 02-07-1973. Advance arrangements had been made for preparation, printing and publication of Text Books, through the Text Book Corporation, so that they are freely available by that date.

    The State Government was served with a stay order of 2nd March, 1973 by the Civil Judge Class II Jabalpur. Even though this order was vacated by the High Court on 28th March, 1973, the Supreme Court on 18th May, 1973 reimposed the earlier restrictions...."

126. *Id.* at 928.

the Supreme Court restricted its application in this case. So also in *Kalyana Sundaram* v. *Karunanidhi.*[127]

The Supreme Court, adopting a restricted interpretation of interfering with the administration of justice, observed:

> The worst that can be said against the publication is that it exposes the respondent to mild ridicule. To say that a publication which exposes a suitor to such mild ridicule in connection with the suit prejudices or interferes or tends to interfere with or obstructs or tends to obstruct, the administration of justice in any other manner is to take a highly sensitive view of the contempt jurisdiction. We do not mean to say that pouring ridicule on a suitor can never interfere or obstruct the administration of justice but we find it impossible to say so in the present case, where the ridicule is not so violent and the parties are well-known public figures well able to bear with equanimity the ridicule poured on them.[128]

Ridiculing the judiciary or party may also amount to contempt of court but it comes under another category of contempt called, 'scandalising the court'. Though it is possible to hold that the publication has the tendency to interfere with the administration of justice, the Supreme Court has not accepted such a wide interpretation by limiting the scope of contempt jurisdiction.

The Supreme Court further considered the effect of interference with the administration of justice in *National Textile Workers Union* v. *P.R. Ramakrishnan*[129] wherein, the

127. AIR 1981 S.C. 1416. In this case Mr. M. Karunanidhi who was then Chief Minister of Tamil Nadu filed a suit in the High Court of Madras claiming compensation of Rs. 10 lakhs as damages for certain alleged defamatory publication made in the Tamil Journal, *Kumudham*. The news was published in other dailies also. The appellant Mr. Kalyana Sundaram published the same with cartoon in 'Janasakthi' of which he was the editor. The respondent filed contempt petition and the High Court found the appellant guilty of contempt. It was held that the news item was likely to interfere with the course of litigation by influencing the mind of the applicant as a party to the suit and hence amounted to contempt of court. Hence this appeal.

128. *Id.* at 1471.

129. AIR 1983 S.C. 759. In this case while special leave petition was being argued the attention of the Supreme Court was drawn to a

court applied the test of serious interference with the course of justice. In this case also the court had not applied the test of tendency to interfere. The writing is said to cause serious interference, because as stated by the court, nothing else will stop this systematic campaign of vilification against the defenceless judges of the High Court.[130] This court is there to protect them from scurrilous accusations, prompted by malice.[131]

According to the Supreme Court the conduct and writings of the contemner constituted serious interference with the administration of justice, since his sole object in giving publicity to the defamatory allegations against the High Court Judge is to deter them from deciding cases against him or against those in whom he is apparently interested.[132]

In this case, the editor misused his position by publishing material which interfered with the administration of justice. The Supreme Court was fully justified in holding the editor liable because the conduct of the editor in publishing the article deserved punishment.

Even then, the Supreme Court had not punished the contemner on the ground of mere tendency to interfere but only on the ground of substantial interference. When there is substantial interference with the administration of justice, the conduct would amount to contempt of court. Thus in this case also the Supreme Court restricted the scope of contempt jurisdiction.

---

certain statement appearing in the press under the name of one P.M. Kumaraswamy alias Kalaimannan. Notice was issued and he submitted a written apology. Apart from other things it was stated: "I further undertake not to write anything against the Madras High Court Judge in my journals 'Sigappu Nada' and 'International Chronicle' in future." Within ten days of this apology he published an article in 'Sigappu Nada'. That showed the hallowness of his apology. In that he mentioned about the direction given by the court, the wild allegation of corruption in the judiciary and his willingness to prove corruption charges. He stated "Kalaimannan is ready to go to jail."

The allegation was to the effect that certain judgment given by the four judges of the High Court of Madras proceeded from corrupt motives. He wanted an opportunity to establish those allegations.

130. *Id.* at 761.

131. *Ibid.*

132. *Ibid.*

Though Sec. 2(c) of the Contempt of Courts Act, 1971 includes "tends to interfere with" and also "tends to obstruct", the judiciary has not applied those principles, so far as editors and publishers are concerned. Supreme Court is reluctant to apply the test of tendency to interfere though it is being put forth in *Naraindas*[133] and in *Karunanidhi.*[134] So for the better maintenance of the freedom of the press, 'real prejudice' and 'actual interference' can be retained as the test for contempt proceedings. 'Tends to interfere' or 'tends to obstruct' need not be taken as the basis for the liability for contempt. So the phrases 'tends to interfere' and 'tends to obstruct' can better be deleted from section 2(c) of the Contempt of Courts Act, 1971 for better protecting the freedom of the press.

4. PREJUDGING THE ISSUE

'Prejudging the issue' as a test of contempt of court has also had its origin in the observation of Lord Hardwickie L.C. in *St. James Evening Post.*[135] It is being followed in subsequent cases and is well explained in *Attorney General* v. *Times Newspapers Ltd.*[136]

> It is easy enough to see that any publication which prejudges an issue in pending proceedings ought to be forbidden, if there is any risk that it may influence the tribunal. But why, it may be said, should such publication be prohibited when there is no such risk? The reason is that one cannot deal with one particular publication in isolation. A publication prejudging an issue in pending litigation which is itself innocuous enough may provoke replies it would seem unfair to restrain. So gradually the public would become habituated to look forward to and resent the absence of preliminary discussions in the media of any case which aroused widespread interest. An absolute rule though it may seem to be unreasonable if one looks only to the particular case is necessary in order to prevent a gradual slide towards trial by newspapers or televisions.[137]

133. *Supra* n. 125.
134. *Supra* n. 127.
135. *Supra* n. 2.
136. (1973) 3 All. E.R. 54.
137. *Id.* at 85.

In pre-independence period in India prejudging the issue has been followed in *Krishna Yachendra* v. *Ram Naidu*[138] *In re Subramaniyan Editor of Tribune*[139] and also in *Emperor* v. *Khushal Chand*.[140] In these cases though the term 'prejudging' was not used, the decisions and observations indicate that the court had applied the test of prejudging the issue.

So when interference by the press reaches such an extent that the press may be taking over the function of the judiciary, such conduct has to be restricted. Opinions of the judiciary after adopting the Constitution also indicate, that there is no change in the approach of the judiciary in this aspect.

An assertion that a fact exists and has established as correct when the existence of the fact is in dispute in a pending case and its correctness is yet to be determined, is likely to prejudice fair trial of the case when the assertion is in the shape of the opinion of persons unconcerned with the case, like the editor of a newspaper.[141]

A decision of the court is to be influenced only by the material and evidence available before the court and not by the private talk or public print.

---

138. AIR 1933 Mad. 2480. The article in question contained a statement that the defendant's case was true and the Raja also had prosecuted false criminal cases against the defendant.

139. AIR 1943 Lah. 329.

140. *Supra* n. 8. In this case it was observed: "Although this article is less harmful in its tone and effect than the other, it is manifest that both the articles are deliberately designed to create an atmosphere of sympathy for the offenders and to mobilise public opinion in their favour. They are unquestionably calculated to produce the impression that the offenders persecuted, as they happen to be, belong to a particular community. As stated above it is a contempt of court to prejudice mankind for or against the party to the cause before the cause is heard" (*Id* at 208).

141. *Lakhan Singh* v. *Balbir Singh* AIR 1953 All. 342, 343. The opposite parties are the editor, the printer and the publisher of the Urdu weekly known as 'Hindustan Weekly' Meerut. While a case under Sec. 61 of the Excise Act was pending the concerned news item was published. It stated: "...that the liquor is being diluted with water is proved by the fact that the liquor which was seized by the Collector in the preceding days contained diluted liquor of the strength of 46 per cent...". The use of words "Liquor is diluted with water" certainly has the effect of asserting a fact which is *subjudice*.

Mohapatra J. in *Harekrishna Mahatab* v. *Balakrishnakar*[142] also applied the test of prejudging the issue and observed:

> This assertion justifying his conduct, which gave rise to cases which are pending decision of the court is to my mind going beyond the permissible law of fair comment and bringing it within the mischief of the law of contempt.[143]

Mere appeal or representation is different from categorical assertion. If there is a categorical assertion as to the truth of the case of the defence, it will be deemed as an impediment to the due course of justice. It amounts to justifying the stand which is nothing but prejudging the issue. But in this case the court refused to take notice of the matter because there was no direct and distinct reference to the case in question. Not only that, though the journalist used the term 'injustice', there was no such categorical assertion as to amount to prejudging. But the use of words "confirmed criminal and notorious history sheeter" while proceedings under Sec. 110 Criminal Procedure Code were pending was held to constitute contempt of court by the Allahabad High Court.[144]

It was stated that use of such words when the matter was being considered by a court of competent jurisdiction would amount to prejudging the issue as it substantially interfered with the proceedings in a court of law.

So also in *Shaminon Rehamaney* v. *Zinab Kansar Dehelvi*[145] it was argued that the writer of the article was doing nothing

---

142. AIR 1954 Ori. 57. The statement for consideration was as follows: Today some newspaper in execution of its duty has become the prey of anger of someone and others will follow suit. In this field newspapers and journalists should unite to resist this injustice.

143. *Id.* at 61.

144. *Rahmat Ali* v. *Beni Madho Baijpal* AIR 1957 All. 457. In *Chunnilalken* v. *Shyamlal Sukhram* AIR 1959 M.P. 50, Madhya Pradesh High Court considered the statement: "There is no substance in the election petition. The idea behind it is to raise money in order to open a big shop in Bhopal" while an election petition is pending. It was held that publication created an atmosphere of prejudice.

145. 1971 Cri. L.J. (Allahabad High Court) 1586. In this case during the pendency of appeal against conviction in a murder case, an article was published in the Bano Magazine in Urdu. It was alleged that the respondents printed and published a highly coloured version of the

short of undertaking a trial of the alleged murderers by contributing an article. After perusing the article the court observed:

> It is the duty of the responsible journalist to realise that it is the function of a court when a case is still not finally decided against an accused person to arrive at the truth and that it is not for the press to hold the trial even for the most heinous crime, before the court has given their final verdict. It may be that this principle is not observed strictly or meticulously in some countries.... It is however clear that, in this country this is not permitted. The courts of justice must not be interfered with by publication which constitute opinion upon the merits of the case or create an atmosphere for or against an accused person before his or her case is finally decided. All that is permitted is fair and accurate reporting of the proceedings of courts of Law.[146]

But the perusal of the publication indicates that there is nothing in the article which prejudiced the issue. The journalist published the statement as given by the parties. If the journalist gives his own conclusion on the basis of the statement given by the parties it can be said to constitute prejudging the issue.

Prejudging the merits of a case by the press has to be prohibited because it would have ulterior effect on the judiciary. The basic function of the judiciary may be side tracked by the one-sided version of the issue by the press based on hearsay versions. So, for vesting the liability, actual prejudging has to be established. Sec. 2(c) of the Contempt of Courts Act, 1971 does not use the term prejudging the issues, but the term prejudicing fair trial includes 'prejudging' the issue also. So any publication which prejudges the issue can be viewed seriously by the court.

---

issue. The article published first states the conversation of eyewitnesses. Then the daughter's answer to the mother. "Doctor had deceived. He has ruined my life, have no wrong in murdering him." It follows: "Bhaiya take this gun and shoot me because I do not want to live any longer...." "Every kind of mischief and deception could be tolerated but not the deception in the name of love which she is not prepared to tolerate at any price."

146. *Id.* at 1588.

5. CONCLUSION

Lord Hardwicke L.C. in *St. James Evening Post*[147] case laid down three different kinds of contempt. They are: (i) scandalising the court; (ii) abusing parties to the proceedings; and (iii) prejudicing mankind against the persons. Those principles are made applicable for indirect contempt or contempt through publication by Wilmot C.J. in *King* v. *Almon.*[148]

The same principles have been applied in India in *R.* v. *Balakrishnakulkarni*[149] and in *Emperor* v. *Khushal Chand.*[150] The test of interference with the course of justice was also recognised by the Privy Council in *Debi Prasad* v. *Emperor.*[151] The tests as laid down by the Lahore High Court in *Emperor* v. *Khushal Chand*[152] are: (a) that something has been published which either is clearly intended or atleast is calculated to prejudice a fair trial which was pending; (b) that the offending matter was published with the knowledge of the pending cause or with the knowledge that the cause was imminent; (c) that the matter published tended substantially to interfere with the due course of justice or was calculated substantially to create prejudice in the public mind.

The principle of substantial interference or real prejudice due to the strict attitude adopted by the judiciary in the post-independent period but before the Contempt of Courts Act, 1971, came to be recognized as likely to prejudice, tendency to prejudice, tend to prejudice, calculated to produce an atmosphere of prejudice, tendency to influence or tendency to interfere, real prejudice or actual prejudice and substantial interference. In case anyone of these elements was present the alleged contemner was held liable. Thus it could be seen that before the passing of the Contempt of Courts Act, 1971, courts in India used to give very strict interpretation to the terms 'substantial interference.' Sec. 2(c) of the Contempt of Courts Act, 1971,

147. *Supra* n. 2.
148. *Ibid.*
149. *Supra* n. 107.
150. *Supra* n. 8.
151. *Supra* n. 4.
152. *Supra* n. 8.

which defines criminal contempt by incorporating the terms "tends to interfere" and "tends to obstruct" gave a wide scope for judicial intervention. But the approach of the courts after the Contempt of Courts Act, 1971, has been very restrictive. Courts, especially the Supreme Court, used to punish the publisher, printer or editor only when there was substantial interference. Courts never punished the editor or publisher on the ground of mere tendency to interfere.

This jurisdiction is applied only to cases of substantial interference. Public discussion on a matter of general or national importance need not constitute contempt unless there is malicious intention of prejudicing fair trial. Such discussion should not be a method of expressing views on a pending case and it should not be prejudging the issue.

7

Scandalising the Judiciary

1. INTRODUCTION

It has long been established that any act or publication which scandalises[1] a court or a judge should not be allowed to interfere with the administration of justice. For maintaining the dignity of the court, it should be protected from any unfounded allegations. But in a democratic society, judiciary being an organ of the state cannot be kept away from criticism, because as stated by Lord Atkin:

> Justice is not a cloistered virtue, she must be allowed to suffer the scrutiny and outspoken comments of ordinary men.[2]

Though constitutional guarantee of freedom of speech and expression[3] can reasonably be restricted on the ground of contempt of court[4] *inter alia*, the democratic right of the citizen

---

1. Scandalising the court means any hostile criticism of the judge as judge, any personal attack upon him unconnected with the office he holds is dealt with under the ordinary rules of slander and libel. Professor Goodhart, "Newspapers and Contempt of Court" 48 *Harv. L. Rev.* 885, 898 (1935).
2. *Andre Paul Terance Ambard* v. *Attorney General Trinidad and Tobago* AIR 1936 P.C. 136.
3. Art, 19(1)(a) — All citizens shall have the right to freedom of speech and expression.
4. Art. 19(2). Nothing in sub-clause (a) of clause (1) shall affect the operation of any existing law, or prevent the State from making any law, insofar as such law imposes reasonable restrictions on the exercise of the right conferred by the said sub-clause in the interest of sovereignty and integrity of India, the security of state friendly relations with foreign State, public order decency or morality, or in relation to contempt of court, defamation or incitement to an offence.

to criticise any organ of the government cannot be prohibited. The same view is emphasised by the Kerala High Court in the following words:

> Healthy and honest criticism of courts and their judgments is an inevitable privilege of the people in a democratic state. But quite often, when the criticism comes from quarters directly affected by the decision, there is likely to be absence of objectivity. The line between permissible criticism of a judgment and scandalous attack on the judge who decided it is thin and when restraint, normally dictated by a sense of prudence recedes to the background there is likely to be trespass.[5]

An attempt is made to ascertain how scandalising the court as a test of contempt of court as laid down by Lord Hardwicke L.C. in *St. James Evening Post*[6] case which has been applied by Justice Wilmot in *Almon's*[7] case for publications also, and as followed in India in *Debi Prasad's*[8] case and *Crown* v. *Amin-ud-Sahrait*[9] before independence has been utilised by the Indian judiciary after the adoption of the Constitution to restrict the freedom of speech of the citizen and that of the press. The approach of the judiciary is analysed, as it was before and after the passing of the Contempt of Courts Act, 1971.

2. SCANDALISING THE JUDICIARY—BY THE INDIVIDUALS

(i) Before the Contempt of Courts Act, 1971

Scandalous statements by individuals may be contained in notices, affidavits, resolutions or public speeches. Irrespective of the method, if the statement has the effect of scandalising, the judiciary has viewed it seriously. What amounts to scandalous statement depends much upon the tone and temper of the language used and not on the material in which it is contained.

---

5. *Advocate General* v. *Abraham George* 1976 Cri. L.J. (Kerala High Court) 158, 161.
6. (1742) 2 Atk. 469. One kind of contempt is scandalising the court itself.
7. 97 E.R. 94.
8. AIR 1943, P.C. 202.
9. AIR 1949, Lah. 266.

Allahabad High Court considered a statement in a resolution passed by the Bar Association to be reported to higher authorities in *State* v. *Brahma Prakash*.[10] The resolution stated that the officers are thoroughly incompetent and intemperate to the litigant public and lawyers. Though the Bar Association has the right to make representations to the government it has no right to make such allegations in an intemperate language. The court expressed the view that even if criticism of the conduct of a judge or magistrate has taken the form of a representation to the government, it was not outside the ambit of the law of contempt of court.[11]

The court further laid down that a criticism must be made in good faith and it must be free from the imputation of improper motives. Also the court's jurisdiction must be exercised with scrupulous care, and that proceedings in contempt ought not to be instituted unless there is a real likelihood of an interference with the due course of justice.[12]

Patna High Court in *In the matter of Basantha Chandra Ghosh*[13] laid down other limitations of scandalous allegations. The author of the article questioned the impartiality and

10. AIR 1950 All. 556. The Executive Committee of the Allahabad Bar Association passed several resolutions. One of the resolutions contained the following statement, "the officers are thoroughly incompetent in law, do not inspire them in their work...intemperate to the litigant public and to the lawyers...."

    The resolution was forwarded to the District Magistrate with a covering letter which stated:

    "...they (Officers) are incapable of improvement and thus instead of proving an acquisition to the Bench as these new cadres are expected to be, they are already discrediting it by deliberately preventing facts whenever it suits them." Statements in the resolution and covering letter were the subject matter of the contempt petition.

11. *Id.* at 561.
12. *Id.* at 561, 562.
13. AIR 1960 Pat. 430.

    In this case one advocate of Patna High Court published an article in the "Search Light" with the following caption "Recommendations of the Law Commission." This article was published soon after the submission of the report by the Law Commission appointed by the Government of India. The article made comments on the judicial independence of the High Court by stating that the judicial decisions are influenced by the executive.

> But the main criterion to be kept in view is that the limits of fair comment must not be exceeded. The language in which the comment is couched should be objective, dignified and there should be no attempt at ridiculing the administration of justice by this court by using language which is likely to shake the confidence of the public in the capacity, impartiality and the fairness of the procedure adopted by this court in the disposal of matters which come up for consideration.[14]

Use of the phrase stultification of justice and the opinion that 'hearing in closed chambers' after independence is really a matter of shame and disgrace, show that the language employed is not respectful and is bound to shake the confidence of the public in the administration of justice by the Patna High Court.[15] But a general reading of the article shows that it only deals with the defects of the existing system without any intention of scandalising it. Viewed objectively the article can only be an academic publication made in the light of the report of the Law Commission.

A letter by an advocate to the advocate of the opposite party with copies to the Chief Justice and Chairman of the Bar Council making allegations of conspiracy, fraud and partiality against the judge who presided over the authority under the Payment of Wages Act,[16] a threat by a party to the advocate

---

administration of the High Court in various matters. One of the passages read as follows: "Very few in this country acquainted with the working of the judiciary would honestly differ from the report of the Law Commission on the unsatisfactory method of recruitment of judges, the lowering of standard of the judiciary and selection of judges on consideration other than fitness as also with that part of the report which deals with the executive influence on the judiciary...."

14. *Id.* at 446.

15. *Id.* at 451.

16. *Registrar High Court A.S. Bombay* v. *S.K. Irani Advocate* AIR 1963 Bom. 254. In this case a wage dispute was pending before the Authority under the Payment of Wages Act. Effort to compromise the matter could not materialise because of difference. While so S.K. Irani (Advocate) wrote a letter to M/s. Garget and Co., which was the subject matter of the contempt petition. A portion of the letter read as follows: "In your

appearing for the other party that he would prosecute him and send him to jail in the course of argument,[17] use of abusive and intemperate language in an affidavit imputing partiality and dishonesty on the part of the Assistant Sessions Judge in disposing judicial work,[18] a statement in the transfer application that a magistrate was friendly with the party who happened to be an advocate and enjoyed his hospitality which imputed motive,[19] use of phrases like dishonest judgment, open dishonesty, misbehaviour, total falsehood, victimising the disliked party, in a pamphlet,[20] are all said to constitute contempt because they scandalised the judge or the judiciary.

(Solicitor's) fraud and cheating, my client says you were actively assisted and aided by the authority Shri Kotwal, in connivance and collusion of the crime, my client states that there was apparent criminal conspiracy between you and...to cheat and commit fraud on the applicant and thus to commit offence against justice, equity and good conscience.

17. *Mrs. Damayanthi G. Chandramani* v. *S. Vaney* AIR 1966 Bom. 19. In this case in connection with the rent suit an affidavit was filed by the plaintiff's advocate. The judge asked the defendant as to whether he got to say anything about the affidavit. The defendant stated that he would see to it that the plaintiff's advocate Mr. Punwani would go to Jail.... This statement was the subject matter of the present contempt proceedings.
18. *Advocate General Andhra Pradesh* v. *Abbaraju Rama Rao* AIR 1968 A.P. 207. The affidavit contained the following paragraph— "...the trying judge being Shri P. Ramachandra Raju, the Ex-Presiding Officer of the Assistant Sessions Judge's Court, Rajahmundry who pronounced judgments in those sessions cases dishonestly and maliciously basing the said three judgments on a forged will known as Ex.-D8.... The whole conspiracy having been positively abetted by the trying judge Sri P. Ramachandra Raju in consequence of which conspiracy...acquittal order of all the accused in sessions cases...were obtained. Ramachandra Raju having dishonestly and maliciously pronounced judgment in those sessions cases, being guilty of committing incidental offences also...."
19. *Gobind Ram* v. *State of Maharashtra* AIR 1972 S.C. 989.
20. *C.K. Daphtary* v. *O.P. Gupta* AIR 1971 S.C. 1132. It was alleged that the respondent with the deliberate design of bringing disrepute to the court printed and published certain statement through a pamphlet. Some portion of the statement was as follows: "Moreover having wrongly persisted in hearing the case, he delivered a demonstrably dishonest judgment which cannot fail to show to any discerning person that he did so only to feed his prejudice and bias. He has gone to the extent of writing total falsehoods in the judgment in the defiant belief that

The Supreme Court in *C.K. Daphtary*[21] viewed that a scurrilous attack on a judge for his judgment or his past conduct has adverse effect on the due administration of justice which will inevitably undermine the confidence of the public in the judiciary.[22]

So, irrespective of the material in which the statement was contained, if the language was degrading the dignity of the court it was held as scandalous allegation. Another way of scandalising the court is by public speeches. The Kerala High Court in *Narayanan Nambiar* v. *E.M.S. Namboodiripad*[23] held E.M.S. Namboodiripad guilty of contempt because, his press statement was not fair and reasonable. Even if it be a defence once the evil tendency of the statement is established it becomes contempt.[24] The court further observed:

> It is a columny calculated not merely in the sense that it tends to, but also, since on the respondent's own showing the statement was a statement deliberately made with the object of educating public opinion—calculated in the sense that it was intended to—to undermine the confidence of the public in the courts of the land than which, since the proper administration of justice depends

there was no one to look into and scrutinise his judgments. His action is highly condemnable and derogatory of a man in his position...he appears to be in the habit of being influenced by extra-judicial considerations and of victimising the disliked party through dishonest means...."

21. *Supra* n. 20.
22. *Id.* at 1134.
23. 1968 KLT 306. In this case question for consideration was whether the statements made by E.M.S. Namboodiripad, the then Chief Minister of Kerala at a Press Conference held at Trivandrum, amounted to contempt of court. In the Press Conference he stated "Marx and Engels considered the judiciary as an instrument of oppression and even today when the State set-up has not undergone any change, and is dominated by class hatred, class interests and class prejudices and where evidence is balanced between a well dressed pot bellied rich man and a poor ill-dressed and illiterate person the judge instinctively favours the former. His party had always taken the view that judiciary is part of the class rule of the ruling classes. And there are limits to the sanctity of judiciary....
24. *Id.* at 318.

so much on such confidence, no greater public mischief can be imagined.[25]

The Chief Minister was punished because his statement substantially undermined the confidence of the public in the judiciary. But if we apply the test as laid down by Lord Atkin,[26] that 'justice is not a cloistered virtue she must be allowed to suffer the scrutiny and outspoken comments of ordinary men,' the words used by E.M. Sankaran Namboodiripad were not calculated to obstruct or interfere with the course of justice, nor was intended to scandalise the judiciary, since he only stated the defects in the existing judicial system.

The dissenting view of Mathew J. throws much light on the subject and is in conformity with the opinion of Lord Atkin. According to him, the law of contempt in relation to scandalising a court is to be read in such a way as to harmonise it with the fundamental right of free speech. That means the operation of this branch of the law of contempt has to be limited to certain definite situation.[27]

They are:

1. Vindictive or scurrilous attack of a court or a judge based on false allegations or made recklessly may amount to contempt by scandalising the court or the judge.
2. In a republican constitution, judges as persons and courts as institutions are entitled to no greater immunity from criticism than any other person or institution.
3. Judges are subject to common human frailties and weaknesses.
4. It is an irrational fear that allegiance and obedience to law would come to an end if the court and judge are freely criticised.
5. *Bona fide* criticism without malice will not amount to contempt.

---

25. *Id.* at 318, 319.
26. *Supra* n. 2.
27. *Supra* n. 23, pp. 332-35.

On appeal,[28] the Supreme Court also held the appellant guilty of contempt, because the statements interfered with the functioning of the courts and the administration of justice. Further the statement was calculated to raise in the minds of the people a general dissatisfaction and distrust of all judicial decisions.[29]

This decision was criticised by scholars like H.M. Seervai[30] and V.G. Ramachandran.[31] H.M. Seervai concluded that the court is correct in its conclusion but unsatisfactory when it attempts to summarise.[32]

The statement of Hidayathullah C.J. that either he does not know or has deliberately distorted the writings of Marx, Engels and Lenin for his own purpose[33] had been repudiated by E.M.S. Namboodiripad himself in his letter to the editor of *Kerala Law Times*.[34]

Even if E.M.S. Namboodiripad's statement was the reproduction of Marx and Engels, it may not have any impact on the decision because the truth of the matter is not a defence for contempt proceedings. The vital question is whether the statement in effect scandalised the court, was answered by the supreme court in affirmative, because the statement had the effect of lowering the prestige of the judges and the courts in the eyes of the people.[35]

28. *E.M.S. Namboodiripad* v. *T.N. Nambiar* AIR 1970 S.C. 2015.
29. *Id.* at 2024.
30. H.M. Seervai 'Supreme Court and Contempt of Court' 73, *Bombay Law Reporter* (Jnl.) 5.
31. V.G. Ramachandran 'Comments on cases' III-II *Lawyer* 33 (1971) *see* also Editorial 74 *Calcutta Weekly notes* No. 38 (1970).
32. *Supra* n. 30.
33. *Supra* n. 28, p. 2023.
34. E.M.S. Namboodiripad "A letter to Editor" 1971 K.L.T. (Jnl.) 2. But since the highest judicial authority in the country has taken up itself the task of trying to find out what the true teachings of Marx and Engels are and to 'expose' my 'error' with regard to them, may I crave the indulgence of your columns to point out that it is not me who is in 'error' about the true teachings of Marx and Engels.' (*Id.* at 4).
35. *Supra* n. 28, p. 2024.

Another important question left unanswered by the Supreme Court was whether criticism of the judicial system will amount to contempt of court?

The criticism by E.M.S. Namboodiripad was a constructive one aimed at modification of the institution, without any intention of bringing disrepute to the judiciary. The Supreme Court changed its view as expressed in *E.M. Sankaran Namboodiripad's*[36] case in *Khadilkar Contempt*[37] case wherein the Court unanimously held Mr. Khadilkar not guilty of contempt. Chief Justice Hidayatullah stated:

> There is no doubt that the court like any other institution does not enjoy immunity from fair criticism. The court does not claim to be always right although it does not spare any effort to be right according to the best of the ability, knowledge and judgment of the judges.... We are constrained to say also that while fair and temperate criticism of this court or any other court even if strong, may not be actionable, attributing improper motives or tending to bring judges or courts into hatred and contempt or obstructing directly or indirectly within the functioning of courts is serious contempt of which notice must and will be taken.[38]

Judicial decisions prior to the Contempt of Courts Act, 1971 generally adopted an approach that allegations which were scurrilous, which imputed motives, or bias constituted scandalising the court.

---

36. *Supra* n. 28.
37. Unreported, as stated by V.S. Mani in his article "Contempt of Court and Democratic Criticism, the Khadilkar Contempt Case". 36 *The Cuttack Law Times* (Jnl.) 53 (1970). In this case soon after the decision in Bank Nationalisation case a meeting was arranged by Blitz National Forum. The speakers included R.K. Khadilkar, Union Minister, Mr. Mohan Kumaramangalam, A.S.R. Chari and S.M. Joshi. At the meeting Khadilkar severely criticised the Supreme Court. He said the judgment in the Bank Nationalisation case will be treated with contempt by ordinary people...ten judges sitting in ivory towers could not sit over the verdict of Parliament which represented the people.
38. *Id.* at 55, 56.

(ii) After the Contempt of Courts Act, 1971

Sec. 2(c)[39] of the Contempt of Courts Act, 1971 which defines criminal contempt widened the scope of scandalising the court by including the terms "tends to scandalise or lowers or tends to lower" and gave wide scope for the judiciary to intervene. But a perusal of the judicial decisions after the Contempt of Courts Act, 1971 shows that judiciary has been very restrictive in its approach. The view taken by the Supreme Court in *E.M. Sankaran Namboodiripad's*[40] case has not been followed in the post Act period. The scope and content of scandalising the court is so taken as to suit the changing social conditions.

Important dignitaries like the Chief Minister and other Ministers were charged for contempt for making comments on the judiciary. The Kerala High Court in *T.A. Rajendran* v. *Vayalar Ravi*[41] the Supreme Court in *M.R. Parashar* v. *Dr. Farooq Abdullah*[42] and *P.N. Duda* v. *P. Shiva Shankar*[43] held the respective Ministers who made the statement not guilty of contempt. But the Bombay High Court in *The State of Maharashtra* v. *Chandrakant Tripathi*[44] found Chandrakant Tripathi, Minister of Urban Development, guilty of contempt. But the court dropped the proceedings by taking a charitable attitude. According to the court, the statement that in the courts an innocent person is convicted and a guilty person is acquitted would constitute an attack calculated to raise in the mind of the general public dissatisfaction about the judiciary.[45] The court gave more importance to the tenor of how the respondent referred to the acquittals of guilty persons.

39. Sec. 2 (c) of the Contempt of Courts Act, 1971 (*See* n. 46 Ch. 6).
40. *Supra* n. 28.
41. AIR 1983 Ker. 105.
42. AIR 1984 S.C. 615.
43. AIR 1988 S.C. 1208.
44. 1983 Cri. L.J. (Bombay High Court) 1841. In this case the Minister severely criticised the judicial system. He stated "under the present judicial system even criminals are given benefit of doubt and are acquitted if there are no witnesses or if they turn hostile. The innocent are sentenced. The Maharashtra Government will soon publish a book showing how many works are lying pending due to stay orders of the court (at 1841).
45. *Id.* at 1844.

A statement of this nature without reference to any particular suit or party cannot be said to constitute contempt. But because of the tenor of the language, the statement was said to constitute contempt.

Contrary to the Bombay High Court, the Kerala High Court in *T.A. Rajendran* v. *Vayalar Ravi*[46] held, a general statement by the Minister that judiciary should not criticise the government in a style more severe than that of the opposition will not amount to contempt because, the court is concerned more with the reasonable and probable effect of what is said or written than with the motives behind what is done.[47]

But the court made a remark that if such seemingly innocent statements are made without good faith and with the evil intention of bringing the courts or the judiciary as a whole into disrepute it will amount to contempt.

So also the Supreme Court in *Dr. Farooq Abdullah's*[48] case adopted a very liberal attitude. In this case the petition was rejected because of lack of evidence as the case was based on the paper report. The need for proving the paper report by further evidence was subsequently emphasised by the Supreme

46. *Supra* n. 41. Ministers Vayalar Ravi and Gangadharan made certain statements at the youth conference held at Mannam Nagar. Vayalar Ravi said: "If judiciary attempts to view the government as political parties do, it would create difficulties for both...government is prepared to recognise the right of judiciary to interpret law; but if things go beyond that limit it cannot be taken lightly". Gangadharan stated: "Considering the national interest, whether it is the judiciary, the government or legislature, in certain matters, boundary bunds have to be erected."

47. *Id.* at 108.

48. *M.R. Parashar* v. *Dr. Farooq Abdullah* AIR 1984 S.C. 615. Dr. Farooq Abdullah, then Chief Minister of Jammu and Kashmir, while addressing the Annual General Meeting of the Institute of Engineers, made certain statements which were alleged to be scandalising the judiciary. He said that the engineers should occupy a certain building forcibly as it would not be possible for them to evict the Amar Singh Club through the normal legal process. Further he said "justice is being bought in the judicial courts...." "I will never honour these stay orders even if I am hanged."

Court in *State of Haryana* v. *Ch. Bhajan Lal* v. *S.A. Khan.*[49] It was observed:

> In the present case, no evidence has been let in proof of the statement of facts contained in the newspaper report. The absence of any denial by Ch. Bhajan Lal will not absolve the applicant from discharging his obligation of proving the statement of facts as appeared in the press report.... Therefore, in the absence of required legal proof, the court will not be justified in issuing *suo motu* notice for contempt of court.[50]

Even though in both the cases the contempt petition was rejected for lack of adequate evidence, it is pertinent to note the liberal attitude of the Supreme Court as evidenced in the following observation in *Dr. Farooq Abdullah's*[51] case:

> The right of free speech is an important right of the citizen, in the exercise of which he is entitled to bring to the notice of the public at large the infirmities from which any institution suffers, including the institutions which administer justice.[52]

The view expressed by the Supreme Court in the above two decisions was followed by the Kerala High Court in *Tharian Joseph* v. *K.P. Viswanathan, Minister of Forests, Government of Kerala.*[53] Since the Minister denied the use of harsh words and

---

49. AIR 1993 S.C. 1348. Certain charges of corruption had been levelled against the Union Minister Bhajan Lal. On the basis of the allegation enquiry was held and F.I.R. was filed. But Bhajan Lal filed a writ petition and obtained a stay of the proceedings. The matter was taken in appeal to the Supreme Court and while it was pending, the Minister made a press statement which was the subject matter of the contempt petition. He alleged that the Deputy Inspector General of Police who considered himself a big officer, was implicating his people in false cases. He vowed to make him rub his nose on the ground, where the meeting was being held, for forgiveness....
50. *Id.* at 1354.
51. *Supra* n. 48.
52. *Supra* n. 48, p. 617.
53. 1994 Cri. L.J. (Kerala High Court) 82. K.P. Viswanathan, Minister for Forests, Kerala during his inaugural address in a function at Ernakulam stated that Forest department was put to lot of troubles because of the verdicts given by the High Court. He further stated that he could not understand the motive and logic underlying the decision.

also because of lack of proof, the court dropped the proceedings by giving benefit of doubt. But the court gave the following warning:

> Of late criticism of the judicial act is on the increase. It has reached a boring point. In as much as the press is too fond of publicity have in our humble view resorted to uncalled for criticism. Several of the articles criticising judges are pedestrian and unscholarly or are exaggerated. Judges do not as per well established conventions, hit back by going to the press. In fact if judges respond they are likely to get embroiled in further controversy of a reply, to a reply which infact is what the critic or the publisher desire for that gives him greater publicity. Judges do not reply. That is not because the allegations cannot be denied and the untruth exposed but because they are hand cuffed by judicial convention, decorum and discipline.[54]

The Supreme Court in *P.N. Duda* v. *P. Shiv Shankar*[55] welcomed criticism about the judicial system or judges so long as such criticism did not impair or hamper the administration of justice.[56] Supreme Court though refused to recognise criticism of the judicial system in its earlier decision in *E.M. Sankaran Namboodiripad* v. *T.N. Nambiar*[57] it respectfully accepted the

54. *Id.* at 89, 90.
55. *Supra* n. 43. In this case Shri P. Shiv Shankar then Law Minister and former High Court judge made the following statement at a meeting of the Bar Council of Hyderabad:

 "The Supreme Court composed of the element from the elite class had their unconcealed sympathy for the haves *i.e.*, the Zamindars. As a result they interpreted the word compensation in Art. 31 contrary to the spirit and the intendment of the Constitution and ruled that compensation must represent the price which willing seller is prepared to accept from a willing buyer. The entire programme of Zamindari abolition suffered a set back.... Now can you tell what that black-robed elites are going to do next. Spring more criminals, abolish more protections. Throw down more ultras.... When the privy purses were abolished the Supreme Court, contrary to the whole national upsurge, held in favour of the Maharajas.... Anti-social elements *i.e.* FERA violators, bride burners and a whole horde of reactionaries have found their haven in the Supreme Court...."
56. *Id.* at 1214.
57. *Supra* n. 28.

ratio in that case, reversed its decision in Shiv Shankar's case because the court accepted that there is change in time and clime in the last two decades.[58] Also there is erosion in human values.

Another reason given by Justice Renganathan was that we must read the speech as a whole and it should be viewed in its face value.[59] The statement of the Minister was a mere theoretical dissertation without any intention to disrespect the court.

The court further observed that in a study of accountability if class composition of the people manning the institution is analysed, it cannot be said that an expression or view or propagation of that view hampers the dignity of the courts or impairs the administration of justice.[60] The question of contempt should depend on the totality of the facts of the case. At places the Minister's statement is little intemperate, but that itself will not interfere with the administration of justice and will not amount to contempt of court.[61]

Though a bare reading of the Union Minister's speech shows that it would lower the authority of the court, the court deterred from holding such a view, because there was change in time and clime in the two decades. In contrast, the court took a stricter view in *E.M. Sankaran Namboodiripad's*[62] case, and punished him, though he also stated the drawbacks of the then existing judicial system. Even if, at places, a statement is intemperate that itself is not sufficient to constitute contempt. The statement as a whole has to be considered for ascertaining its contemptuous nature.

Whether the alleged statement is contained in representation[63]

---

58. *Supra* n. 43, p. 1215.
59. *Supra* n. 43, p. 1229.
60. *Id.* at 1215.
61. *Id.* at 1220.
62. *Supra* n. 28.
63. *Mulkhraj* v. *State of Punjab* 1972 Cri. L.J. (Punjab High Court) 754. Mulkhraj, the defeated party in a civil suit made an application to the Chief Justice of India. It contained the following allegation: "That against this decision of Shri J.P. Gupta (officiating) District Additional Judge, the plaintiff applicant has filed an appeal in the Punjab High

or appeal memorandum[64] or false averments in the affidavit[65] if the language used is offensive casting aspersions on the judges and lowering the dignity and esteem of the judiciary it constitutes a clear case of contempt.[66] Though section 6[67] of the Contempt of Courts Act, 1971 protected complaints made to the higher court, if such complaint contained offensive language, Sec. 6 is of no rescue. In *Baradakanta Misra's*[68] case Orissa High Court after considering the statement contained in the appeal memorandum and in a representation observed:

> The allegations in the petition not only scandalised the learned Chief Justice and the other learned judges, but

---

Court...which appeal was dismissed unjustifiably by the Honourable justice Harbans Singh simply to suppress my case...dismissing my application of letters patent appeal unjustifiably and forcibly and just to suppress my case and did not allow to file a letters patent appeal. This resulted in my full destruction and disaster. The defendant party is too rich and has many approaches."

High Court held that the appellant maliciously endeavoured to impair the image of the Judicial integrity of the High Court.

64. *Advocate General Orissa* v. *Baradakanta Misra* 1974 Cri. L.J. (Orissa High Court) 70. In this case disciplinary proceedings were initiated by the High Court against Baradakanta Misra, then District Judge. Against the finding of High Court, he preferred an appeal to the Governor and also to the Supreme Court. The Statement in the representation and appeal were the subject matter of contempt.

    The contemner alleged that the learned Chief Justice and other learned judges had committed contempt of court by disposing of an administrative proceeding against the contemner while Special Bench was still hearing the contempt matter against him. The contemner further alleged that the charges in the administrative proceeding and in the contempt case were common. The Bench approached the issues which arose for consideration therein with preconceived notions.

65. *Afzal and another* v. *State of Haryana* (AIR 1996 S.C. 2326).
66. *Supra* n. 63 p. 756.
67. Sec. 6: A person shall not be guilty of Contempt of Court in respect of any statement made by him in good faith concerning the presiding officer of any subordinate court to—

    (a) any other subordinate court, or

    (b) the High Court to which it is subordinate.

    Explanation:

    In this section, subordinate court means any court subordinate to a High Court.
68. *Supra* n. 64.

> clearly interfered with the administration of justice. A bare reading of the text of the petition would lead to the indisputable conclusion that the remarks are scurrilous, motive has been imputed and the integrity of the judges have been doubted.[69]

Copy of the appeal given to the Governor was sent to the High Court with a covering letter which constituted another case of contempt[70] because the letter substantially interfered with the due course of justice.

On appeal,[71] the Supreme Court considered two important questions: (i) whether criticism of the administrative act of the High Court Judge would amount to contempt; (ii) whether prejorative imputations about a court or a judge however offensive, true or honestly held even if contained in an appeal to higher court or in a remedial representation to correctional authority, constituted contempt.

Justice Krishna Iyer considered the first question elaborately and tried to make a distinction between judicial function and administrative function of a judge. According to him judicialisation as a functional limitation on contempt jurisdiction must exclude from its ambit interference with purely administrative acts of courts and non-judicial functions of judges.[72] Though the personality of a judge is an integrated one, the purely administrative function cannot be the subject matter of contempt.

But Justice Palekar is of the view that if the attack on a judge affected the administration of justice, it became punishable for contempt and it did not matter whether such an attack related only to the administrative functions of a judge or not.[73]

Justice Krishna Iyer further observed:

> Judges and courts have diverse duties. But functionally, and jurisprudentially, the value which is dear to the

---

69. *Id.* at 73.
70. *Registrar of the Orissa High Court* v. *Baradakanta Misra* AIR 1973 Ori. 244.
71. *Baradakanta Misra* v. *Registrar Orissa High Court* AIR 1974 S.C. 710.
72. *Id.* at 729.
73. *Id.* at 722.

> community and the function which deserves to be cardoned off from public molestation is judicial. Vicious criticism of personal and administrative acts of judges may indirectly mar their image and weaken the confidence of the public in the judiciary but the counterveiling good not merely of free speech but also of greater faith generated by exposure to the atnic light of *bona fide* even if marginally overzealous criticism cannot be overlooked. Justice is no cloistered value.[74]

Though the majority opinion had not accepted the distinction between administrative and judicial functions of a judge, it was further considered by the Allahabad High Court in *G.N. Verma* v. *Hargovind Dayal.*[75]

In this case it was argued that the principle laid down in *Baradakanta Misra* v. *The Registrar, Orissa High Court*[76] should not be taken to be an authority for the view that intemperate language used about an administrative or legislative act of the Chief Justice as distinguished from that of the court shall also amount to contempt.

It was further argued that when the Chief Justice was acting under Clause 14 of the High Court Amalgamation Order, he exercised a legislative power and that anything said in exercise of such a power of the Chief Justice could amount to contempt.

But the Allahabad High Court refused to make any distinction between the administrative and the judicial acts of the judge and held whether the act was administrative or legislative in nature, if the imputations made against the Chief Justice in that regard fall within the definition of criminal contempt as

74. *Id.* at 733.

75. AIR 1975 All. 52. The subject matter for consideration was the resolution passed by the Avadh Bar Association. The material portion read as follows:

"The Action Committee is of the opinion that the Chief Justice is acting in the discharge of administrative power under Clause 14, of the Uttar Pradesh High Court's Amalgamation Order, 1948, in a most partisan manner under the influence of Allahabad Bar, quite unbecoming of the office which he holds."

76. *Supra* n. 71.

contained in the Act of 1971, it would be punishable by this court.[77]

The contempt jurisdiction is exercised for protecting the authority of the court and not for protecting the person. The wording used in Sec. 2 (c)[78] of the Act is also that, lowering the authority of any court. Though the personality of a judge is an integrated one, this extra-ordinary jurisdiction is not to be used if he exceeds the limits of a judge.

The Supreme Court in *Ram Pratap Sharma* v. *Daya Nand*[79] refused to extend the protective veil of contempt jurisdiction when a judge addressed a public meeting. The reason is that the judge travels from his judicial work and descends into the arena of politics and parties. The judge cannot in such cases take shelter behind his office if the public discussed his views. Because it is no part of the duty of judge nor it is a duty in the discharge of office of a judge to address a political meeting to redress grievances of the people.[80] The court further observed:

> We wish to make it clear that if on facts it appears that the judge did say things or matters about politics, such utterances or views or observations will be the personal opinions expressed by the judge and therefore, the protective umbrella of the court cannot be used by way

77. *Supra* n. 75, p. 60.
78. *Supra* n. 39.
79. AIR 1977 S.C. 809. The subject matter of contempt was the letter written by the Bar Association to the President of India with copies to the Prime Minister, Chief Justice of India, Chief Minister of Haryana, and Chief Justice of Haryana. The letter stated: "The learned judge met the members of the Bar on 15th Feb., 1975 in the Bar room, Bhivani. During the course of the meeting, the learned judge criticised the government's policy in regard to its attitude towards the judiciary. Besides, the learned judge was openly attacking the government in its political as well as administrative decision. On the whole he gave an impression that he was not a Judge but a politician who had come to Bar room.... He suggested the members of the Bar to revolt against the present government.... The judge further said that the prevailing system of government was not good in this country and we must adopt the communist form of government which can save the nation...."
80. *Id.* at 812.

of bringing the critics on the charge of contempt of court.[81]

The opinion of the Supreme Court in *Baradakanta Misra's*[82] case that the personality of a judge is an integrated one, was criticised in the *Calcutta Weekly Notes*[83] as the judgment proceeded on a misconception of the contempt jurisdiction.

Use of words maliciously in bad faith and sidetracking the issue in a notice,[84] sending threatening notices to the judges imputing *mala fides* and lack of *bona fides* in them,[85] squarely fall within the ambit of criminal contempt.

On appeal[86] the Supreme Court also accepted the above view given by the Andhra Pradesh High Court and held the respondents guilty of contempt. Unfounded imputation of *mala fides*, bias, prejudice or ridiculing the performance of a

81. *Id.* at 812, 813.
82. *Supra* n. 71.
83. 78 *Calcutta Weekly Notes* No. 8 (1973) "With all respect to the learned judge, we think the judgment proceed on a misconception of the contempt jurisdiction of the High Court." The reasoning of the author is that the High Court derives its powers of punishing for contempt from Art. 215 which says that the High Court shall be a court of record and shall have all the powers of court of record including the power to punish for contempt. It follows that only when the High Court is acting as a court of record it has the power to punish for contempt. In appointing, dismissing or taking disciplinary action against members of subordinate judiciary under Art. 234, or 235, the High Court does not act as a court of record.
84. *Advocate General Andhra Pradesh* v. *Rachapudi Subba Rao* 1976 Cri. L.J. (Andhra Pradesh High Court) 745. A civil suit filed by the respondent was dismissed by the Subordinate Judge's Court, Vijayawada. The decree holder filed an execution petition and the same was stayed. While so, the respondent sent a notice to the Additional Subordinate Judge which contained scandalous allegations. The relevant portion of the notice reads as follows: "Your honour has intentionally with bad faith and maliciously discorded the existing oral and documentary evidence with a view to help the plaintiff.... Your honour has maintained different standards in the same judgment.... Your honour has side tracked the binding direct decision of the High Court and Supreme Court...."
85. *Id.* at 748.
86. *Rachapudi Subba Rao* v. *The Advocate General A.P.* AIR 1981 S.C. 755.

judge or casting aspersions on his integrity,[87] reckless allegations made without good faith against the District and Sessions Judge by a defeated party in a suit, to the Chief Justice of India,[88] imputations of partiality, if not dishonesty by the defeated party to the judge who heard and decided the case[89] are also instances of scandalising the court. Imputation of unfairness, bias or dishonesty to the judge would undermine the confidence of the people in the courts and the judicial system of the country.[90] So also a notice drafted by an advocate attributing motives to the judicial officer is said to amount to contempt of court.[91]

Subsequent decisions also indicate that so far as complaint letters or petitions made to higher authorities are concerned, the court will extend the contempt jurisdiction if the tone and temper of the language scandalises the judge or judiciary or it

87. *Id.* at 759.

88. *State* v. *R.N. Patra* 1976 Cri. L.J. (Orissa High Court) 440, 445. The Contemner addressed a petition to the Hon'ble Chief Justice of the Orissa High Court. It contained certain allegations against the District and Sessions Judge. The relevant portion is "this judge gives all to understand that no one can stop his present activities so long as Shri G.K. Mishra the Chief Justice of Orissa was there to protect him. He also alleged that the District and Sessions Judge was visiting freely the residence of counsel for parties whose case he was hearing while in circuit and was obliging a group of lawyers.

89. *Advocate General* v. *Abraham George* 1976 Cri. L.J. (Kerala High Court) 158. In this case a civil suit was decided by the Alleppy Sub-Court. The matter was taken in appeal to the High Court and the Division Bench of the High Court dismissed the appeal. Soon the respondent addressed a petition to the Chief Justice of the High Court making certain allegations against the judges who decided the appeal (Allegations in the letter are made in Malayalam). He alleged that the court held a farce making up before hearing and decided the case without recognizing the principle that before the court the priest and the respondents are equals. Thus it is said the court has conducted itself in such a way as to sell its prestige. Reference was made in the petition of the Advocate General to several similar petitions having been sent by the respondent to the High Court when the original suit was pending at the court in Alleppy.

90. *Id.* at 161.

91. *Shamsher Singh Bedi* v. *High Court of Punjab and Haryana* (AIR 1995 S.C. 1974).

imputes improper motives or malicious intention to scandalise the court. Thus in *State of Rajasthan* v. *M.R. Mitruka*[92] a letter written by the President of the Rajasthan Judicial Service Association to the Hon'ble Union Home Minister in respect of alleged corruption in judiciary, was held not to constitute contempt because the letter was not actuated by any improper motive or malicious intention to scandalise the court[93] and has been written with a zeal and fervour of an idealist acting on the spirit of a crusade against the evil of corruption.[94] Accusations, attributions and aspersions made against a judge will malign the court and undermine the dignity and authority of the Court.[95]

Casting aspersions on the judge in a transfer application had been viewed seriously by the court because it brings the court into disrepute and is an affront to the majesty of law and offends the dignity of the court.[96]

The court observed:

> No system of justice can tolerate such unbridled licence on the part of a person, be he a lawyer, to permit himself the liberty of scandalising a court by casting unwarranted, uncalled for and unjustified aspersions on the integrity, ability, impartiality or fairness of a judge in the discharge

---

92. 1978 Cri. L.J. (Rajasthan High Court) 1440. The respondent stated in the letter that he had highest respect for the judges of that court and judicial officers of all courts and that he had no intention of scandalising them. He had further stated that the reference to corruption in the letter in question was in reference to officials working in the judiciary and not to any of the judges of that court or the judicial officers. According to the respondent his sole object in writing the letter was to invite the attention of the Union Home Minister to the increase in corruption and to help him to root out corruption in Rajasthan.

93. *Id.* at 1444.

94. *Ibid.*

95. *In Re: Sanjiv Datta* (1995 Cri. L.J. 2910).

96. *Jeswant Singh* v. *Virendra Singh* AIR 1995 S.C. 520, 536. Contempt petition arose because of allegations contained in the stay petition and transfer application in connection with an election petition. The transfer petition cast aspersions on the learned judge in the discharge of his judicial functions and had the tendency to scandalise the court.

of judicial functions as it amounts to an interference with the due course of administration of justice.[97]

So also in *Rajiv K. Garg* v. *Shanti Bhushan*[98] the Supreme Court refused to take *suo motu* action to initiate contempt proceedings, taking into account larger interest of the Bar. It could be remembered that when the Allahabad Bar Association passed a resolution to be sent to the higher authorities which stated the inefficiency of the judicial officers it was said to constitute contempt because the language used was scandalous and abusive. But that attitude has been changed and the court will take action if the complaint is couched in intemperate or scurrilous language. Thus the Madhya Pradesh High Court in *In Re Ananddhar Diwan, the contemner,*[99] viewed that unfounded imputation of *mala fides*, bias, prejudice or ridiculing the performance of a judge or casting aspersions on his integrity are considered to mean scandalising the court.[100] So also use of coloured flare of language, and unhealthy expressions in an article though tantamount to contempt, would not by itself be the ground to take any serious view of the matter.[101] Any scurrilous, offensive, intimidatory or malicious attack on the

97. *Id.* at 536.

98. AIR 1995 S.C. 573: With a view to remove a sitting judge, a committee of lawyers called "Sub Committee on Judicial Accountability" was formed in order to maintain purity of legal profession. The allegations in the petition were that the members of the legal profession who were members of the so-called sub committee on judicial accountability...were using legal profession as a shield and committing of the grossest criminal contempt and this honourable court must take serious note.

99. 1982 Cri. L.J. (Madhya Pradesh High Court) 1744. During the pendency of a revision petition based on a money suit the contemner who was not a party to the suit sent an application to the Chief Justice of India with copies to the Chief Justice of High Court, the President, the Prime Minister etc. (Application is in Hindi). The contemner pleaded that, what he stated was a fair and reasonable comment on the order and made in the public interest without any intention to scandalise the court.

100. *Id.* at 1746.

101. *Bhal Chandra Gangadhar Ghate* v. *Pralhad Saduji Raghute* 1977 Cri. L.J. (Bombay High Court) 1490, 1491. The opponent published an article in a souvenir called "Prema", in which certain disrespectful references were made about a decision of the Bombay High Court (Article not reproduced).

judicial officer/authority beyond condonable limits amounts to scandalising the court.[102] So also a party who lost his case (Public interest litigation), when makes false allegations against the Chief Justice of India, in the writ petition, in most scurrilous terms, it will amount to contempt of court.[103]

Use of insulting language in the face of the court,[104] and issuing a prepared statement commenting on an interim stay of a court[105] will amount to contempt of court. Because such acts will have ulterior effect on the authority and dignity of the court. So also attempt to attack Judicial Magistrate and chasing him to his chamber hurling abuses in filthy language as

---

102. *U.P. Sales Tax Service Association* v. *Taxation Bar Association, Agra,* AIR 1996 S.C. 98 at 101.
103. *In Re Dr. Saxena and Dr. D.C. Saxena, Contemner* v. *Hon'ble the Chief Justice of India* AIR 1996 S.C. 2981.
104. *Court on its own motion* v. *Bansilal* 1979 Cri. L.J. (Notes on cases p. 76) 165. The contemner in a crowded court room contemptuously shouted in the face of the Presiding Officer that he was a party to the conspiracy hatched by certain executive authorities to kill him and also insultingly levelled the charge that he had prejudged the issue of his remand and agreed with the police authorities to entrust his personal custody to them for a period of five days and that he was convinced that the presiding officer was going to do so.... The accused declared that the presiding officer was a liar and criminal, and concluded that no justice would be expected from such a liar and a criminal.
105. *Vincent Panikulangara* v. *Gopala Kurup* 1982 Cri. L.J. (Kerala High Court) 2094. The respondent Gopala Kurup was a member of the Syndicate and also President of non-teaching gazetted officers Association of the University of Kerala. Consequent on the allegation of malpractices, criminal cases were filed against some members of the association and interim stay order was obtained. During the pendency of the stay order, the respondent issued a statement to the press in Malayalam. The translated version is as follows:

    "The university had done whatever is possible this year to see that the valuation in the Pre-Degree examination was perfect. Our belief is that we have succeeded in this. Some of the irregularities at certain examination centres are under enquiry. We have already taken steps to see that such things are not repeated. In these circumstances while it would have been sufficient to call for the mark lists of 400 students, to direct that all the answer papers of all these students have to be carried to Ernakulam and further to find fraud in three papers when checking exactly 30 books is suspicious."

reaction of unfavourable decision given in a case is said to amount to contempt and the contemner was punished.[106]

Advocate slapping judge in open court is guilty of criminal contempt.[107] Supreme Court observed:

> A slap on the face of the judicial officer is in fact a slap on the face of the justice delivery system in the country as such question of acceptance of any apology or an undertaking does not and cannot arise, neither there can be any question of any leniency as regards the sentence.[108]

The Kerala High Court though accepted the right to make fair criticism of all organs of the state wanted to have a limitation when it relates to the judiciary. It was observed:

> This does not mean that the right to commit for any contempt by scandalising the court has become obsolete. The question would still be whether the publication alleged to be offending is by way of fair comment on the merits of the case. Comment not made honestly and in good faith would not be a fair comment. Comment not intended to promote public interest could not be a fair comment.[109]

So also use of terms such as a misconduct of the presiding judge, and most illegal and unconstitutional legal process, which are unwarranted are scurrilous, highly offensive, vicious, intimidatory, malicious and beyond condonable limit.[110] Such

---

106. *In Re: Tapan Roy and others, Contemners* 1997 Cri. L.J. (Calcutta High Court) 2166.
107. *Prem Surana* v. *Additional Munsif and Judicial Magistrate* (AIR 2002 S.C. 2956).
108. *Id.* at 2959.
109. *Id.* at 2098.
110. *Pritam Pal* v. *High Court of Madhya Pradesh, Jabalpur* AIR 1992 S.C. 904, 916. The appellant joined the Bar after serving in the defence service. Since there was delay in accepting his resignation, he filed a writ petition which was ultimately dismissed. Being aggrieved, he filed a contempt petition which was also dismissed. Allegations contained in the contempt petition were drawn up by the High Court and contempt proceedings were taken up. The appellant used the terms "misconduct of the presiding judge and most illegal and unconstitutional legal process adopted by the Hon'ble Judge." The petitioner charged the Hon'ble Court especially justice J.S. Verma for adopting most illegal and unconstitutional judicial process.

allegations are most fatal and dangerous obstruction of justice, shaking the confidence of the public in the administration of justice calling for more rapid and immediate punitive action.[111]

Any liberal attitude of the courts should not be misconstrued as an allowance for advocates to use intemperate language against the judiciary. Advocates being an integral part of the judicial system should have a greater sense of responsibility than ordinary citizen.

In *S.P. Sawhney* v. *Life Insurance Corporation of India*[112] the Supreme Court refused to invoke contempt proceedings in view of the age and physical condition of the contemner though the statements were sufficiently malicious.

The same view was followed by the Rajasthan High Court in *Dalpatraj Bhandari* v. *The President of India.*[113] The court though dropped the proceedings taking into account the obsession and frustration of the advocate viewed that the advocate should have refrained from making such indiscreet and despicable remarks about the judgments of the Supreme Court and the manner in which their Lordships decide matters pending before them.[114]

111. The same view was expressed by the Supreme Court in *M.B. Sanghi, Advocate* v. *High Court of Punjab and Haryana* AIR 1991 S.C. 1834. The appellant, a practising Advocate having failed to persuade the subordinate judge to grant an *ad interim* injunction pending filing of a counter by the opposite party, resorted to derogatory remarks on the subordinate judge. He made the remarks with the intention of casting aspersions on the integrity and to lower him in the esteem of others. The court observed: "when there is a deliberate attempt to scandalise which would shake the confidence of the litigating public in the system, the damage, caused is not only to the reputation of the concerned judge but also to the fair name of the judiciary."
112. AIR 1991 S.C. 661. A series of litigations between the respondent and the L.I.C. were pending and some of them were dismissed by the respective courts. The present contempt petition was the result of statement contained in a petition filed by the respondent in the Supreme Court.
113. AIR 1993 Raj. 1. The alleged contemner, the advocate, questioned the validity of appointment of Chief Justice and Judges of the High Court and Supreme Court. He claimed that he fulfilled all the qualifications required for a judge but his application was not considered. The allegations by the advocate in the writ petition were the subject matter of the contempt petition.
114. *Id.* at 29.

But in *Mohd. Zahir Khan* v. *Vijai Singh*[115] it was held that the statement "either he is an antinational or the judges are antinationals" has the effect of scandalising the court.[116]

So also, the contemner, an advocate questioning the conduct of the Supreme Court judges and demanding apology and compensation from the judges are said to amount to contempt of court.[117] Same view was followed by Delhi High Court in court on its own Motion, *Petitioner* v. *H.L. Sehgal Respondent* and *H.L. Sehgal, Petitioner* v. *J.D. Kapoor, Respondent.*[118]

Another instance of scandalising the judge by an advocate is considered by the Supreme Court in *In Re S.K. Sundaram.*[119] A case in which Advocate S.K. Sundaram made scandalous allegations against the former Chief Justice of India A.S. Anand.

The contemner first made an objection as to the appointment of Solicitor General by the court to assist the court. This objection is negatived by the court and held, the power of the court to make such appointment is thus unrestricted and it can be ordered at any stage. The contemner further putforth the claim that the statement is only a libel and also it lacks communication. The court found no difficulty in finding the contemner guilty of contempt because the allegations are undermining the authority of the court and the majesty of law and also expressed the view that the telegram also involves communication to third party.

Court observed:

> On the part of this court we may observe that if the contemner had stopped with his telegram we would have persuaded ourselves to ignore it as a case of ranting gibberish. But when he followed it up with lodging of a criminal contempt before the criminal court in which

115. AIR 1992 S.C. 642. When the judge made an order that the petitioner's miscellaneous application be heard by a Bench consisting of Ratnavel Pandian and Jayachandra Reddy JJ. The petitioner addressed the court in loud tones "Either he is antinational or the Judges are antinationals." This statement was the subject matter of the contempt petition.
116. *Ibid.*
117. *In Re: Ajay Kumar Pandey* (1997 Cri. L.J. 231).
118. 1997 Cri. L.J. 1472 (Delhi High Court).
119. AIR 2001 S.C. 2374.

> Chief Justice of India was arrayed as an accused having committed offences of cheating, criminal breach of trust and falsification of records, we realised that he seriously meant to malign and undermine the dignity and authority of this court.[120]

Though the legislature gave a broad scope for judicial interference by using the terms "tends to scandalise, lowers or tends to lower," judiciary had adopted a restrictive attitude and interfered only when there was allegation of bias, dishonesty, malice, partiality or imputation of motive, or when the language used was scurrilous, abusive or intimidatory. The court adopted a liberal attitude taking into account the condition of the alleged contemner.

3. SCANDALISING THE JUDICIARY—BY THE PRESS

(i) Before the Contempt of Courts Act, 1971

The basic principles as applied in the case of individuals are normally applied in the case of contempt by press also. Supreme Court followed the principle laid down by Hardwickie L.C. in *St. James Evening Post*[121] case and as applied by Wilmot, J. in *Almon's*[122] case and as followed by Lord Atkin in *Debi Prasad* v. *Emperor*[123] in *Bathina Ramakrishna Reddy* v. *State of Madras.*[124] In this case the court observed:

> The article in question is a scurrilous attack on the integrity and honesty of a judicial officer. Specific instances have been given where the officer is alleged to have taken bribes or behaved with impropriety to the litigants who did not satisfy his dishonest demands. If the allegations were true, obviously it would be to the benefit of the public to bring these matters into light. But if they were false, they cannot but undermine the confidence of the public in the administration of justice and bring the judiciary into disrepute.... As the appellant did not act with reasonable care and caution, he cannot be said to

120. *Id.* at 2382, 2383.
121. *Supra* n. 6.
122. *Supra* n. 7.
123. *Supra* n. 8.
124. 1952 I MLJ S.C. 736.

have acted *bona fide*, even if good faith can be held to be a defence at all in a proceeding for contempt.[125]

Scandalising the court by subsequent judicial interpretation as it relates to the press has become the embodiment of various other forms, such as distorted version of judgment, allegation of corruption, unfounded and scurrilous abuse and the like. So scandalising the court by the press is analysed under these categories.

(a) *Distorted version of judgment*

It is an accepted principle that true and faithful report of judicial proceedings and publication of a final judgment will not amount to contempt of court. But in some cases editors and publishers with a view to attract the public may twist the facts or misinterpret the verdict. In such cases of deliberate distortion the editors and publishers cannot escape liability.

A specific instance of such distorted version of judgment was considered by the Assam High Court in *Registrar, Assam High Court* v. *Frank Moraes, Resident Editor, Times of India.*[126] 'Times of India' published a news item which gave an impression that at the instance of the court a failed candidate was given

---

125. *Id.* at 740, 741.

126. AIR 1954 Ass. 201. A student of B.Sc. (Agriculture) of Gauhati University filed a writ against the university for a declaration of pass in the examination because it was alleged that there was some discrepancy in applying the division rules. After hearing the parties the court gave a judgment in favour of the student. Court directed that the rules and regulations framed by the university should be strictly followed. Subsequently a news item appeared in *Times of India* with the following headlines. "Failed candidate to get his degree."

Assam High Court's writ to Gauhati University. *The Times of India* News Service...A candidate of the Jorhat Agriculture College who was declared failed in the B.Sc. (Agri.) Examination, 1952 (Gauhati University) was to be granted his degree, according to a writ issued by Assam High Court on Tuesday.

On an *ex parte* application of the petitioner, Mr. Hemendra Chandra Das, Chief Justice, Sarjoo Prasad and Mr. Justice Habiram Deka of Assam High Court issued the writ, declaring the petitioner to have passed the examination.... The petitioners case was that he sat for the examination in 1952 and obtained an average of 48.8 per cent of aggregate total marks for all subjects, but failed to obtain 33 per cent in one subject alone.

the degree by the university. The caption of the article, "Failed candidate to get his degree", in capital letters is by itself somewhat intriguing and sensational.

The court viewed that the article was presented in a manner to create the opinion that the university was correct in not passing the candidate and the court without any reason compelled the university to give pass to a failed candidate. The publication has therefore, distorted the essential facts and presented them in such a garbled manner as to make it appear that the decision of the university in failing the candidate was quite justified, and that the action of this court was arbitrary in directing the failed candidate to get his degree.[127]

The facts and contents of the judgment, as published in the report were totally incorrect and misleading. Hence the court observed:

> It may ill-accord with the respectability of a responsible journal to cater for sensation mongering items of news, but the temptation is venial, no serious exception could be taken to it unless what follows thereafter is actually bound to be objectionable and constitutes contempt.[128]

The court further observed:

> Where the publication creates a mischievous effect on the public mind leading to the impression that the Chief Justice was or the judges were acting like arbitrary despots in order to enforce their authority, and that, although under the rules, the action of the university was justified, yet this court interfered in its extraordinary powers in order to assist a person who was not entitled to it, this court could not, with equanimity ignore the publication as some thing innocuous and innocent.[129]

From this decision the following guidelines to be followed by an editor and publisher can be derived:

1. The publication should not indulge in sensation mongering when reporting on a judgment.

---

127. *Id.* at 204.
128. *Id.* at 203.
129. *Id.* at 205.

2. The publication should not create a wrong impression that the judges are acting as arbitrary despots in enforcing their authority.
3. The editor and publisher should have a better sense of responsibility and verify the facts before reporting the judgment.
4. Their claim of excuse on the basis of inaccuracy or mistake cannot be admitted.

By a majority opinion given by Chief Justice Sarjoo Prasad and Ram Lahaya J. the rule has been made absolute.

But Deka J. gave a dissenting opinion. The learned judge considered one important question. Whether the report of the case was published in the "Times of India" has any tendency to interfere with the due course of justice or whether it amounts to scandalising the court? Assuming that there was any such attempt, whether it is of such a character as justifies and requires interference of the court by a summary jurisdiction in contempt.[130]

According to him there was not the slightest material in the article which would suggest that the writer had any such intention of imputing improper motives to the judges who decided the particular matter.[131] He concluded that the report undoubtedly to some extent, is misleading as far as facts are concerned, but it was not in any sense malicious or intended to throw any reflections on the judges of this court or the administration of justice by this court to merit punishment for contempt. The article was more or less a confused and half-digested matter written by an inexperienced correspondent hastily without due care.[132]

The Chief Justice viewed that the news report was bound to create a misapprehension in the minds of innumerable readers on the action of the court and accordingly brings into disrepute the decision of the court and tends to scandalise the court by false imputations. Moreover the publication is said to have the mischievous effect on the public.

130. *Id.* at 207.
131. *Id.* at 208.
132. *Ibid.*

While the Chief Justice gave more importance to the effect of the publication, Deka J. gave importance to the motive of the publisher.

Law of contempt is concerned more with the effect of the publication than with the motive. In that sense the approach of Deka J. cannot be said to be totally correct. Moreover as stated by Mukherjee J. in *Bathina Ramakrishna Reddy's*[133] case, a reasonable man should verify facts before resorting to publication. In the present case the editor failed in that duty also. So the majority opinion seemed to be right.

The right of fair and *bona fide* criticism given to editors and publishers cannot be misused. Publishing without ascertaining the facts, imputing motives to the judge, or ridiculing the judge,[134] cannot be said to be fair and *bona fide* criticism.

(b) *Allegation of corruption*

Allegation of corruption on the part of the judge is a serious instance of contempt of court. *In Sukh Raj* v. *Hemraj,*[135] a pamphlet addressed to the President and the Prime Minister, published by a person who lost his case in the High Court and the Supreme Court, is said to constitute contempt. Because as stated by the court:

---

133. *Supra* n. 112.

134. *State of Kutch* v. *Saifuddin Kharawala* AIR 1956 Kut. 7. A man was sentenced to eight years rigorous imprisonment for having committed a theft, which was published in the daily newspaper called 'Vatan' with the title "What is more important—a man's moustache or a cow's tail." This article severely criticised the punishment and mentioned that lesser sentences are imposed for murder and culpable homicide. A sentence of eight years imprisonment was given to a man of Kutch for slaughtering a cow of another person.

135. AIR 1967 Raj. 203. A pamphlet was published purporting to be addressed to the President of India and the Prime Minister containing charges of corruption against judges and requesting them to take action. It contained the following statement: "Inspite of the fact that we had a very strong case, its decision went against us and the reason for that, we believe, was that Poonamchand Narasinghi is a relative of Heerachand and he has amassed great wealth amounting to 50 to 60 lakhs of rupees by dishonest means and by resorting to smuggling and black marketing activities. These dishonest people have in this case justice massacred by black money, and therefore it is prayed that suitable action be taken...."

> If however the language used is fairly capable of an innocent interpretation, the court will not be astute to read an import into it. But if on the other hand, the language is fairly clear, liability to punishment cannot be allowed to be avoided by the use of a cloak or an artifice. Likewise the intention or the motive of the contemner is immaterial if the publication is calculated to impede the fair trial of a case or bring the administration of justice into contempt.[136]

(c) *Unfounded and scurrilous allegations*

Unfounded allegations, which are detrimental to the fair administration of justice has also been viewed seriously by the court. If not, such allegations may degrade the image of the judiciary.

In *In re Hiren Bose*[137] the Editor of 'Darpan' Bengali weekly published an article giving a dismal picture of the judiciary. Banerjee J. holding it as scandalising the court, observed:

> I do not doubt that the press is free to criticise a system. A free press stands as one of the great interpreters between the government and the people. To allow this to be fettered is to fetter ourselves.... In the garb of criticism, the press cannot commit contempt of court.[138]

As stated by Lord Atkin in *Debi Prasad's*[139] case the test is whether the words were calculated to obstruct or interfere with the administration of justice. No wrong is committed by any member of the public who exercise the ordinary right of criticising in public or private, the public act done in the seat of justice. In this case also the author of the article fairly

136. *Id.* at 206.

137. *In the matter of Hiren Bose, the contemner,* AIR 1969, Cal. 1, Hiren Bose, Editor of 'Darpan' was charged for contempt for publishing an article. The relevant portion was as follows: "It is just the same legal system which in the pre-independence days helped the judiciary to stifle the just demands of man and the freedom of movement.... We feel interested to know how many judges resigned their office in protest against this legal system. They claim to be educated person, the elite of society. There is no necessity for this education and these elites...."

138. *Id.* at 3.

139. *Supra* n. 8.

criticised the judicial system. Since no specific motive has been imputed to any member of the judiciary, it cannot be said to be scandalous. It was further considered by the Supreme Court in *Perspective Publications (P) Ltd.* v. *The State of Maharashtra.*[140] In this case the Supreme Court considered the effect of an article published in the weekly 'Main Stream' which discussed the necessity to have a code of conduct for judges, and held that imputations of dishonesty and lack of integrity on the part of a judge would amount to scandalising the judge and the judiciary.

The Supreme Court further laid down the following principles[141]:

1. The summary jurisdiction by way of contempt must be exercised with great care and caution and only when its exercise is necessary for the proper administration of law and justice.
2. It is open to anyone to express fair, reasonable and legitimate criticism of any act or conduct of a judge in his judicial capacity or even to make a proper and fair comment on any decision given by him.
3. A distinction must be made between a mere libel of a judge and what amounts to contempt of the court. The test in each case would be whether the impugned publication is a mere defamatory attack on the judge or whether it is calculated to interfere with the due course of justice or the proper administration of law by this court. It is only in the latter case that it will be punishable as contempt.

---

140. AIR 1971 S.C. 221. An article was published in the weekly "Main Stream" under the title "Story of a loan and Blitz Thackersay libel case." It mentioned that there was the code of conduct for university and college teachers, but there was no such code of conduct among judges." Referring to the integrity and reputation of judges of Bombay High Court the author stated "...there must not be allowed to be raised even the faintest whisper of any misgiving on that score...." Also it mentioned the involvement of the relative of Justice Tarkunde as a beneficiary in the loan case.

141. *Id.* at 230.

(ii) After the Contempt of Courts Act, 1971

The definition of criminal contempt as contained in Sec. 2(c) of the Act does not include distorted version of judgment, scurrilous abuse and allegation of corruption, but it only used the terms 'scandalise or tends to scandalise'. It signifies that scandalising the judiciary can be by any method and it is not restricted to those instances as laid down by the judiciary. The scope of the term 'scandalising' is further widened by the expression 'tends to scandalise'. The defences available to an alleged contemner is dealt with in sections 3 to 8 of the Act. The Supreme Court[142] as well as the High Courts[143] considered different instances of scandalising the judiciary by the press.

The object is to ascertain as to what extent freedom of the press is protected by the judiciary, after the statutory definition of criminal contempt. Scandalous allegations include the most reckless and *mala fide* allegations made without verification and personal knowledge;[144] use of intemperate language in a reckless manner,[145] allegation of partiality,[146] baseless allegation of corruption,[147] questioning the integrity of the judge, publication of one-sided version of judgment and so on.

In *State of U.P.* v. *D.K. Das Vidhi*[148] the question considered

---

142. *In re Mulgoakar* AIR 1978 S.C. 727; *In re Shamlal* AIR 1978 S.C. 489.

143. See e.g., *State of U.P.* v. *Das Vidhi* 1973 Cri. L.J. (Allahabad High Court) 1271; *S.C. Tyagi* v. *N.C. Gupta* 1974 Cri. L.J. (Allahabad High Court) 428; *Manikchand Gupta* v. *Virendra Kumar* 1979 Cri. L.J. (Allahabad High Court) 1637; *Mohammed Vamia and others* v. *Om Prakash Bansal* 1982 Cri. L.J. (Rajasthan High Court) 322. *V.M. Kanade* v. *Madhav Gadkari* 1990 Cri. L.J. (Bombay High Court) 190.

144. *State of U.P.* v. *Das Vidhi* 1973 Cri. L.J. (Allahabad High Court) 1271.

145. *S.C. Tyagi* v. *N.C. Gupta* 1974 Cri. L.J. (Allahabad High Court) 428.

146. *Manikchand Gupta* v. *Virendra Kumar* 1979 Cri. L.J. (Allahabad High Court), 422.

147. *State of U.P.* v. *Narendra Pal Singh* 1990 Cri. L.J. (Allahabad High Court) 1637.

148. 1973 Cri. L.J. (Allahabad High Court) 1271. D.K. Das Vidhi, the Editor of 'Shoorvir', during the pendency of a criminal case under Sec. 411 of the Indian Penal Code, published a news item which stated that the magistrate changed the decision at the instance of a lady being arranged by the accused.

was whether the news item[149] published in the local newspaper of Meerut "Shoorvir" interfered with the administration of justice. The News item directly attacked the morality of the magistrate. According to justice Shukla, it amounted to contempt of court because:

> The news item published by him had unmistakably the effect of undermining the prestige of the court and bringing the Munsiff—Magistrate into disrepute.... Judicial administration would topple down if impassioned litigants were allowed to arraign the character of presiding officers of the courts on the basis of street gossip or yarns spun out in the market place and retailed as cheap fare for public consumption.[150]

A similar case of personal attack was considered by the same High Court in *State of U.P.* v. *Narendra Pal Singh*[151] which involved a specific allegation of corruption and also the allegation that the law is sold in the Sessions Court. The court took a serious view of the matter and observed:

> Nothing should be done which impairs the dignity of the court in the minds of the public. It will be a sad day if open scandalisation of courts lowering the authority of courts and interference with the administration of justice are left to go unpunished even when it is found that the said item of publication regarding the court concerned was *per se* scandalous, contemptuous and derogatory. No one, much less the court, is averse to legal and legitimate

149. Specific portion of the news item—"From the side of the accused, Om Prakash, a lady went to the house of Jain and met him secretly. She stayed there for the whole night...the higher authorities should make a thorough enquiry in the matter...."

150. *Supra* n. 136, p. 1273.

151. 1990 Cri. L.J. (Allahabad High Court) 1637. Narendra Pal Singh Chauhan, proprietor, editor and publisher of a local weekly newspaper 'Hamraj Express' published an editorial which was the subject matter of the contempt petition. Translated version of the editorial is as follows: The Additional District and Sessions Judge is sliding on the path of corruption : (1) Law is sold there, (2) law is torn into pieces there, (3) Law is always shelved there.... The Additional District and Sessions Judge Sri 'X' had taken lakhs of rupees as bribe and has thereby undermined the prestige of law....

> criticism of a judgment. To level charges of corruption, accompanied with baseless allegations and disrespectful remarks, which have neither any foundation nor base much less any truth, has to be seriously condemned.[152]

Though legitimate criticism of a judgment can be permitted baseless allegation and disrespectful remarks on a judge has to be condemned.

Attacking the integrity of a judge by attributing motives like dishonesty or incompetence, arbitrariness or want of independence, would be exceeding free and fair criticism by the press,[153] because it is a remark on a judge and it is not a legitimate criticism of a judgment. Distorted version of a judgment when published by Assistant Director of Public Relations and Information it is said to amount to contempt of court.[154]

So also when partiality is attributed to a court in passing an order or deciding a case through a newspaper article the limits of fair comment on the merits of the case are clearly crossed and gross contempt is committed, as impartiality is a basic characteristic of a court and any attack on it seriously affects its prestige and dignity.[155] Fair criticism of a judgment and fair appreciation of law have always been recognised.

But when it questions the integrity and independence of judges it is not a fair comment as it amounts to scandalising

---

152. *Id.* at 1640.

153. *Mohammed Vamin and others* v. *Om Prakash Bansal*, 1982 Cri. L.J. (Rajasthan High Court) 322, 333. A weekly newspaper 'Prasant Jyoti' (Hindi) published a news item. It was alleged that it scandalised the former and the present judges of the High Court. The news item was the representation given by 25 advocates of Jaipur in 1977 to the President of India. The copies of the representation were given to high dignitaries also.

154. *Sadhvi Ritumbhara* v. *Digvijay Singh and another* 1997 Cri. L.J. (S.C) 1905.

155. *Manikchand Gupta* v. *Virendrakumar* 1979 Cri. L.J. (Allahabad High Court) 412, 414. In the contempt petition it was alleged that after the Sub. Divisional Magistrate Mechhilisha passed an order releasing the land in dispute in favour of the petitioner under Sec. 146 Criminal Procedure Code the opposite parties with a view to scandalise the magistrate, published an article alleging partiality in 'Deshdoot' in collusion with the Editor of the said paper (Article is reported in Hindi).

the judiciary. The Supreme Court in *In re Mulgoakar*[156] considered the effect of an article published in the 'Indian Express' entitled "Behaving like a judge," and another publication which discussed and criticised the proposed code of ethics for judges.

Chief Justice Beg, viewed that apart from general allegations of corruption and inefficiency, suggestion of lack of moral courage to the extent of having disowned what had been done,[157] would amount to scandalising the judiciary. He concluded:

> National interest requires that all criticism of the judiciary must be strictly rational and sober and proceed from the highest motives without being coloured by any partisan spirit or tactics. This should be a part of national ethics. Newspapers, in particular ought to observe such a rule imbued with what Montesquieu considered essential for a healthy democracy; the spirit of virtue.[158]

Further:

> When there appears some scheme and a design to bring about results which must damage confidence in our judicial

---

156. AIR 1978 S.C. 727. The Supreme Court considered a publication in the 'Indian Express' dated 13th Dec., 1977. The following sentence appeared regarding the supposed code of judicial ethics assumed wrongly to have been drafted by some judges of the Supreme Court. "So adverse has been the criticism that the Supreme Court Judges some of whom had prepared the draft code have disowned it...." The Registrar of the Supreme Court, wrote to inform the editor about the misstatement. Instead of publishing the correction, the editor offered to publish the whole material in his possession, as though there was an issue to be tried between the editor of the newspaper and this court and the readers were there to try it and decide it. Soon after the incorrect stand taken by the editor, there appeared on 21-12-1977 an article entitled "Behaving like a Judge" in the same newspaper. The suggestion that a code of ethics should be formulated by judges themselves was characterised in this article as "So utterly inimical to the independence of the judiciary, violative of the constitutional safeguards in that respect, and offensive to the self-respect of the judges as to make one wonder how it was conceived in the first place. The above article ends, by attempting to make a distinction between the wonderful performance of High Court judges and the disappointing record of the Supreme Court.
157. *Id.* at 733.
158. *Id.* at 734.

> system and demoralize judges of the highest court by making malicious attack, anyone interested in maintaining high standards of fearless, impartial and unbending justice will feel perturbed.... Although the question whether an attack is malicious or ill-intentioned, may be often difficult to determine yet, the language in which it is made, the fairness, the factual accuracy, the logical soundness of it, the care taken in justifying and properly analysing the materials before the maker of it, are important considerations.[159]

Justice V.R. Krishna Iyer who gave separate but concurring judgment laid down the following tests to be followed in case of contempt by scandalising the judiciary:

1. Wise economy in use by the court of this branch of its jurisdiction. The court will act with seriousness and severity where justice is jeopardised by a gross and/or unfounded attack on the judges, where the attack is calculated to obstruct or destroy the judicial process.
2. The second principle must be to harmonise the constitutional values of free criticism, the fourth estate included, and the need for a fearless curiel process and its presiding functionary.
3. The third principle is to avoid confusion between personal protection of a libelled judge and prevention of obstruction of public justice and country's confidence in that great process. The former is not contempt the latter is, although overlapping spaces abound.
4. The fourth principle which channel discretionary exercise of the contempt power is that the fourth estate which is an indispensable intermediary between the state and the people, should be given free play within responsible limits.
5. The fifth guideline for the judges to observe in this jurisdiction is not to be hypersensitive even when distortions and criticism over step the limits.

159. *Ibid.*

6. The sixth consideration is that after evaluating the totality of factors, if the court considers the attack on the judge or judges scurrilous, offensive, intimidatory or malicious beyond condonable limits, the strong arm of the law must in the name of public interest and public justice, strike a blow on him who challenges the supremacy of the rule of law by fouling its source and stream.[160]

Though Beg C.J. and V.R. Krishna Iyer J. gave different judgments, the approach and attitude are the same. Thus according to Beg C.J., the judiciary cannot be immune from criticism. But, when that criticism is based on obvious distortion or gross misstatement and made in a manner which is designed to lower respect for the judiciary and destroy public confidence in it, it cannot be ignored.[161] He further stated that confidence in them cannot be permitted to be impaired by attack upon them.[162] So also, it may be better in many cases for the judiciary to adopt a magnanimously charitable attitude even when utterly uncharitable and unfair criticism of its operation is made out of *bona fide* concern for improvement.[163]

The same approach could be seen in a different language used by V.R. Krishna Iyer J. In contempt jurisdiction, silence is a sign of strength since our power is wide and we are prosecutor and judge.[164] Further he said "to criticise the judge fairly, albeit fiercely, is no crime but a necessary right, twice blessed in democracy."[165] However, if the court considers the attack on the judge or judges scurrilous, offensive, intimidatory or malicious beyond condonable limits, contempt proceedings can be instituted in the interest of maintaining the supremacy of the rule of law.[166]

Both the judges unanimously directed that the proceedings be dropped. So also the court dropped the contempt proceedings

160. *Id.* at 736, 737.
161. *Id.* at 733.
162. *Id.* at 734.
163. *Id.* at 733, 734.
164. *Id.* at 736.
165. *Ibid.*
166. *Id*, at 737, 738.

in *In Re: Chandigarh News Line* 'Indian Express' Group[167] when the contemners published an apology realising the mistake, even before service of notice and tendered unconditional apology in the court.

So far as allegation of corruption, partiality and personal weaknesses are concerned the judiciary generally follows the view that such allegations have to be sternly dealt with. It may be because the aggrieved party has the remedy to complain to the High Court under the Contempt of Courts Act, 1971. Judiciary is hesitant to permit the press to act as an arbitrator. Under the Contempt of Courts Act, 1971 grievances against the lower judiciary can be put to the High Court. But there is no provision in the Contempt of Courts Act so far as allegations against the judges of High Court and Supreme Court are concerned.

Unfounded allegations have to be prohibited because the dignity of the judiciary depends upon the respect and confidence of the people in the institution. The judiciary should adopt a charitable attitude in ascertaining what kind of allegation would constitute a scurrilous one. For ascertaining that, wide experience, vast knowledge and pious attitude of the judge should play a vital role. It is not possible to suggest with any precision as to what kind of language would constitute scurrilous abuse.

The Supreme Court considered a specific instance of distorted version of judgment in *In re Shamlal,*[168] wherein a newspaper published one of the two views possible on a question. Majority judges (Untwalia and Kailasam JJ) took the view that it was not a fit case where formal proceeding should be drawn up and so the proceedings had to be dropped. No reason has been adduced by the majority of judges. Chief Justice Beg who gave the dissenting view was forced to speak

167. AIR 1999, S.C. 144.

168. AIR 1978 S.C. 489. The Editor of 'Times of India' was charged for contempt of court in respect of the news items in which the *Habeas Corpus* case (*A.D.M. Jabalpur* v. *Shukla*. AIR 1976 S.C. 1297) was the subject matter. The news item used the word 'misdeed' and also stated that judges should have held what they could not honestly believe to be correct in law.

because he was also a party to the earlier decision,[169] which was being criticised. He viewed that there was a consistent scheme or design to malign the court and the judges, which would shake the confidence of the public in the administration of justice and hence the publication amounted to contempt of court.

Chief Justice applied the test of tendency to lower the authority of the court to ascertain whether there was contempt of court or not. But it was clear from the publication, that there was nothing in it which would lower the authority of the judiciary and hence the dissenting opinion did not seem to be accurate.

Of late, because of the callous and indifferent attitude of the editors and publishers towards judiciary, the court expressed its concern in maintaining its dignity and had to lay down certain guidelines to be followed in reporting judicial matters. In *D.K. Paliwal* v. *Editor, Dainik Bhaskar newspapers,*[170] the news item published related to issue of bailable warrant by the Railway Magistrate to one of the booking clerks. The court asserted that the content and scope of the freedom which the contemners possess is no better than the right possessed by a citizen of this republic.

If the publication is neither innocent nor a fair comment but is an attempt to scandalise the court then action has to be taken. Because only a fair and accurate report can be published with regard to judicial proceedings.[171]

Further:

> Liberty of the press is subordinate to the independence of the judiciary and the proper administration of justice.

169. *Additional District Magistrate, Jabalpur* v. *S. Shukla* AIR 1976 S.C. 1207.

170. 1994 Cri. L.J. (Madhya Pradesh High Court) 2933. There was a controversy in reserving the railway ticket, and on complaint by one R.K. Mishra, the aggrieved person, Railway Magistrate issued a bailable warrant against S.S. Sharma, the booking clerk. In the evening station Superintendent, presented an application, praying for a stay of the bailable warrant. Hence the Railway Magistrate deferred the execution of the warrant. All these events were published in the newspaper and that gave way for the contempt petition.

171. *Id.* at 2945.

> We are conscious of the fact that the liberty of the press is equally important but this cannot be permitted to subvert usefulness and efficiency of the courts.[172]

So also Jammu and Kashmir High Court in *B.A. Rather* v. *H.K. Dua*[173] though accepted the apology, gave a warning that the editor should be careful in future while discharging his professional duties as an editor of a newspaper especially when these related to the material concerning the institution of the judiciary in the country.[174]

The court further observed:

> In a country totally wedded to democracy and rule of law, where freedom of expression, the most cherished ideal of social ethos apart from being a guaranteed fundamental right under the constitution, a corresponding obligation is not only always expected, but is actually cast upon this pillar of democracy, the fourth estate and its esteemed members not only to respect functioning of other institutions but to be fair and objective while reporting about the events and the people and to use circumspection while dealing with sensitive issues.[175]

Supreme Court also punished an editor for publishing an article when the whole trend, tenor and content of the article tend to shake the confidence of the public in the High Court and leads the public to believe that even in High Court one is highly doubtful of getting justice.[176]

---

172. *Ibid.*

173. 1994 Cri. L.J. (Jammu and Kashmir High Court) 3414 Contempt petition arose in this case because of the publication contained in 'Hindustan Times'. The headline was "Jagmohan faces acid test." The publication revolves round the terrorism, military and other forms of widespread disturbances prevalent in Kashmir valley. The publication also alleged relation between High Court Judges and the militants. It stated: "Even the judiciary at the tehsil level and High Court level as well is infiltrated by subversives. A singular example of such infiltration is the manner in which two judges of the Srinagar Bench of the Jammu and Kashmir High Court granted stay to some local newspapers against the decision of the state government."

174. *Id.* at 3418.

175. *Id.* at 3420.

176. *Vishwa Deva Sharma* v. *State of Rajasthan* 1994 Cri. L.J. (Supreme Court) 1223.

Supreme Court reinstated the need for the editor and publisher to ascertain and evaluate the correctness and credibility of information published by them in *In Re Harijai Singh and another, In Re: Vijay Kumar.*[177] In this case incorrect news item was published relating to allotment of petrol outlets. Though the court accepted the unconditional apology tendered by them made the following observation:

> If it (Press) were wholly free even from reasonable restraints it would lead to disorder and anarchy. The freedom is not to be misunderstood as to be a press free to disregard its duty to be responsible. Infact the element of responsibility must be present in the conscience of journalists. In an organised society the rights of the Press have to be recognized with its duties and responsibilities towards the society. Public order, decency, morality and such other things must be safeguarded. The protective cover of press freedom must not be thrown open for wrong doings. If a newspaper publishes what is improper, mischievously false or illegal and abuses its liberty it must be punished by court of law.[178]

4. CRITICISM OF THE JUDICIAL SYSTEM

Healthy criticism aimed at modification of the institution has to be permitted because it helps in the development of the institution. In *E.M. Sankaran Namboodiripad* v. *T.N. Nambiar*[179] though it was argued that the statement made by E.M. Sankaran Namboodiripad at the press conference was aimed at modification of the institution, Supreme Court rejected the argument. He has not mentioned any particular case pending before the court or any particular judge, but only stated the defects in the then existing judicial system. Even then the statement was said to constitute contempt of court.

But later the judiciary changed its attitude and recognized the right to make fair appraisal of the institution. In *S.C. Tyagi* v. *N.C. Gupta*[180] since the language used was intemperate and

177. 1997 Cri. L.J. (S.C.) 58.

178. *Id.* at 62.

179. *Supra* n. 28.

180. 1974 Cri. L.J. (Allahabad High Court) 428. The Editorial published in

reckless it was held to constitute contempt of court. The publication stated that wealthy persons could secure favourable verdicts by means of money. Poor persons who have no money could not expect any justice. It also stated that there is a conspiracy between the judges and the lawyers. The court made the following observation:

> None can justify an abridgement of the right of fair criticism or an objective appraisal of any institution existing in the country. At the same time scurrilous remarks which on the face of them tend to pour ridicule on the judiciary or for that matter on any institution are not to be overlooked. A person cannot be allowed to indulge in such wild allegations with impunity. There is not the least doubt that the above remarks have the effect of bringing into disrepute the bench and the bar of India.[181]

Similar situation arose before the Bombay High Court in *V.M. Kanade* v. *Madhav Gadkari*.[182] In this case it was argued that the object of the article was to highlight the view of the author regarding the defects in the working of the judicial system and in the working of the High Court and to suggest remedies. But the court refused to accept the argument because most of the statements in the article were aimed at sensationalism. To suggest that a particular judge of the High Court does not give judgment on the basis of the merits of the case before him but decides the case being influenced by the charm of a particular lady advocate is nothing but to scandalise this court.[183] Similarly the allegations against the members of the Motor Accident Claims Tribunal were also of such a nature that they scandalise all the members of the said Tribunal.

---

the Hindi Daily "Vidambana" was the subject of contempt proceedings. The editorial stated among other things that wealthy persons were able to secure verdicts in their favour from judges by means of money. How a poor man who has no money to spend in these courts expect justice from them. At some places there is sent ganth (conspiracy) between lawyers and judges; other courts are offered the temptation of wine and women.

181. *Id.* at 427. Calcutta High Court also expressed the same view in *In re Hiren Bose* AIR 1969 Cal. 1.

182. 1990 Cri. L.J. (Bombay High Court) 190.

183. *Id.* at 194.

To say that one third of the compensation amount awarded by the members of the Tribunal not only does not reach the claimants but is swallowed by the members of the Tribunal itself is a statement which holds the members of the Tribunal to ridicule in the eyes of the public.[184]

But when the language used is fair and reasonable the judiciary used to be liberal. Thus the Kerala High Court in *T.A. Rajendran* v. *Vayalar Ravi*[185], Supreme Court in *M.R. Parashar* v. *Dr. Farooq Abdullah*[186] and in *P.N. Duda* v. *P. Shiv Shankar*[187] held the respective ministers not guilty of contempt though they criticised the judicial system.

Criticism aimed at ridiculing the institution through the use of intemperate language is nothing but scandalisation.

Thus healthy criticism of the judicial system has always been permitted, though not encouraged, provided the language is fair and temperate, because development of any institution depends upon healthy criticism.

5. CONCLUSION

Scandalising the court as a test of contempt laid down by Hardwicke L.C. in *St. James Evening Post*[188] case was made applicable to publications also by Justice Wilmot in *Almon's*[189] case. The same principle is adopted by the Indian Judiciary too. There is no definite periphery for this concept and judiciary in the pre-Contempt of Courts Act, 1971 period very strictly construed the term. Though the judiciary recognized that the court, like any other institution, does not enjoy immunity from fair criticism, attributing improper motives or tending to bring judges or courts into hatred are something serious which may amount to contempt. So also distorted version of judgment, allegation of corruption, unfounded and scurrilous abuse are also said to be instances of scandalising the court. Even after the passing of the Contempt of Courts Act, 1971 there is not

184. *Id.* at 194, 195.
185. *Supra* n. 41.
186. *Supra* n. 42.
187. *Supra* n. 43.
188. *Supra* n. 6.
189. *Supra* n. 7.

much change in this branch of law. Because the definition of criminal contempt in Sec. 2(c) of the Act uses the terms 'scandalise' or 'tends to scandalise' 'lowers' or 'tends to lower' the authority of any court.

After the passing of the Contempt of Courts Act, 1971, though the judiciary is very liberal in its approach, it could not specifically lay down what constitutes scandalous allegation, but could indicate only the broad spectrum of this branch of law. Accordingly unfounded imputation of *mala fides*, bias, prejudice, ridiculing the performance of a judge, scurrilous allegations, reckless allegation of corruption, imputing motives, imputing unfairness, or dishonesty are said to constitute scandalising the court.

A review of the decisions shows that the judiciary is not averse to legal and legitimate criticism of a judgment. Generally courts used to adopt a charitable attitude, even when utterly uncharitable and unfair criticism of its operation is made out of *bona fide* concern for improvement. Fair criticism without any reference to the pending suit has always been recognized. Courts have given more importance to the tone and temper of the language than the material in which such statements are contained.

The conclusion which emerges from the foregoing discussion is that a criticism of the judgment or the judicial system is tolerated provided the language used is temperate and fair and the criticism is motivated by *bona fides*.

PART 3

8

Civil Contempt— Disobedience by Administrative Authorities and Corporations

1. INTRODUCTION

The law relating to contempt of court has developed over the centuries as a means whereby the courts may act to prevent or punish conduct which tends to obstruct, prejudice or abuse administration of justice either in relation to a particular case or generally.[1]

In its origin all legal contempts will be found to consist in an offence more or less directed against the Sovereign himself as the fountain head of law and justice or against his place, where justice was administered.... Court cannot function properly unless it has the power to enforce discipline within its precincts and punish those who fail to comply with its orders.[2]

This early origin of contempt of court by disobedience has been recognized by authors.[3]

Disobedience of the orders of the court is generally termed as civil contempt, which, appears to have originated in the

1. *Report of the Committee on Contempt of Court*, 2 (1974). This committee was constituted in England in the year 1971, and was required to consider whether any change was required in the law relating to contempt of court.
2. Oswald, *Contempt of Court*, 1 (1910).
3. "Judges are therefore in a position to command dutiful and prompt obedience. The judge is the mouth-piece of the king and the judge's judicial pronouncements are the utterances of the Sovereign." Tek Chand, *The Law of Contempt of Court and Legislature*, 7 (1949). *See* also Joseph, H. Beal, *Contempt of Court Criminal and Civil* 21 Harv. L.R. 161 (1980).

seventeenth century from the practice of the Court of Chancery which used to enforce its orders in person.[4]

The English law of contempt which itself had a haphazard growth came to be introduced in our country in a yet haphazard manner. Power to punish for contempt being an attribute of court of record, the setting up of such courts by the British in India necessarily meant the introduction of English law of contempt in some measure. This is how English law of contempt came to be introduced in India, first.[5]

Thus the Mayor's Court established by the Charter of 1726 was treated as a court of record. The Mayor's Court was succeeded by the Supreme Court constituted in pursuance of the Regulating Act of 1773 which was also a court of record. Different Supreme Courts were replaced by the High Courts established under the High Court's Act of 1861 and they were also made courts of record.

This inherent jurisdiction to punish for contempt was recognized by the Calcutta High Court in *Martin* v. *Lawrence*[6] (1879). In this case Justice White observed:

> The jurisdiction of the High Court to imprison for contempt, is a jurisdiction that it has inherited from the old Supreme Court and was conferred upon that court by the Charters of the Crown which invested it with all the powers and authority of the then Court of King's Bench and of the High Court of Chancery in Great Britain.[7]

Privy Council also accepted the same view in *Surendranath Banerjee* v. *The Chief Justice and Judges of the High Court at Fort William in Bengal.*[8] According to Justice Peacock contempt of court is an offence which by the common law of England is punishable by the High Court in a summary manner by fine or imprisonment or both.[9] Madras, Bombay and Calcutta High

4. *Martin* v. *Lawrence,* ILR 4 Cal. 444.
5. *Report of the Committee on Contempt of Court,* 4 (1963).
6. *Supra* n. 4.
7. *Id.* at 445.
8. ILR 10 Cal. 109.
9. That part of the common law of England was introduced into the presidency towns when the late Supreme Court was respectively established by the Charters of justice. The High Court in the Presidencies

Courts also exercised this jurisdiction. In order to remove the doubts as to the power of High Court to punish contempt of lower court, Contempt of Courts Act, 1926, and Contempt of Courts Act, 1952 were enacted.

Any kind of interference with the due administration of justice is treated as contempt of court. This interference can be caused by disobedience of the orders of the court by the executive authority, by an individual or by the judiciary itself. In this chapter the matter for consideration is interference by the administrative authority including corporation.

Our constitution provides for three organs[10] of the State which put together perform the sovereign functions. They are not put in water-tight compartments, but are so placed that no one organ can perform the function that essentially belongs to another.[11] In practice the judiciary often uses its contempt jurisdiction to make others obey its orders.[12]

The Contempt of Courts Act, 1971 made certain changes with regard to criminal contempt by providing a clear definition and certain defences. But, so far as civil contempt is concerned, no change is effected except providing a good definition. Sec. 2(b) of the Act states "civil contempt means wilful disobedience to any judgment, decree, direction, order or other process of a court or wilful breach of an undertaking given to a court."

What constitutes disobedience has not been precisely stated in the Act. Hence the principle of law as laid down by the

---

are superior courts of record and the offence of contempt and the powers of High Court for punishing it are the same there as in this country not by virtue of the Penal Code for British India and the Code of Criminal Procedure 1882, but by virtue of common law of England. (*Id.* at 132).

10. The three organs are the executive, the legislature and the judiciary. In our Constitution, Chapter I of Part V deals with Union Executive, Chapter II of Part V deals with Union Legislature, Chapter IV of Part V deals with Union Judiciary. So also Chapter II of Part VI deals with State Executive. Chapter III of Part VI deals with State Legislature. Chapter V and VI of Part VI deal with State Judiciary.
11. *Ram Jawaya* v. *State of Punjab* AIR 1955 S.C. 549; also *Indira Gandhi* v. *Raj Narain*, AIR 1975 S.C. 260.
12. *The State of Bihar* v. *Rani Sonabati Kumari* AIR 1961 S.C. 221; *Subodh Gopal Bose* v. *State of Bihar* AIR 1969 P and H 435; *Aligarh Municipal Board* v. *Ekka Tonga Mazdoor Union* AIR 1970 S.C. 1767.

judiciary prior to the passing of the Act continues to be the good law and so the subject is analysed without making any distinction between the position before and after the enactment of the Contempt of Courts Act, 1971.

The exercise of contempt jurisdiction against administrative authority is analysed under the categories listed below:

(a) Disobedience of the orders of the court;
(b) Non compliance with the orders of the court;
(c) Disciplinary proceedings and contempt jurisdiction, and,
(d) *Hebeas Corpus* and contempt jurisdiction.

2. DISOBEDIENCE OF THE ORDERS OF THE COURT

Wilful disobedience of the orders of the court by the executive is viewed seriously by the judiciary and the court resorts to contempt jurisdiction to ensure due compliance with its orders. What constitutes wilful disobedience has not been specifically defined by any statute, and so the principles laid down by the judiciary remain the only guiding factor. The Calcutta High Court, in *Tarafatulah Mandal* v. *S.N. Maitra*[13] considered the matter and held that the continued interference by the executive authority with the peaceful possession of the petitioner during the existence of a stay order will amount to wilful disobedience and thus constitute contempt of court. Chakravarthi J. observed:

> It is true that when an injunction is granted against a corporation, which afterwards does or permits an act in breach of the injunction, there is a wilful disobedience of the order and it will be no answer for the corporation to say that the act was done or the omission allowed to

13. AIR 1952 Cal. 919. In this case the petitioners were the owners of certain land and proceedings were taken by the respondents, namely the Collector and State of West Bengal, under an ultravires Act to deprive the petitioners of their property. So the petitioners filed a writ petition and a rule *nisi* was obtained. While so, the respondents continued their interference and hence this petition. The petitioners prayed that the State of West Bengal as represented by Sri Banerjee should be committed to prison. Contempt petition failed because the alleged act of disobedience was committed before the interim order had been served on the respondents.

occur unintentionally or through carelessness, or through dereliction of duty on the part of servants of the corporation. The same principle, I imagine, would apply in the case of a Government or a State, but before an individual officer of the Government can be held to be liable, it must be established that he was the person in charge of the subject matter to which the injunction or order alleged to have been disobeyed related and unless that is established no case against an individual officer can succeed.[14]

In *Miss Sumedha Kaha* v. *State of Haryana*[15] the question for consideration was whether giving of provisional admission during the pendency of writ petition will amount to wilful disobedience. Court held that there was no disobedience of the orders of the court[16], because there was confusion in ascertaining the quota. In *K.V. Venkatesh* v. *Taluka Executive Magistrate, Magadi Taluk, Magadi*[17], Karnataka High Court by its order in 1985 directed the respondents to hold an enquiry. But till 1990 no enquiry was conducted. This was construed as unreasonable delay in carrying out the order, even though no time limit was fixed, and hence it was held as contempt.

But in *Maniyeri Madhavan* v. *Inspector of Police Cannanore,*[18] though the situation was similar, the Supreme Court had not

14. *Id.* at 924.
15. AIR 1990 P. and H. 239. In this case a writ petition was pending questioning the reservation policy for admission for MBBS of Maharshi Dayanand University, Rohtak. During the pendency of writ petition some of the petitioners were given provisional admission. Hence the contempt petition.
16. *Id.* at 242. The same view was followed in *Tapan Kumar Mukherjee* v. *Sri Heramoni Mondel,* AIR 1991 S.C. 281, and the court found that the disobedience was not wilful and held the respondents not guilty of contempt. In this case the appellant signed a memo overlooking that the lands in issue were covered by an interim order of stay.
17. AIR 1990 Kant. 86.
18. AIR 1993 S.C. 356. In this case a journalist complained of misbehaviour and attack by police. In a writ petition High Court directed the matter to be enquired by the Deputy Inspector General of Police. Petitioner went to the Supreme Court to get the matter to be enquired by the Central Bureau of Investigation. But the Supreme Court appointed another D.I.G. to investigate the matter and submit the report within 3 months. After a lapse of one year State Government moved the Supreme Court for an extension of time. Not only that enquiry was not

made any finding on contempt, though it is a clear case of contempt because no enquiry was conducted within the time prescribed by the court.

The court viewed the matter seriously and directed the enquiry to be conducted by the Central Bureau of Investigation within 3 months.

But when there is a compelling circumstance under which it was not possible for the contemner to comply with the orders of the court,[19] or when there is genuine difficulty in implementing the order[20] there is no wilful disobedience.

In case of impossibility of compliance it is the duty of the aggrieved party to take the matter in appeal or express the difficulties to the court in advance. Impossibility should not be a defence for contempt proceedings.

If there is violation of the order issued by the Supreme Court it will amount to contempt of court. But if the order is susceptible to two interpretation—one in favour of the contemner and another in favour of the complainant—the contemner is entitled for the benefit of doubt.[21]

---

conducted but also the concerned D.I.G. was transferred to some other department.

19. *Niaz Mohammed* v. *State of Haryana* AIR 1995 S.C. 308, 311. In this case there was disparity in the scale of pay of instructors working under adult and non-formal education and those of squad teachers. On writ petition court regularised the salaries and gave three months time for payment of arrears. Total arrears come to rupees 28 crores and the State of Haryana could make up only 20 crores and remaining had to be granted by the Union of India. Since the State of Haryana had shown its willingness to pay the amount, it was held that there was no wilful disobedience.

20. *Mohd. Iqbal Khanday* v. *Abdul Majid Rather* AIR 1994 S.C. 2252, 2254. In this case a lecturer, Faculty of Medicine, Medical College, Srinagar, who was denied promotion got a direction from the High Court to promote hirn to the post of Associate Professor. Contempt arose because of the non-implementation of the order of the court. It was argued that the petitioner did not possess the required qualification and also promotion matters were to be considered by the Departmental Promotion Committee.

21. *Mritynjoy Das* v. *Sayed Habibur Rahaman* AIR 2001 S.C. 1293 at 1297.

So also non-compliance under the guise of getting directions from the government[22] or unreasonable delay in implementing the order[23] will amount to wilful disobedience. Allahabad High Court in *Lakhan Singh* v. *Ram Bahadur Srivastava*[24] explained wilful disobedience in the following words:

> What is meant by wilful disobedience is nothing but deliberate disobedience and not disobedience with a particular motive. It is the act of disobeying the injunctions that must be done wilfully or deliberately, it is not the requirement that it must be done with a criminal intention or motive.[25]

Further, even if the alleged contemner had no intention to disobey the order passed by the court, yet it has to be held that the person was guilty of wilfully disobeying the orders of the court.[26] The same view was expressed by the Punjab and Haryana High Court in *N.S. Kanwar's case*:[27]

---

22. *Lakhan Singh* v. *Ram Bahadur Srivastava* 1994 Cri. L.J. (Allahabad High Court) 2997 in this case one Ram Bahadur Srivastava, Gram Vikas Adhikari filed a writ petition, seeking the relief that the order by which he had been removed from service be quashed. Court by its *ex parte* order directed to reinstate the petitioner with arrears of salary within one month. Non-compliance of the order gave way for contempt petition.
23. *Court on its own motion* v. *N.S. Kanwar* 1995 Cri. L.J. (Punjab and Haryana High Court) 1261.
    Certain temporary workers who served for more than 10 years filed a writ for regularisation of their services and court directed to regularise their service if they fall within government regulations. While so, Chief Secretary to Government of Haryana issued directions to regularise services of certain other persons who had served for 5 years. But persons directed to be considered by the court had not been considered. The reason adduced was that they did not comply with the government regulations. So two affected persons filed another writ petition. Court when enquired about the earlier order it was answered that the claim of the petitioners for regularisation had been rejected. Since there was no proper reply for the improper delay in executing the earlier order of the court, court took *suo motu* contempt action.
24. *Supra* n. 21.
25. *Supra* n. 21 p. 3002.
26. *Id.* at 3003.
27. *Supra* n. 22.

> ...term wilful disobedience used in Sec. 2(b) of the Contempt of Courts Act, 1971 cannot be construed to mean that an act must in all cases be designed and deliberate to be held as civil contempt. If a party who is fully in know of the order of the court or is conscious and aware of the consequences and implications of the court's order ignores it or acts in violation of the court's order it must be held that disobedience is wilful.[28]

In *Tarafatulah Mandal's case*[29] P.B. Mukherjee J. laid down certain pre-requisites for contempt by disobedience of the orders of the court:

> Before a proceeding for contempt can succeed it is of paramount importance to establish first, the service of the order of the court said to have been disobeyed upon the person alleged to have committed contempt thereof; secondly the precise act of contempt, thirdly the precise responsibility of the contemner in the act of contempt, and fourthly the date of the alleged contempt being subsequent to the service of the order said to have been disobeyed. These are the four indispensable requisites and failure to establish anyone of them must mean dismissal of the petition for contempt.[30]

Each of these ingredients is considered in detail below:

(i) Personal service

It was laid down by the Calcutta High Court, that service of the order of the court was a fundamental postulate for contempt.[31] A person who was not aware of the order could not be said to have disobeyed the order and committed contempt of court. This principle was followed by the Nagpur High Court in *Pitrus Lahra* v. *R.V. Dalal*.[32] Accordingly the sale of

28. *Id.* at 1268.
29. *Supra* n. 13.
30. *Id.* at 927.
31. *Ibid.*
32. AIR 1953 Nag. 179. In this case the First Class Magistrate of Jashpur convicted and sentenced Pitrus and Boka each to undergo four months rigorous imprisonment under Sec. 7 of the Essential Supplies (Temporary powers) Act, 1946 for contravention of Food Grains Control Order, 1945. 68 bags of grains weighing 170 maunds were also ordered to be forfeited. On appeal the Additional Sessions Judge set aside the

grains (170 maunds) without the personal knowledge and that too prior to the receipt of the copy of the order of the Additional Sessions Judge was held not contempt of court:[33]

> The contempt here was not, however, the result of wilful disobedience or wilful disregard of the order in question, and as such it should not be visited with a penalty.[34]

In this case though we can infer the existence of the knowledge of the order, there is no personal service. The Calcutta High Court further clarified the circumstances in which personal service would be required in *Nabakumar Saha* v. *S. Banerjee.*[35]

In this case, though Mr. S. Banerjee had not implemented the court order within the prescribed time limit, he was discharged on the ground that the order of the court, was not personally served to none of the opposite parties before the rule was issued by the court.[36] But the following principle is of much importance:

> But disobedience, if it is to be punishable as a contempt, must be wilful. Disobedience cannot be held to be wilful until the order is served. Hence the judgment or order must be shown to have been served on the party

order and acquitted the accused. The state appealed against the order of the Sessions Judge and the same was dismissed. After one month of the disposal of the appeal; the State Government sold the grains without the knowledge of the petitioner. Hence, the contempt petition.

33. *Id.* at 180.

34. *Ibid.*

35. AIR 1953 Cal. 96. The petitioner Mr. S. Banerjee applied for a writ of Mandamus and for *ad interim* injunction. The court after hearing the parties made the following order: "For the reasons given by me in civil revision case No. 1678 of 1950 disposed of by me today, I make the rule absolute in terms similar to those of the said rule." The order passed in civil revision case was as follows: "I accordingly direct that the state do restore possession forthwith of the lands which are in their possession to the petitioners after giving them notice of the date on which possession would be restored. I also direct that the State will supply, to the petitioners within one month from this date, the names of the persons to whom possession was made over by the state of the lands which are covered by notification and the description of such lands as far as possible...."

36. *Id.* at 97.

> personally, except in the following cases: (1) prohibitive orders the drawing up of which is not completed; (2) orders embodying an undertaking to do an act by a named day; (3) orders to answer interrogatories or discovery or inspection of documents; (4) where an order for substituted service has been made; where the respondent has evaded service of the order.... Personal service of the judgment or order may be dispensed with (1) if it be made to appear to the court or a judge that prompt personal service of the judgment or order cannot be effected, in such a case substituted or other service of the order or merely giving notice of the order may be directed; (2) if it is shown that the person to be served has evaded services.[37]

In case the authority avoids knowledge by evading acceptance of the injunction order the concerned party is guilty of contempt of court.[38] The court made a distinction between summons and injunction as follows:

> Refusal to accept, or evade service of a summons may not be contempt, but refusal to accept, or evade service of, an injunction order is contempt because there is fundamental difference between summons and an injunction order. A summons does not require obedience. The party summoned is at liberty not to appear in court because the proceeding can still be taken *ex parte* against him. An injunction requires obedience and since there can be no obedience unless the contents of the order are brought home to the person, the injunction must be accepted when offered. To refuse to accept an injunction order is to interfere with the course of justice by refusing to acquire the knowledge

37. *Id.* at 98.

38. *Ramcharan* v. *Debi Dayal* 1955 Cri. L.J. (Allahabad High Court) 1223. In this case applicant filed a suit against the Municipal Board of Etawah and got an injunction restraining the Municipal Board from constructing certain shops at the back of the applicant's shop. When the suit was dismissed the Municipal Board started construction. The applicant took the matter in appeal and got an injunction at the appellate court. Though the applicant informed the Board of the injunction, they continued the construction and evaded service of the injunction order by the process server.

> without which the Court's order cannot be complied with.[39]

In this case the respondent without just cause refused to accept the service of the injunction order and also interfered with the process server's duty of serving it upon him and so he was found to be guilty of contempt of court.[40]

Punjab High Court in *Gurbachan Singh, Lachhman Singh* v. *Ch. Hoshiar Singh*[41] expressed the view that official communication is not necessary for vesting the liability, but the officer should credibly be informed of the passing of a stay order and he may be guilty of contempt if he persists in carrying out the action which has been ordered to be stayed.[42]

On appeal,[43] the Supreme Court also accepted the opinion expressed by the High Court.

But Justice Raghubir Dayal expressed the view that, no question of wilful disobedience can arise when the very existence of the order is not believed.[44] Further:

> Conviction for contempt of court must depend on unimpeachable evidence of the knowledge of the alleged contemner about the order said to have been disobeyed.[45]

Though by majority opinion the appeal was dismissed, the opinion of Justice Raghubir Dayal is correct, because as stated

---

39. *Id.* at 1229.
40. *Id.* at 1230.
41. AIR 1959 Punj. 205. In this case the petitioner was in unlawful possession of certain land and authorities had taken a decision to dispossess the petitioner. So he filed a petition under Art. 226 and got a stay order. But the Tehsildar formally dispossessed the petitioner and gave the property to some other person. The principle laid down in this case was followed by the Patna High Court in *Ramroop Yadav* v. *State of Bihar* AIR 1969 Pat. 151. In this case it was further stated that in case the court had special reason to doubt the authenticity, the court can insist on filing an affidavit in support of the certificate. Further it was followed by the same High Court in *Dr. Dukhan Ram* v. *State of Bihar* AIR 1972 Pat. 465 wherein knowledge of the order was not denied but delivery of official communication was denied.
42. *Ibid.*
43. *Hoshiar Singh* v. *Gurbachan Singh* AIR 1962 S.C. 1089.
44. *Id.* at 1095.
45. *Id.* at 1098.

by the learned Judge himself, the question of obedience or disobedience of an order can arise only when there is knowledge of the order. But Justice Raghubar Dayal has also not insisted upon official communication, but only insisted upon existence of knowledge.

The same view was held by the Supreme Court in *The Aligarh Municipal Board* v. *Ekka Tonga Mazdoor Union,*[46] wherein Aligarh Municipal Board collected stand fees even after the Mazdoor Union got an interim stay from the High Court. Collection of stand fees even after knowing the existence of stay order constituted contempt even though there was no official communication.

In case the person alleged to have disobeyed the order was a party to the proceedings no further personal service of the order was necessary.[47]

It is not a condition precedent that a person who disobeyed the order should be a party to the proceedings and a person who is a party to the proceedings should have personal service of the order. In *Narain Singh* v. *S. Hardayal Singh Harika Executive Officer Municipal Committee Patiala,*[48] it was argued

46. AIR 1970 S.C. 1767. In this case there was a dispute in regard to the realisation of fees claimed by the Municipal Board of Aligarh from Ekkawalas and Tongawalas for the use of the Municipal stand at various places in the Aligarh city. Two suits filed by the Ekka Tonga Mazdoor Union in this connection had been decided in its favour. As the Board still persisted in realising the fees the said union along with six of its members filed a writ petition in the Allahabad High Court and got an interim stay order. The stand fee was continued to be collected as usual till 7th April, 1965 even though the Municipal Board and the concerned officers of the Board had been appraised of the order as early as 31st March, 1965.

47. *In re K.E. Johnson Commissioner of Income Tax, Assam, Tripura and Manipur* AIR 1964 Assam and Nagaland 92, 96. In this case the respondents Mr. Johnson and others purposely dodged the compliance of the order of the court directing them to return the register and other goods seized in pursuance of Sec. 37 (2) of the Income Tax Act.

48. AIR 1958 Punj. 180. In this case notice had been issued by the Municipality to remove the encroachment by the petitioner. So the petitioner filed a suit in the subordinate judge's court and got an injunction. Soon the Municipality sent another notice for which the petitioner claimed that it was in disobedience of the order issued by the court.

that the respondent was not a party to the suit and he had no knowledge of pending proceedings. But it was held:

> In order to render a person amenable to an injunction it is not indispensable, that he should have been a party to the suit in which the injunction was issued or that he should have been served with a copy of it. Such a person is amenable where with actual knowledge in his possession of the injunction he defied the injunctive order. A stranger is not punishable for contempt for an act, with which he had no connection, for which he was not responsible, or for acts done without his knowledge or consent.[49]

Delhi High Court also held the same view in *Nand Kishore Chela Mal* v. *Commissioner of the Municipal Corporation of Delhi*,[50] and observed:

> In order to sustain the charge of contempt of court for disobeying the court's order, knowledge of such order has to be proved beyond all reasonable doubt and in case of doubt benefit ought to be given to the person charged.[51]

Since there was no evidence to disobey or flout the orders of the court,[52] on the part of the contemner, he was held not guilty of contempt.

But in this case the authority cannot claim lack of knowledge, because as a responsible officer he is expected to know what is going on in his office. If he is not informed the officer responsible should be held liable. In *Isaac and Sons Pvt. Ltd.* v. *K. Prathodhanan*[53] the respondent was found guilty of contempt

---

49. *Id.* at 182.
50. AIR 1969 Del. 137. In this case Single Judge dismissed a writ petition filed against the corporation and the corporation was directed to carry out the demolition work. This decision was reversed by the Division Bench in the Letters Patent Appeal. But the advocate of the respondents requested for time and so the case was adjourned. On the date of hearing it was stated in the court that the demolition had been completed. This was the cause of contempt petition.
51. *Id.* at 140.
52. *Id.* at 141.
53. 1992 Cri. L.J. (Kerala High Court) 2587. The petitioners in this case were the Managing Director and Manager of Hotel Residency in Munnar.

because he flouted the orders of the court even after having had the knowledge of the order.[54] Court directed the respondent to make an open apology as punishment, on a specified date.

Personal service which was laid down by the Calcutta High Court as an indispensable pre-requisite of contempt by disobedience was very much diluted by subsequent decisions and reached the stage of knowledge of the order except in the case of prohibitory orders. In the case of prohibitory orders also, if the concerned person is a party to the proceedings, personal service can be dispensed with. The only pre-requisite is that knowledge should be established. This is welcome change because the authority may not dodge due compliance of court order under the guise of lack of official communication.

(ii) Precise act of contempt

What constitutes disobedience depends on the facts of each case and also the orders passed. Sale of grain in contravention of the court order,[55] issuing notification acquiring certain properties in contravention of the court order,[56] direction by the Under Secretary to the Magistrate to ignore the decision of the High Court[57] issuing licence in disobedience of the stay order of the High Court,[58] collection of stand fees by the Municipal Authority during the pendency of stay order[59] are some instances of such disobedience. But precise act of contempt as laid down by the Calcutta High Court in *Tarafatulah Mandal*

The Hotel was assessed for building tax. Petitioner moved the High Court questioning the assessment order. But the High Court directed the petitioners to move the government to get a reassessment and for that five weeks time was granted. After knowing the order the respondents, Tahsildar and Deputy Tahsildar immediately attached the movable property of the hotel. Hence the contempt petition.

54. *Id.* at 2589.
55. *Pitrus Lahra* v. *R.V. Dalal* AIR 1953 Nag. 179.
56. *The State of Bihar* v. *Rani Sonabatikumari* AIR 1961 S.C. 221.
57. *Dibarkar Satpathy* v. *Hon'ble the Chief Justice and his Companion Justices of the Orissa High Court* AIR 1961 S.C. 1315.
58. *Subodh Gopal Bose* v. *State of Bihar* AIR 1969 P. and H. 435.
59. *The Aligarh Municipal Board* v. *Ekka Tonga Mazdoor Union* AIR 1970 S.C. 1767.

v. *S.N. Maitra*[60] should be established before finding an authority guilty of contempt.

In *Messers Bhatnagar and Co. Ltd.* v. *Union of India,*[61] it was held that the existence of an undertaking should first be established before committing a breach of it.

So also when the commissioner of a corporation granted permission to construct a theatre to a person other than the one to whom the High Court directed the commissioner to grant licence, he is committing contempt of court,[62] as there is disobedience of a precise direction.

But in case the government had revised the scale of pay detrimental to the petitioner who obtained a writ of mandamus directing the government to avoid discrimination between

---

60. *Supra* n. 13. This principle was well recognized by the Calcutta High Court itself in *Taradas Dutt* v. *Administrative Officer of the Corporation of Calcutta* (AIR 1951 Pat. 451). In this case it was held: "To me it appears that from the very inception he was trying to undo the order passed by the learned Munsiff/Magistrate for the removal of Rasdhari Singh to jail custody. In my judgment his action amounts to a clear disregard of the court's order. He has, therefore, committed the offence of contempt of court (at 452).
61. AIR 1957 S.C. 478. In this case a group of petitions were filed by the petitioners Messers Bhatnagar and Co., for appropriate writs. The petitioners had the licence to import soda ash. The customs authorities charged the company for violations of Customs Act, and confiscated certain goods. In the suit the Solicitor General made a statement indicating that the goods confiscated by customs authorities would not be sold or otherwise dealt with for a month from the date of the communication to the petitioner of the final order that the Central Government may pass in the revision petition preferred by him before them. Acting on this undertaking court allowed the petitioners a period of one month from the date of communication to him of the final order which the Central Government might pass on this revisional petition. Breach of undertaking given by the Solicitor General was the subject matter of the contempt petition.
62. *Fatima Begum* v. *The Commissioner of the Hyderabad Municipal Corporation* AIR 1958 A.P. 170. The petitioner was a lessee of a plot of land and applied to the corporation for the licence to construct a theatre. The corporation refused to grant licence. So she made an appeal to the High Court. High Court directed the corporation to grant licence subject to compliance of other conditions. But the corporation not only refused to grant licence to the petitioner but granted licence to construct a theatre in the same plot to another person.

graduate inspectors and postgraduate inspectors the government was not disobeying the orders of court and did not commit any contempt of court,[63] when they were not given the same scale of pay because there was no wilful disobedience.

A similar situation was considered by the Supreme Court in *Niaz Mohammed* v. *State of Haryana*,[64] wherein contempt arose because of non-payment of arrears of salary as directed by the court. State of Haryana expressed its inability to pay and also stated that it is waiting for the grant from Union of India. Though, a decree once passed is to be executed, if there is compelling circumstance under which it is not possible to comply with the order of the court it may not amount to contempt of court.[65]

But as stated by the court, once a decree is passed it is to be executed. If there is any difficulty, it should be brought to the notice of the court in advance and should get necessary modification. The plea of inability need not be considered when contempt proceedings have been taken up.

For constituting contempt of court deliberate disobedience of the stay should be established,[66] and disobedience

---

63. *Aswini Kumar Rath* v. *P.C. Mukherjee* AIR 1965 Cal. 484. In this case there was a discrepancy between the scale of pay of Inspectors of schools who are ordinary graduates and that of honours degree holders or postgraduates. So a writ of mandamus was filed and the High Court allowed the writ and directed the government to avoid discrepancy. In pursuance of the order of the High Court, government fixed the scale of Sub Inspectors of schools at 175-7-245. The petitioner's case was that, their prayer in the original case was that their pay scale should be raised from Rs. 225 to Rs. 475 and the rule *nisi* issued according to that prayer was made absolute, and there had been wilful violation of the rule by fixing the scale at 175-7-245.
64. AIR 1995 S.C. 308 (For facts *see* n. 19 *Supra*).
65. *Id.* at 311.
66. *Rameshwar Singh* v. *A.N. Choubey* AIR 1954 Pat. 554. In this case proceedings under Sec. 133 Cr. P.C. were pending in respect of a well on the public road. During the pendency of the proceedings Second Officer made an order that the alleged encroachment should be removed by filling up the well. So a title suit was filed in the Munsiff Court which restrained the Second Officer from filling the well. The matter ultimately went to the High Court. The High Court issued a stay order. Because of the delay in getting the order the party informed the Second

on the part of any agency will amount to contempt of court.[67]

But compliance of a statutory duty, though in contravention of court's order will not amount to contempt of court.[68] Thus the issue of show cause notice in good faith in obedience to the Sea Customs Act cannot amount to contempt of the criminal court.[69]

A peculiar situation arose in *J. Vasudevan* v. *T.R. Dhananjaya.*[70] In this case an I.A.S. officer met the Supreme Court judge in order to seek the mercy of the court in a contempt matter relating to his colleague. This meeting of the I.A.S. officer was viewed seriously by the court and disapproved in strong terms by the court. But the court closed the matter by ordering that an entry would be made in his CCR about the gross impropriety committed.

Officer of the stay order by letter supported by a letter from the advocate. But the Second Officer rejected the letter and filled the well. Hence the contempt petition.

67. *The State* v. *Bhawani Singh* AIR 1968 Del. 208. In this case contemner No. 1, raided the house of the petitioner and took possession of two keys. Since no incriminating document was available no F.I.R. was filed. Since the contemner (1) had not returned the key the Magistrate ordered the production of the material. But the contemner refused to appear. On notice, Superintendent of police also ignored the matter. Non-compliance of the order of the court was brought to the notice of the High Court and hence the contempt proceedings. The same view was expressed by the Madras High Court in *Mottur Hajee Abdul Rahman and Co.* v. *Deputy Commercial Tax Officer, Vaniyambadi* AIR 1969 Mad. 232.
68. *Tukaram G. Gaokar* v. *R.K. Shukla* AIR 1968 S.C. 1050. In this case customs authorities raided the house of John D'Sa and confiscated certain gold. Charges were framed under Sec. 120 B and Foreign Exchange Regulation Act and the proceedings were imminent. While so Assistant Collector of Customs issued a show cause notice as to why the gold confiscated should not be sold and why penalty should not be imposed under the Sea Customs Act. This show cause notice was the subject of the contempt petition.
69. *Id.* at 1052. The same view was followed by the Gauhati High Court in *Bibekananda Bhawal* v. *Santosh Mohan Dev.* 1977 Cri. L.J. NOC P. 101 Gau., wherein it was held that a person cannot be committed for contempt for doing an act in accordance with law or rules.
70. AIR 1996 Supreme Court 137.

Though the same principle may be applied in case of granting of pardon by the executive head, because he is exercising the constitutional right, there is no direct authority for the proposition. Pardon can be granted either after the final verdict is given by the court or during the pendency. In the case of the former there is no interference because the matter is not pending before the court. But in the case of the latter there is the possibility of interference. In such cases of conflict Supreme Court[71] adopted the principle of harmonious construction to avoid a conflict between the two powers and held that Art. 161 does not deal with the suspension of sentence during trial and that Art. 142 is in operation when the matter is *subjudice*.[72] An advocate writing on pardoning power suggested that neither the executive nor the judiciary need be impatient and/or over-jealous and if both have respect for each others rights a conflict can be avoided and the so-called problem, which otherwise appears to be baffling will never arise necessitating a solution and/or affirmative decision of this question.[73]

It is suggested that in the light of the opinion of the Supreme Court in *In re Vinaya Chandra Misra*[74] and also that executive power is co extensive with that of the legislative power,[75] in the case of direct conflict, the power and authority

71. *K.M. Nanavati* v. *The State of Bombay* AIR 1961 S.C.112. In this case K.M. Nanavati was charged for murder and found guilty by the High Court and sentenced him to life imprisonment. On the same day Governor in exercise of his powers under Art. 161 suspended the sentence until appeal intended to be filed by him. Hence the conflict. The matter went to the Supreme Court by special leave and because of the importance of the matter it was considered by the Special Bench.

72. *Id.* at 122.

73. Nalin Chandra Banerjee "Whether it will amount to contempt of court if an accused is granted pardon by the Executive during the pendency of Judicial Proceedings." 12, (No. 2) *Law Quarterly* 94, 98 (1975).

74. (1995) 2 SCC 584. The Parliament's power to legislate in relation to law of contempt relating to Supreme Court is limited, therefore the Act does not impinge upon this courts power with regard to the contempt of subordinate courts under Art.129 of the Constitution (*Id.* at 605).

75. Art. 73 (1): Subject to the provisions of this Constitution the executive power of the Union shall extend — (a) to the matters with respect to which Parliament has power to make laws....

Art. 162: Subject to the provisions of this Constitution the executive

of the Supreme Court and High Courts will prevail over that of the executive power.

In *State of Bihar* v. *Rani Sonabati Kumari*[76] the Supreme Court explained the need for each and everyone including the executive to obey the orders of the court:

> When once the order has been passed which the court has jurisdiction to pass, it is the duty of all the persons bound by it to obey the order so long as it stands and it would tend to the subversion of orderly administration and civil government if parties could disobey orders with impunity. If such is the position as regard private parties the duty to obey is all the more imperative in the case of governmental authorities, otherwise there would be a conflict between one branch of the state polity, *viz.* The executive and another branch the judiciary.[77]

This rule as laid down by the Supreme Court was followed by the Allahabad,[78] Rajasthan,[79] Jammu and

power of state shall extend to the matters with respect to which the legislature of the state has power to make laws.

76. AIR 1961 S.C. 221. The Bihar Land Reforms Act, 1950 provided for the transference to the State of the interests of proprietors and tender holders in estates within the state. Rani Sonabati Kumari questioned the validity of the Act and got an injunction restraining the defendant (State) its officers, servants, employees and agents from issuing any notification for taking over the possession of the suit properties. Subsequently the state filed an application for vacating the order on the ground that the validity of the Act had been upheld in another suit. Before disposing of this application, State of Bihar issued a notification acquiring certain properties. This notification was the subject matter of the contempt petition.

77. *Id.* at 231.

78. *Lakhan Singh* v. *Ram Bahadur Srivastava* 1994 Cri. L.J. (Allahabad High Court) 2997. (For facts *see* n. 22 *Supra*) *Dr. Rohat Gupta* v. *The Principal S.N. Medical College* AIR 1995 All. 52. A student of J.L.N. Medical College, Belgaum got transferred to S.N. Medical College, Agra on recommendation of the Medical Council and also on direction by Allahabad High Court. During the internship period Principal, Medical College, Agra discontinued the petitioner by a letter on the basis of a judgment from Supreme Court. Thereafter Full Bench of the Allahabad High Court directed the Principal to permit the petitioner to continue the internship. He refused to comply with it and wanted to get a direction from the government of Uttar Pradesh.

79. *Jaipur Development Authority* v. *Harinath Sharma* 1995 Cri. L.J.

Kashmir[80] and Punjab and Haryana[81] High Courts. Allahabad High Court in *Lakhan Singh's*[82] case further directed that the copy of the judgment should be send to the Chief Secretary for circulation among the concerned.

But the Supreme Court in *Mohd. Iqbal Khanday* v. *Abdul Majid Rather*[83] recognized an exception that if there are genuine difficulties in implementing the order that can be considered while imposing the punishment. But the Supreme Court had not recognized it as a ground for non-compliance of the order. In this case court accepted the apology because there is genuine difficulty in implementing the order.

So also if the order passed by the court is without jurisdiction, the disobedience of the order will not amount to contempt of court.[84] It is not binding on the parties. In the same manner if the parties carry on the construction work after the expiry of the period of stay, then also there is no wilful disobedience of the orders of the court because no order is in existence.[85]

The Punjab and Haryana High Court in *Chhotta Singh* v. *Pritam Singh*[86] held that the contempt petition must fail on merits as it had not been proved that any of the respondents

---

(Rajasthan High Court) 1290: In this case land was acquired and compensation was given. After 22 years the proceedings have been questioned by a writ petition and the Division Bench of the Rajasthan High Court dismissed the writ and justified the acquisition. In spite of that, land acquision officer dropped the acquisition proceedings by unilateral order contrary to the finding recorded by the court.

80. *Miss Baljeet Oberaia* v. *The State* AIR 1985 J. & K. 16.
81. *Court on its own motion* v. *N.S. Kanwar* 1995 Cri. L.J. (Punjab and Haryana High Court) 1261.
82. *Supra* n. 78.
83. *Supra* n. 20.
84. *K.S. Jhunjhunwala* v. *Tayebhai Mohammedbhai Bagasapwalla* 1997 Cri. L.J. 1953 (Bombay High Court).
85. *B.N. Rathinasabapathy* v. *K.S. Palaniappa Kandar* [1995 Cri. L.J. 3622 (Supreme Court)].
86. AIR 1969 P. and H. 435. In this case Chhotta Singh and others complained of disobedience of the orders of the court and orders of Financial Commissioner passed in proceedings between the parties under the Tenancy and Agricultural Lands Act. Actual dispossession had not taken place because of the standing crop.

had flouted or acted in disobedience of the relevant orders of the court.

In a mining licence case, it was observed that wilful disobedience of the stay order would constitute contempt.[87] When the licence was issued, the suit as well as the stay order were pending, and so the state and its officers were liable for contempt in case of disobedience and violation of the order of injunction.[88]

But refusal to pay arrears of salary to a government servant illegally dismissed from service and directed to be reinstated by the High Court would not amount to contempt of court because the order of the High Court was silent on payment of arrears of salary.[89]

The court did not issue any direction to the state government to pay the arrears of salary and as such it cannot be held that the state government or its officers had committed contempt

---

87. *Subodh Gopal Bose* v. *State of Bihar* AIR 1969 Pat. 72. In this case the State of Bihar acquired certain lands over which the petitioner was doing mining business after attaining the proper licence. A portion of the said property was likely to be leased out to another. So the petitioner filed a suit and got a stay order restraining the State from granting any lease or permit in respect of the limestone quarries in favour of any person or body. The State of Bihar referred the matter to the Mines Tribunal, a writ petition was filed in the High Court and from there an appeal was preferred to the Supreme Court. While so government issued a notification for granting mining lease over the same property and the lease was granted. In these circumstances the petitioner alleged that the opposite party had deliberately and wilfully violated the order of injunction.
88. *Id.* at 76.
89. *Ratan Narain Mulla* v. *The Chief Secretary Government of U.P.* 1975 Cri. L.J. (Allahabad High Court) 1283. The petitioner in this case was an employee of the state government and was working as a Jail Superintendent. He was suspended from service because of misconduct and after enquiry dismissed from service. The petitioner filed a writ petition and the same was dismissed. The petitioner filed a special leave to appeal which was allowed mainly on the finding that the petitioner had not in the circumstances of the case received opportunity to show cause as contemplated by Art. 311 of the Constitution. The order of dismissal was accordingly quashed. As regards arrears of salary, the state government took the view that the conduct of the petitioner did not entitle him to the same and finally refused to pay it on the ground that the claim, had become time barred.

of court, by not paying the amount.[90] So also when there is substantial compliance of the court's order there is no wilful disobedience.[91]

The contempt jurisdiction cannot be used as an indirect method of executing decree, or as a means of getting any ancillary order.[92]

In *Parkash Chand* v. *S.S. Grewal*[93] it was claimed that the failure to reinstate the petitioner and non-payment of arrears of salary amounted to gross contempt of the court. But it was contended that the matter had been taken in appeal to the Supreme Court, depending on its decision action would be taken.

In this case the court considered two important questions.

(i) Whether the refusal or failure of the government or its servants to take any action to reinstate such a decree holder and grant him all benefits and privileges of his service amounted to contempt of court; and

(ii) If the above question was found in the affirmative whether the state or its officials could take shelter behind the legal advice tendered to them or the fact that an appeal was pending though no stay order had been obtained.[94]

---

90. *Id.* at 1287.

91. *Nias Mohammed* v. *State of Haryana* AIR 1995 S.C. 308. (For facts *see* n. 19 *Supra*).

92. *S. Teja Singh* v. *Ram Lal* 1978 Cri. L.J. (Punjab and Haryana) 612. In this case the learned single judge while finding that the respondent is not guilty of contempt stated: "The authorities concerned are directed to hand over the physical possession to the petitioner in Village Bassi Daulat Khan as well as to the respondents in village "Marauli Brahmanan." The single judge's ancillary order directing the change of physical possession was held to be invalid because there was no provision in the Contempt of Courts Act for doing that.

93. 1975 Cri. L.J. (Punjab and Haryana High Court) 679. The petitioner was a head clerk in the Punjab Government Service. He was dismissed from service. He filed a declaratory suit and the trial court decreed it. Appeal filed by the state and the Letters Patent Appeal were dismissed. But the state had not reinstated and has not paid the arrears of salary. Hence the contempt petition.

94. *Id.* at 683.

The first question was answered by the court in the following terms:

> Mere inaction on the part of the government or its servants to take any action to reinstate a decree holder whose dismissal has been declared to be void or ineffective and grant him all the benefits and privileges of his service will not amount to contempt of court, but, if the conduct of the particular government servant, whose duty it is to give effect to the decree, shows that he has wilfully and deliberately refrained from giving effect to the decision of the civil court, a case of contempt of court may arise.[95]

These powers have to be used only in serious cases where deliberate contempt is clearly established on the part of the contemner.

Regarding the next question it was held:

> If the court comes to the conclusion that the conduct amounts to wilful disobedience of the court's decree, or order, the obtaining of legal advice or the pendency of an appeal will not ordinarily constitute a good defence.[96]

But in *Kashinath Kher* v. *Dinesh Kumar Bhagat*,[97] Supreme Court expressed the view that when the contemner, officers of the Bank acted on the faith of the advice of the counsel and the counsel took the responsibility for the advice, the court held that there is no wilful disobedience of the orders of the court.

Principle as laid down by the Allahabad High Court[98] in answer to the first question had not been followed by the Himachal Pradesh High Court in *Hans Raj Dhir* v. *Himachal Pradesh*.[99] Though special leave to appeal was granted, no stay

---

95. *Id.* at 684, 685.
96. *Id.* at 687.
97. 1998 Cri. L.J. 666 (Supreme Court).
98. *Ratan Narain Mulla* v. *Chief Secretary, Govt. of U.P.* 1975 Cri. L.J. (Allahabad High Court) 1283.
99. 1985 Cri. L.J. (Himachal Pradesh High Court) 1030. Petitioner, who was in the service of the state government was first placed under suspension and subsequently terminated from service. So the petitioner filed a writ petition for various remedies including reinstatement, arrears of salary etc. and the same was allowed by the High Court. But the state government filed an appeal. As soon as the order was issued

was obtained. So it is the duty of the authorities to reinstate the petitioner and pay arrears of salary. If not, the authority should be held liable for contempt. Once a case is decided, it is the bounden duty of the state and its subordinates to implement with utmost expedition the said decision. It was observed:

> It requires to be emphasised, in this connection, that mere preferment of an appeal does not automatically operate as a stay of the decision under appeal and that till an application for stay is moved and granted by the appellate court, or, in the alternative, the court which rendered the decision is moved and grants an interim stay of the decision pending the preferment of an appeal and grant of stay by the appellate court, the decision continues to be operative.[100]

In *Union of India* v. *M/s. Oswal Woollen Mills Ltd.*[101] Supreme Court expressed the view that mere failure to take action by the Chief Controller of Imports and Exports within a prescribed time while no such time limit was prescribed by the court, will not amount to contempt of court.[102]

The Supreme Court considered the question of wilful breach of an undertaking and direction in *Union of India* v.

---

by the single judge of the High Court, the petitioner presented himself for duty but was not permitted to join duty and arrears of salary was not paid because of the Letters Patent Appeal. This action of the state was the subject matter of the contempt petition.

100. *Id.* at 1033. Punjab and Haryana High Court also expressed the same view in *Parkash Chand* v. *S.S. Grewal.* 1975 Cri. L.J. (Punjab and Haryana High Court) 679.

101. AIR 1984 S.C. 1264. In this case M/s. Oswal Woollen Mills Ltd. having its registered office at Ludhiana filed a writ petition against Union of India, the Chief Controller of Imports and Exports, the Collector of Customs, and the State Trading Corporation seeking various remedies and got injunctions. An application to vacate the stay order was made. In the meantime Oswal Woollen Mills Ltd. kept on writing letters and sending telegrams complaining that the interim orders of the High Court had not been obeyed and threatened with action for contempt of court. So an application to commit the Chief Controller of imports and exports and others for contempt was made and the High Court issued a rule. Hence the appeal.

102. *Id.* at 1267.

Mario Cabral e sa[103] and expressed the view that the order claimed to be disobeyed should be an enforceable order and then only there can be disobedience of the order.

The need to comply with the undertaking given by the government was further considered by the Supreme Court in *Mohd. Aslam alias Bhure* v. *Union of India,* and *Acchan Rizvi* v. *State of U.P.*[104]

Two important questions considered in this case are: (i) whether the undertaking given by the Chief Minister is a personal one or on behalf of the U.P. Government, and (ii) whether the state government and Chief Minister were not liable for contempt for any alleged wilful disobedience of the orders of the court.

Supreme Court relying on the opinion given in *State of Bihar* v. *Rani Sonabati Kumari*[105] held that a minister or officer of government is also either in his official capacity or if there is any personal element contributing to contempt in his personal capacity, liable for contempt.[106] The court observed:

> We find that the undertaking given by Shri Kalyan Singh was both in his personal capacity and on behalf of his government. There has been a flagrant breach of that

103. AIR 1982 S.C. 691. In this case Mario Cabral e sa applied for grant of accreditation to the Government of Goa Daman and Diu. The accreditation Committee also recommended the same. But the Government of Goa refused to grant accreditation. So the respondent moved an application before the Court of the Judicial Commissioner under Art. 226. On the basis of the undertaking given by the government advocate the application was disposed of on April 29, 1980. On June 9, 1980 the respondent moved the learned Addl. Judicial Commissioner for taking action under Contempt of Courts Act, 1971 against Union of India, Director of Information etc. for breach of undertaking given to the Judicial Commissioner.

104. AIR 1995 S.C. 548. This contempt case arose out of the Ram Janma Bhoomi Babri Masjid incident. Kalyan Singh, then Chief Minister of Uttar Pradesh was charged for breach of undertaking and also for permitting construction work in violation of court order.

105. Supra n. 76. Which followed the opinion of Chakravarthi C.J. in *Tarafatulah Mandal and Others* v. *S.N. Maitra* (AIR 1952 Cal. 919, 921) "I do not say that in fit cases a writ for contempt may not be asked for against a corporation or against a government."

106. *Supra* n. 104 p. 557.

undertaking. There has been wilful disobedience of the order.[107]

In *R.M. Ramaul* v. *State of Himachal Pradesh*[108] the Supreme Court held:

> Withholding of the monetary benefits in respect of this period [period for which promotion was not granted] is inconsistent with what was decided in the judgment and what complainant was clearly entitled to. Since there was no specific direction in this behalf in the order technically there may be no case for punishment for contempt.[109]

So also it has been held that a mistake in interpretation of the order of the court, did not amount to wilful or deliberate or contemptuous flouting or disobeyance of the orders of the court.[110]

In *V.G. Nigam* v. *Kedarnath Gupta*,[111] the court observed:

---

107. *Ibid.*

108. AIR 1971 S.C. 1171. In this case, the petitioner who was serving in the Tourism Department of Himachal Pradesh was denied promotion. So on writ petition High Court directed the department to give promotion. But the department gave only notional promotion and denied the monetary benefit. Hence the contempt petition. Court directed the department to give monetary benefit and also to consider the petitioner for further promotions.

109. *Id.* at 1172.

110. *Ashok Kumar Singh* v. *State of Bihar* AIR 1992 S.C. 407. The petitioners are primary school teachers who had been terminated from service. They filed a writ petition and got a direction from the court that these teachers should be absorbed after screening test and they should be given full benefit. After the decision, Human Resource Department passed an order determining the categories of persons eligible for reappointment. The Commissioner took the view that as per the executive direction only trained teachers were eligible for reappointment and accordingly only 81 teachers were found eligible for reappointment. It was claimed that the order of the Commissioner was contrary to executive direction and also in contravention of this court order.

111. AIR 1992 S.C. 2153. In this case a petition was filed before the Madhya Pradesh State Administrative Tribunal by the respondent, an Assistant Director-cum-Project Officer for his suppression and denial of promotion, which was allowed by the Tribunal. Since there was some delay respondent invoked the contempt jurisdiction of Tribunal. Tribunal found the appellants guilty of contempt. Hence the appeal.

> As regards the order of the tribunal sentencing the appellants for not complying with the order in letter and spirit while depreciating the practice or any attempt to ignore or by-pass the order passed by courts or tribunals it would be too hazardous to sentence in exercise of contempt jurisdiction on mere probabilities. The wilful conduct is the primary and basic ingredient of such an offence.[112]

Deliberate and wilful disobedience of the order,[113] or long delay in implementing the order of the court[114] may amount to wilful disobedience. But when there is no evidence of violation of injunction order[115] or when there is no violation at all[116] or when there is substantial compliance of the order[117] there is no contempt of court by disobedience.

---

112. *Id.* at 2155.
113. *Amar Bahadur Singh* v. *P.D. Wasnik* 1994 Cri. L.J. (Bombay High Court) 1359. Petitioner, a teacher promoted as headmaster, was prematurely ordered to be retired by the education officer on the basis that the petitioner was born on 21-09-1930. Petitioner claiming his date of birth as 30-06-1934 filed a civil suit and got a stay of the order of the education officer. Contempt arose because in the pay bills petitioner's name was scored and some other person was put in charge.
114. *Hari Shankar Bhandari* v. *Secretary, Public Health and Family Welfare Department* 1994 Cri. L.J. (Madhya Pradesh High Court) 3518. Petitioner, a retired radiographer, got his pension settled by a writ petition. Court directed to settle the matter within 3 months and pay arrears within one month thereafter. No action was taken even after 3 years.
115. *A. Dharmarajan* v. *Collector of Kamarajar District* 1994 Cri. L.J. (Madras High Court) 3585. In this case contempt petition arose because it was claimed that the quarry licence holder violated the injunction order of the court. Single judge held the appellant guilty of contempt of court based on the report of the Deputy Director of Geology and Mining. But the Division Bench found that no credence can be given to the report and the appellant was not guilty of contempt.
116. *Jabhiulla* v. *The Chief Engineer, Karnataka Electricity Board* 1995 Cri. L.J. (Karnataka High Court) 718. Petitioner sought an appointment in the Karnataka Electricity Board on compassionate ground. Since his request had not been complied with he got a direction from the High Court to consider his request sympathetically within 3 months. Board considered and rejected the matter taking into account monthly income of the petitioner. Contempt petition had been filed because the petitioner had not been given the appointment. Court held that there was no disobedience as the matter had been considered.
117. *Niaz Mohammed* v. *State of Haryana Supra* n. 19.

(iii) Responsibility to obey

The authority to whom the court has issued the order should have the responsibility to obey, that means a stranger to proceedings or a person who has no duty to obey, is not bound by the orders issued by the court.

The responsibility of a third party to obey an injunction order was considered by the Punjab and Haryana High Court in *Narain Singh* v. *S. Hardayal Singh Harika, Executive Officer, Municipal Committee, Patiala.*[118]

It was held:

> In order to render a person amenable to an injunction, it is not indispensable, that he should have been a party to the suit in which the injunction was issued or that he should have been served with a copy of it. Such a person is amenable where with actual knowledge in his possession of the injunction, he defied the injunctive order. A stranger is not punishable for contempt for an act, with which he had no connection, for which he was not responsible, or for acts done without his knowledge or consent.[119]

So even if a person is not a party to the proceedings, if he has the responsibility to obey he is liable for contempt if he disobeys. In *Santhosh Kumar Samant* v. *Raja Sri Bira Chandra Jadumania Deo*[120] the question was whether the Sarpanch of the Panchayat of Rampur was guilty of disobedience of an order of injunction in an arbitration case in which he was not a party.

The Orissa High Court held:

---

118. AIR 1958 Punj. 180. In this case it was alleged that the executive officer of the Municipal Committee had committed contempt of court.

119. *Id.* at 182.

120. AIR 1965 Ori. 222. In this case under an agreement between the Raja of the State Rairakhole and Union of India, the State was ceded to the Union of India and the Raja was given full ownership to the private properties including the village of Rampur. Subsequently the Raja was informed that the village except the building used for public purpose was only ceded. So the Raja filed a suit and got an injunction. Contempt petition arose because the Sarpanch disobeyed the injunction order. But he was not a party to the original suit.

> In view of the position that the injunction was issued by the court against the Union of India and the State of Orissa alone, in respect of the plots in dispute and further that the injunction order made no mention of their servants and agents, the appellant Sarpanch cannot be found guilty of disobeying the injunction.[121]

But in this case the decision is not correct because once an order is issued against the government it will bind its servants and agents also.

A person who is not a party to the injunction cannot be held liable for breach of injunction or disobedience. The third principle as laid down by the Calcutta High Court[122] was also invariably followed.

(iv) Contempt subsequent to disobedience of order

It is necessary that the alleged act of contempt must be after the date of the order of the court. In other words, on the date of contempt, the order should have been in existence.

In *Deben Adhicary* v. *State of West Bengal,*[123] it was claimed that the respondents disobeyed the order of the Calcutta High Court. But the order was not served on the concerned respondent, and that the alleged act of contempt was anterior to the service of the order. Further, the order was communicated to the respondent by the petitioner's advocate on August 31, 1967 even though the alleged act of contempt was committed on the 19th July, 1967.[124] Thus the last requirement as laid down in *Tarafatulah Mandal's*[125] case, had not been complied with and so there was no disobedience of the order of the court.

---

121. *Id.* at 224.
122. *Supra* n. 13.
123. 1972 Cal. 84. Due to labour unrest there was a gherao by the workers in the factory and the residence of the petitioner. So he filed a writ and got an interim order restraining the respondents (Employees and Trade Union leaders) from interfering with the functioning of the factory. Subsequent to this order the workers and leaders interfered with the functioning of the factory and hence the contempt petition.
124. *Id.* at 87.
125. *Supra* n. 13.

The same view was upheld by the Supreme Court in *The State of U.P.* v. *M.V. Siddiqui.*[126] In this case the date on which the professor (petitioner) was relieved no injunction order was in force. The court observed:

> The *status quo* which obtained then was that the respondent had already been relieved of his charge and we feel that in the absence of an order from the court directing the respondent being put back to his earlier position no contempt can be said to have been committed by the government or its officers.[127]

But when the officers of the state government misread the orders of the Supreme Court in such a way that the quota of non resident Indians in professional colleges were affected, the court felt that it is a deliberate subversion of the orders of the court and punished the officers for contempt.[128]

When an interim order is passed by the court it is to be obeyed. In case of disobedience whether it amounts to contempt of court or not depends upon the nature of order passed by the court. The particular point was considered by the Jammu and Kashmir High Court in *Miss Baljeet Oberaia* v. *The State.*[129] The petitioner claimed that non-compliance of the interim order amounted to contempt of court and until they purge the

---

126. AIR 1980 S.C. 2052. In this case a research professor was reverted and he filed a suit and got an interim injunction. On a particular date of posting neither the advocate nor the party was present and so the court dismissed the suit. When the suit was dismissed the Professor was reverted. So the professor again moved the court for setting aside the order of the court and for the maintenance of *status quo.* The court passed an order for maintenance of *status quo.* But on the date of this order the professor had already been reverted. So he claimed that there was disobedience of the order and thus it amounted to contempt of court.
127. *Id.* at 2053, 2054.
128. *T.M.A. Pai Foundation and others* v. *State of Karnataka and others* (AIR 1995 S.C. 1938).
129. AIR 1985 J. & K. 16. In this case an application was made by the acting principal, Medical College, Srinagar, seeking clarification/modification of the order passed by the court. J. & K. High Court earlier passed an order directing the principal to provisionally admit the petitioner. But he was not admitted. Hence the contempt petition.

contempt they should not be heard. On this particular point the court observed:

> This aspect of the case needs fuller consideration and I for one with great respect cannot subscribe to the view that in all cases where an interim order is not immediately complied with by the party against whom it is passed he commits contempt.... Simply because a party chooses to file a contempt application, the alleged contemner does not become disentitled to plead his cause before the court.[130]

In case of contempt by disobedience the alleged contemner should have the knowledge of the order. To constitute knowledge, official communication of the order is not necessary. The alleged contemner should be informed of the order from reliable sources. Further, the order alleged to have been disobeyed should be an enforceable order. If the order is issued by an officer who had no authority to issue such order, it cannot be an enforceable order.

The question whether a state law officer be permitted to appear for and on behalf of the officer or employee of the state who disobeyed the court order was considered by the Supreme Court in *Commissioner, Agra and another* v. *Rohtas Singh and others*[131] and held that they can.

3. NON-COMPLIANCE OF ORDERS OF COURT

Wilful disobedience of the court's order amounts to contempt of court. But difficulty arises when non-compliance is concerned. In some cases the concerned officer, instead of obeying the order, may seek clarification, make suggestions or keep it pending.

In *State* v. *Radhagobinda Das*,[132] the question considered was whether the demi-official letter written by the Deputy Secretary, Government of Orissa to the District Magistrate would amount to interference with the course of justice. Considering the position of the respondent and the endorsement

130. *Id.* at 18.

131. AIR 1998 S.C. 685.

132. AIR 1954 Ori. 1.

on the letter it was held that the letter had the effect of interfering with the administration of justice.

So also when an Under Secretary, Board of Revenue circulated a circular containing the opinion of Legal Remembrancer and directed the Magistrate to ignore the decision of the High Court though it was binding on them, it was held that the Under Secretary had committed flagrant interference with the administration of justice.[133]

The same principle was followed even after the enacting of the Contempt of Courts Act, 1971. Thus in *Gouri Shankar Jain* v. *State of Bihar*,[134] when an officer of the police station instead of complying with the direction of the munsiff-magistrate, made certain suggestions to the magistrate, the officer had committed contempt. So the conclusion is that non-compliance of the order amounts to disobedience, which is contempt.

Kerala High Court also followed the same view in *M.C. Joseph* v. *The State of Kerala*.[135] In this case the High

---

133. *Dibakar Satpathy* v. *Hon'ble the Chief Justice and his Companion Justices of the Orissa High Court.* AIR 1961 S.C. 1315. The appellant was Under Secretary Board of Revenue. He was admonished by the Orissa High Court in a contempt petition for circulating the opinion of Legal Remembrancer and of Advocate General in which it was stated that no special authorisation was necessary to empower the magistrate to take cognizance under Sec. 20 of the Cattle Trespass Act.
134. 1973 Cri. L.J. (Patna High Court) 137. In this case Gouri Shankar, petitioner was a mining lease holder. A temple, situated in the mining land was likely to be damaged. So there was a public protest. The resident magistrate visited the spot for lodging a first information report. The magistrate was annoyed at the behaviour of the petitioner and so he issued a warrant of arrest. Since the petitioner was not present orders under sections 87 and 88 of the Criminal Procedure Code were issued and the officer in charge of the police station, attached and seized the properties. Subsequently the petitioner appeared before the court and was released on bail. The court also allowed the request for release of seized articles. On receipt of this direction from the learned munsiff-magistrate the officer in-charge did not carry out the order but he wrote a letter addressed to the resident magistrate expressing some doubt about the order of the court. This was the cause of contempt petition.
135. AIR 1973 Ker. 216. The petitioner in this case was a godown keeper and he was being directed by the government to pay for the loss arising due to shortage in the stock of rice at the godown. The petitioner filed

Court directed the government to reconsider the request of the petitioner. The government in turn replied that no reconsideration of the petition was necessary. The court observed:

> To say that on reconsideration of the matter the previous decision cannot be altered is one thing, but to say that no reconsideration is necessary at all is another. It was because this court found that reconsideration was necessary, that was ordered. Refusing to reconsider saying it is unnecessary is flouting the order of court and showing scant respect to court.[136]

Though non-compliance of a direction of the court amounts to contempt of court, if the direction itself is premature the non-compliance of such direction will not amount to contempt. Thus in *State of Jammu and Kashmir* v. *Mohd. Yaqoob Khan*,[137] Supreme Court held that so long as the stay matter in the writ petition was not finally disposed of, the further proceeding itself was misconceived and no order therein should have been passed.[138]

Supreme Court further held that the orders passed in the contempt proceedings were not justified being premature and must therefore be entirely ignored. High Court should first take up the stay matter in the writ case and dispose it off by an appropriate order. Only then it should consider whether the state and its authorities could be accused of being guilty of having committed contempt of court.[139]

---

a writ and the court directed the government to reconsider the matter. Government in reply informed the petitioner that no reconsideration was necessary.

136. *Id.* at 217.

137. (1992) 4 SCC 167. In this case contempt proceedings were initiated against the state and its officers for non-compliance of the direction given by the court. In a writ petition filed by the petitioner a compromise was reached and as per the compromise, the court directed the government to give 50% of the timber to the petitioner which was the subject matter of the dispute on furnishing a bond by the petitioner. But the government did not comply with the direction thinking that they were not required to obey the interim direction immediately. So also there was no specification of time for the compliance of the direction. On non-compliance of the direction, the petitioner filed the contempt petition. The same was allowed by the High Court.

138. *Id.* at 170.

139. *Id.* at 171.

But showing indifference to the court's direction will amount to contempt of court.[140]

Calcutta High Court in *S.K. Samsudin (Petitioner)* v. *Ravikant and another*,[141] refused to accept the plea that there is confusion in the order of the High Court, which directed the Regional Transport Authorities to consider the petitioner's prayer for temporary permit, and held the authority guilty of contempt. The court further held that if there is any confusion in the order, the party can in advance very well approach the court and get the clarification.

Non-compliance of the court's order is viewed similar to disobedience. It is suggested that in case there is a genuine reason, acceptable to the court for non-compliance, that should not be treated as contempt. But in such circumstances, the concerned person has to approach the court well in advance and not to plead inability when contempt proceedings are taken up.

4. CONTEMPT OF COURT AND DISCIPLINARY PROCEEDINGS

For the efficient functioning of the administrative machinery proper discipline is necessary. Often authorities will initiate

---

140. *M.L. Sachdev* v. *Union of India* AIR 1991 S.C. 311. In this case, the petitioner by a writ under Art. 32 got a direction from the Supreme Court to fill up the post of Chairman and Members of the Commission under the Monopolies and Restrictive Trade Practices Act, 1969. Even after one extension of time the direction was not complied with. Hence the contempt petition. Supreme Court found the respondent, Union of India in the Ministry of Industries represented by Shri A.N. Verma, Secretary in the Ministry, guilty of contempt of court.
Recently Supreme Court punished Mr. Vasudevan, an I.A.S. Officer, Secretary, Housing and Urban Development, Karnataka Government, with one month simple imprisonment for disobeying its orders which directed the State Government to create a supernumerary post of Engineer-in-chief in the Bangalore city corporation for Mr. T.R. Dhananjaya, giving him all the consequential benefits (*See* 'Indian Express' 15th September, 1995). So also Madras High Court imposed a fine of Rs. 1000 on three I.A.S. Officers for disobeying the orders of the court (*See* 'Indian Express' 15th September, 1995). But it was subsequently stayed by the Division Bench of the same High Court (*See* 'Indian Express' 23rd September, 1995).
141. 1997 Cri. L.J. 1603 (Calcutta High Court).

steps against the subordinates for misbehaviour in relation to which a suit may be pending. Such disciplinary proceedings are show-cause notice, parallel enquiry, charge sheeting and the like. So the question is to what extent such administrative actions interfere with the administration of justice and constitute contempt of court.

The question of show-cause notice was considered in *Shankarlal Sharma* v. *M.S. Bisht,*[142] wherein the superior officer issued a notice to the subordinate staff as to why he filed a writ before the High Court. Allahabad High Court was of the opinion that there is no doubt that if any kind of threat or action is held out to a person, for having approached the civil court with a view to refrain him from seeking assistance, will amount to contempt of court.[143]

Any hindrance to administration of justice is an interference and hence contempt proceedings can follow. Even if the authorities are competent to prescribe certain pre-conditions that should not interfere with the administration of justice.

The issue of show-cause notice for approaching the court of law without exhausting departmental enquiry was also held to be contempt of court in *Gurbakhsh Singh* v. *S. Pratap Singh.*[144] In this case the petitioner claimed that, as a citizen of India he

---

142. AIR 1956 All. 160. In this case one Shankar Lal Sharma an employee in the public works department of Uttar Pradesh moved an application to grant a writ against Shri M.S. Bisht, Chief Engineer praying for a direction to the opposite party to forward to the Public Service Commission U.P. his application for employment in some higher post, which he had sent to the Commission through the opposite party. While so M.S. Bisht asked for an explanation from Shri Shankarlal as to why he had submitted a writ to the High Court. This notice was the subject of the contempt petition.

143. *Ibid.*

144. *Gurbakhsh Singh* v. *S. Pratap Singh* AIR 1959 Punj. 182. The petitioner in this case was a forester and the respondents were Chief Conservator of Forests and Divisional Forest Officer. The respondents directed the petitioner to pay a sum of money for short supply of timber failing which the sum was to be deducted from salary. The petitioner filed a suit for a declaration that the order was void. It was followed by a writ petition under Art. 226 and was dismissed. While the suit was pending, the charge sheet and show-cause notice were issued to the petitioner and that resulted in the contempt petition.

had every legal right to go to the court of law, for redressal of his grievances and the respondent tried to punish him for exercising that right. The respondent submitted that the government had no desire to interfere with the administration of justice and was only anxious to ensure that the remedies available under the departmental rules are exhausted by him before approaching the court of law. The court held:

> A government servant like any other citizen of this country, has a right to invoke the authority of the court at any time he chooses to ask for it, and it seems to me therefore that a person who deters him from exercising this right when he wishes to exercise it, commits contempt of court.[145]

It was also argued that every public servant holds office at the pleasure of the state and was not wrong or improper in informing the employees that it would not hesitate to exercise its legal right in terminating the services of its employees if the employees assert their right of seeking the intervention of court of law. It was held:

> It is true that government has a right to take disciplinary action against its own employees but it has no right to interfere with the administration of justice, and if in exercising its own rights it interferes with the course of justice it commits contempt of court. There can be no manner of doubt that the communication which was addressed by the Chief Secretary to government was issued with the object of preventing government servants from seeking redressal at the hands of courts of law at their own sweet will and pleasure and must therefore be deemed to have been issued with the object of diverting the course of justice.[146]

This decision poses questions like, what is the exact scope of departmental and disciplinary proceedings? Can the aggrieved servant directly approach the court without exhausting departmental proceedings? Can the aggrieved person during the pendency of disciplinary proceedings file a suit and stall the disciplinary proceedings? To a limited extent, the Supreme

145. *Id.* at 184.

146. *Id.* at 185.

Court answered these questions when the matter was taken in appeal.[147] Before the Supreme Court it was contended *inter alia* that on a fair construction of the terms of the circular letter on which the two appellants took action against the respondent, it should be held that it did not constitute an interference with the course of justice in as much as it did not impose any absolute ban on a government servant to have recourse to a court of law for the redressal of his grievances but merely imposed an obligation on him to exhaust his departmental remedies before approaching a court of law. The court, after referring to similar service rules, negatived the contention and held that the notice did interfere with the administration of justice. But it is pertinent to note the following observation made by Justice S.K. Das:

> If the circular letter merely lays down that ordinarily a government servant should exhaust his departmental remedies before going to a court of law, no objection can be taken to it. Speaking generally, a government servant does not ordinarily go to court, unless and until he fails to get what he considers to be justice from the departmental authorities. But we have to consider in this case a somewhat different problem, namely, the action taken against the respondent during a pending litigation, as though going to a court of law before exhausting departmental remedies must in all cases be visited with punishment.[148]

The learned judge held that the circular letter had the effect of interfering with the course of justice.

But Justice Raghubir Dayal declined to follow the majority view. He stated:

> If an employee acts against the directions contained in the circular, it is just and proper that action be taken. If action is taken and that be considered *per se* to amount to the commission of contempt of court, the directions in the circular can be disobeyed with impunity and the circular, though valid would remain a dead letter. It would then be incongruent to hold that any action taken

147. *Pratap Singh* v. Gurbakhsh Singh. AIR 1962 S.C. 1172.

148. *Id.* at 1177.

> in pursuance of it would *per se* amount to contempt of the court to which the government servant had gone for adjudication.[149]

Further:

> Contempt of court proceedings are in public interest and so are departmental proceedings against government employees for any act of indiscipline committed by them. It is therefore only when departmental action directly affects the course of the judicial proceeding that it can amount to interfering with the course of justice and, consequently, to contempt of court. If it does not do so, there can be no case of contempt of court.[150]

Justice Raghubir Dayal was of the opinion that if the circular be considered as constituting interference then any action taken by the authorities on the basis of the circular letter would be out of place and hence amount to contempt of court.

But both the judges are of the opinion that the action taken by the authorities on the basis of the circular letter would amount to interference with the administration of justice and hence it would be contempt of court.

For the purpose of avoiding conflict and for maintaining the authority of the judiciary it is suggested that the following principles may be followed:

(a) Departmental proceedings *ipso facto* cannot be held to interfere with the administration of justice.

(b) Once cognizance of the matter is taken up by the judiciary, departmental proceedings should be stopped.

(c) Judiciary, before taking cognizance of the matter, should confirm that the departmental remedies are exhausted.

(d) If the remedy is sought in the judiciary, against the disciplinary proceedings, the administrative department should not take any further action in the matter.

---

149. *Id.* at 1179.

150. *Id.* at 1181.

In *Giani Ram* v. *Ramnath Dutt*[151] Rajasthan High Court considered the effect of the charge sheet and the show-cause notice served by the Superintendent of post offices, the official superior to the petitioner who appeared as a witness for the prosecution. In this case Rameshwar Prasad, the prosecution witness was under the control of the Superintendent of post offices, the opposite party. Therefore the action taken by the opposite party was certainly, that of interfering with the course of justice.

The court observed:

> Witnesses no less than judges and counsel are an integral part of this process and they must be left unhampered to perform their respective duties with frankness and without interference of any kind.[152]

The Supreme Court in *Gurucharan Dass Chadha* v. *State of Rajasthan*,[153] while holding that the department had every right to take action against its employee, made the following observation:

> If the petitioner was guilty of any lapse under the services (conduct) rules or even guilty of an offence the action to which he would be otherwise subject could wait till the present proceedings had terminated and there was really

---

151. AIR 1955 Raj. 123. The petitioner in this case was a Sub-Post Master in Bikanar city and was under suspension and was being prosecuted under Sec. 400 I.P.C. for having embezzled some money. The opposite party Ramnath Dutt was the superintendent of post offices. At the trial Rameshwar Prasad was examined as prosecution witness. So the opposite party served a charge sheet on him to show cause why he gave false statement in court and why disciplinary action should not be taken against him for, what the opposite party characterised in the charge, to be a vicious statement. Hence the contempt petition.
152. *Id.* at 127.
153. AIR 1966 S.C. 1418. The petitioner was tried for charges under Sec. 120-B/161 of the Indian Penal Code and Sec. 5 (1)(a)(d) and 5(2) of the Prevention of Corruption Act. While the transfer application under Sec. 527 was pending, the petitioner was served with a show-cause notice and charge sheet; because he had communicated "directly/indirectly official documents and information to government servants/other persons to whom he was not authorised to communicate such documents/information...." This charge sheet and show-cause notice were the basis of the present contempt petition.

> no reason to hurry with a charge against the petitioner which charge would have put him under duress of some kind.[154]

But the court accepted the unconditional apology tendered by the party.

So also conduct of parallel enquiry by the administrative authority will amount to contempt of court because such conduct will undermine the prestige of the court.[155]

Appointment of a commission of enquiry during the pendency of a civil suit may not amount to contempt of court, if the scope of the trial by the court of law and the commission of enquiry is altogether different.[156]

---

154. *Id.* 1420.
155. The question of parallel enquiry arose before the Andhra Pradesh High Court in *D. Jones Shield* v. *N. Ramesan* 1955 Cri. L.J. (Andhra Pradesh High Court) 1028. The petitioner was a surveyor of Sattanepollic village. The petitioner's case was that pending the revision petition filed by him, the three respondents did some acts interfering with the course of justice and that therefore they were liable to be punished for contempt.

    On the hearing date when the matter was about to be taken up, respondent 3 rose up and with the permission of the court stated that the contents of the revision petition against the Sub-Magistrate were false, that respondents (1) and (2) in their departmental capacity enquired into the matter and came to the conclusion that they were false, that they had intimated the said fact to the government and that they had also intimated to him and asked him to represent the said facts to the Session's Judge. The first two respondents with the knowledge that the matter was subjudice communicated the aforesaid facts to the government and to respondent 3 and thereby prejudiced the mind of the judge and obstructed the course of justice.
156. *P.V. Jagannath Rao* v. *State of Orissa* AIR 1969 S.C. 215. In this case it was alleged that Sri Biju Patnaik, Biren Mitra and Tripathy who served as Chief Ministers of Orissa committed certain acts and commissions which resulted in the appointment of a commission of enquiry. But the daily newspaper, the 'Eastern Times,' published a memorandum containing the allegations presented to the President for which a defamation suit was filed and it was pending in appeal at the High Court. The question for consideration was whether the appointment of commission of enquiry amounted to contempt of court. "The scope of the trial by the courts of law and the commission of enquiry is altogether different. In any case it cannot be said that the commission of enquiry would be liable for contempt if it proceeded to enquire into a matter referred to it by government notification" (*Id.* at 226).

But the Calcutta High Court expressed the view that even if the subject matter was the same or identical, the question of contempt did not arise, because they are performing a statutory duty.[157]

5. CONTEMPT OF COURT AND *HABEAS CORPUS*

One of the important features of our Constitution is that the right to enforce a fundamental right is also made a fundamental right.[158] The Supreme Court and the High Courts are empowered to issue writs including a writ of *habeas corpus*. Writ of *habeas corpus* is resorted to, to compel the production of a unlawfully detained person before the court of law. In some cases it may not be possible to produce the person for various reasons, like the deliberate detention by the executive. Here, a question may arise whether the non-compliance of such a writ issued by the court will constitute contempt of court. In *Amarnath Sawan Mal* v. *Joginder Singh*,[159] the respondent gave a false statement in a *habeas corpus* petition that the person concerned was not in his custody. It was held that the act of the respondent, amounted to perjury, as well as obstruction

---

157. *Gokulananda* v. *Tarapada Mukherjee* AIR 1973 Cal. 233. In this case soon after the resignation of Ajay Kumar Mukherjee as Chief Minister, hartal and violent incidents took place and that resulted in the death of three persons. Soon after the resignation of Ajay Kumar Mukherjee, the President issued a proclamation taking over the administration of the state government, visited those places and a commission was appointed to enquire into those incidents. Appointment of the commission was questioned as interfering with the course of justice.
158. Art. 32(1). The right to move the Supreme Court by appropriate proceedings for the enforcement of the rights conferred by this part is guaranteed. (2) The Supreme Court shall have power to issue directions or orders or writs, including writs in the nature of *habeas corpus, mandamus, prohibition*; *quo warranto* and *certiorari*, whichever may be appropriate for the enforcement of any of the rights conferred by this part.
159. AIR 1961 Punj. 18. In this case the petitioner's son Sukhdev Raj had been illegally detained by the Sub Inspector of Police and Staff of CIA. So the petitioner filed a *habeas corpus* petition. On notice the respondent filed an affidavit and in that the respondent denied the allegations and stated that they have not taken Sukhdev Raj into custody and he could not be traced even after search. Hence this contempt petition, alleging falsity of the statement.

to court in the performance of its duties. The fact that perjury is also a substantive crime under the Indian Penal Code does not prevent conviction for a contempt under the Contempt of Courts Act.[160] Since the false statement deprived the courts in properly hearing the matter, the statement is said to constitute contempt.

But when the statement or act has no such effect of interference there is no contempt of court.[161] In *Sukhvinder Singh's case*[162] it was alleged that the sub inspector, interfered with the functioning of the warrant officer appointed by the court. But it was held that, since sub inspector and the constables have not interfered with the functioning of the warrant officer and have not flouted the orders of the court, they have not committed any contempt of court.

Mere failure to obey the writ may not constitute civil contempt. It depends upon the facts and circumstances of each case. But wilful disobedience to a writ issued by a court constitutes civil contempt. Again it is well settled that the appropriate mode of enforcing obedience to a writ of *habeas corpus* is by committal for contempt. A committal order may be made against a person who intentionally makes a false return to a writ of *habeas corpus*, but an unintentional misrepresentation on a return is not a ground for committal.[163]

When there is a wilful disobedience to the writ of *habeas corpus* by misleading the court by presenting a distorted version of facts not borne out by the records it amounts to contempt of court.[164]

---

160. *Id.* at 20, 21.

161. *Court on its own motion* v. *Sukhvinder Singh* AIR 1981 P. and H. 361. In this case a writ of *habeas corpus* was filed by Shrimathi Jito alleging that her husband Bookal Ram had been detained in the police station illegally. Court appointed Shri Gurdev Singh as warrant officer.

162. *Ibid.*

163. *Sebastian M. Hungray* v. *Union of India* AIR 1984 S.C. 1026, 1028. In this case a writ of *hebeas corpus* had been filed by a party and the Supreme Court allowed the writ and directed the production of C. Danial and C. Paul. Ministry of Defence informed the court that in spite of best efforts the respondents were unable to produce S/Shri C. Danial and C. Paul.

164. *Id.* at 1028.

So also when a public limited company (Mohan Meakins Ltd.) disobeyed the order issued by the Supreme Court that the company should not be operated until the removal of deficiencies in the effluent treatment plant of the company and the company operated the plant, it was held to be a disobedience and imposed a compensatory fine.[165]

6. CONCLUSION

Contempt jurisdiction has been utilised by the judiciary as an effective means of enforcing its orders and directions even against the administrative authorities. Any kind of disobedience of any judgment, direction or order is used to be punished summarily by availing contempt jurisdiction. Even after the passing of the Contempt of Courts Act, 1971, the law is the same because the definition of civil contempt as contained in Sec. 2(b) only states, wilful disobedience of any judgment, decree, direction or order...or breach of any undertaking given to the court. What constitutes disobedience depends upon the tests laid down by the Calcutta High Court in *Tarafatulah Mandal* v. *S.N. Maitra*.[166] Those tests are: personal service of the order, act of disobedience, responsibility to obey and the act of disobedience should be subsequent to the date of order. By subsequent judicial decisions the requirement of personal service has been very much diluted and an alternative requirement, *viz.* knowledge of the order has been laid down. So before an authority could be held liable for contempt by disobedience, knowledge of the order should be established. A third party can also be held liable if his act actually results in the disobedience of a prohibitory order.

Non-compliance of the order should also be treated in the same manner as disobedience of the order. But if there is reasonable ground because of which the concerned authority could not comply with the order, it is the duty of the concerned authority to approach the court and get necessary orders. The same principle can be applied in the case of *habeas corpus* petition also.

---

165. *Vineet Kumar Mathur* v. *Union of India and others* (1996) 7 Supreme Court cases 714.

166. *Supra* n. 13.

Administrative authorities have every right to take disciplinary proceedings against their subordinates. But they have no right to interfere with the administration of justice. Thus prescribing certain conditions before seeking judicial remedies, will not interfere with the administration of justice provided the conditions are reasonable. But once the person has approached the court for redressal of grievances, any kind of administrative action against the concerned person will interfere with the administration of justice and thus will result in contempt proceedings.

For better application of the law these principles may be incorporated in the Contempt of Courts Act, 1971, so that the authorities could know their limitations and the possibility for further extension of the law of contempt can be restricted.

9

DISOBEDIENCE—BY INDIVIDUALS

1. INTRODUCTION

Power to punish for contempt, disobedience being the reason, is a necessary complement of the court of record. Creation of different courts of record through different Charters[1] led to the exercise of contempt jurisdiction by such courts, on the basis of disobedience generally termed civil contempt. "Civil contempt of court exists, therefore, to provide the ultimate sanction against one who refuses to comply with the orders of a properly constituted Court."[2]

The court's jurisdiction in respect of civil contempt is primarily remedial, "the basic object being to coerce the offender into obeying court's judgment or order. Committal is granted mainly for the purpose of enforcing judgment in civil disputes."[3] This jurisdiction is used against the authorities and the individuals. Individuals can commit contempt by disobeying the court's order or by committing a breach of an undertaking given to the court.

2. DISOBEDIENCE OF JUDGMENT, DECREE, ORDER

Due obedience to the orders of the court is a compulsive duty of every individual. Disobedience usually results in

1. First court of record was created by East India Company's Charter of 1687, followed by Mayor's Court created by Charter of 1727, it was modified by Charter of 1755; Charter of 1774 created Supreme Court. Charter of 1801 created Supreme Court in the place of Recorder's Court, Charter granted under the statute of 1823 created Supreme Court at Bombay; High Courts were created under the High Courts Act 1861. All these courts were courts of record.
2. C.J. Miller, Contempt of Court, 2 (1976).
3. *M/s. Indo-Keniyan Industrial Enterprises* v. *M/s. Metal Forgings (P.) Ltd.* 1986 Cri. L.J. (Delhi High Court) 1592, 1601.

punishment for contempt. In case of misconduct, contempt bears a twofold character. One is as between parties a right to exercise and the liability to submit to a form of civil execution. The other is as between party in default and the state, a penal or disciplinary jurisdiction to be exercised by the court in public interest.[4]

It is a subsidiary jurisdiction punitive in nature exercised for the public good that the orders of the court should not be permitted to assist in the breach of these orders.[5] The same principle was followed in subsequent decisions also. It was held in *Phonographic Performance Ltd.* v. *Amusement Caterers Ltd.*[6] that deliberate defiance of an order constitutes contempt of court notwithstanding that the order is subsequently complied with.

In India, disobedience to the court's orders is treated as wrong against the State and compliance of the order is obtained by resorting to contempt jurisdiction. What constitutes contempt by disobedience was explained by the Madras High Court in *Sadhu Venkayya* v. *Colla Meenakshamma*:[7]

> For constituting disobedience it is absolutely essential that it should be proved beyond doubt that the persons who are charged with contempt did really disobey an order validly passed by court and which was brought home to them and a copy of which was personally served in the manner required by the procedure.[8]

So it is clear that there has to be personal service of the order, the order under which contempt is charged should be valid and the liability has to be vested in the person charged and not on third party and the disobedience must be wilful one. These conditions have to be satisfied for vesting the liability for contempt by disobedience of the court's order.

---

4. 8 *Halsbury's Laws of England*, 20-21 (Third edn.).
5. *Seaward* v. *Perteson* (1897) I Ch. 545.
6. (1963) 3 All E.R. 493.
7. AIR 1952 Mad. 180. It was a case involving disobedience of orders passed by the District Munsiff, Guntur, restraining the party from cutting and removing the crop, standing on the disputed land. In this case the respondents were held not guilty of contempt because the defendants had not wilfully disobeyed the order of the District Munsiff.
8. *Ibid.*

Further, Calcutta High Court considered the question of disobedience in *Dulal Chandra Bhar* v. *Sukumar Banerjee*[9] wherein the cause of contempt petition was the alleged disobedience of the order made by the High Court on revision petition which directed that the possession of the tenants should not be disturbed. Court observed:

> The order actually made, however, is an order in the passive voice, merely declaring that the possession of the respondents be maintained and it appears to me that whatever other proceedings may rightly be taken for non-compliance with or violation of an order of that kind, it is impossible to found on it a proceeding for contempt, when the party concerned had not been disturbed or obstructed in exercising his rights of an existing possession.[10]

No proceedings for contempt can be initiated on the alleged violation of an order which is not clear, specific, and which is contingent in character.[11]

The Supreme Court also expressed the same view in *Smt. Ram Pyari* v. *Jegadish Lal*[12] wherein also it was held that the respondent was not guilty of contempt because there was no violation of any specific order.[13] So also a mere inaction on the part of the alleged contemner may not amount to wilful disobedience of the order.[14]

---

9. AIR 1958 Cal. 474. The order said to be violated was an order passed in a criminal revision case arising out of a proceedings under Sec. 145 of the Criminal Procedure Code. There was a dispute over 9 bighas of property with structures in it between two branches of a family. The Magistrate passed an order declaring the first party to be entitled to possession and forbidding all disturbance of such possession. On revision the High Court affirmed the order of the magistrate.
10. *Id.* at 480.
11. *Id.* at 481.
12. AIR 1992 S.C. 1537. It was also an eviction suit in which the respondent undertook to vacate the premises on a specified date. But it had not been complied with.
13. *Id.* at 1538.
14. *Dr. Laxmi Narain* v. *Jia Lal Jain*. AIR 1975 All. 213. In this case the plaintiff (the principal) instituted a suit for permanent injunction to restrain the defendant from interfering with the plaintiff's functioning as Principal. The suit was dismissed, but the lower appellate court

In *Trikain Lal Manilal Shah* v. *Musamiya Isan Haider Bux Razvi*,[15] the Gujarat High Court considered the question whether the tenant had wilfully disobeyed the injunction order restraining him from erecting a permanent structure. The tenant put up a new wall replacing the dilapidated and ancient one. Since there was a mere replacement, it was held that there was no wilful disobedience of the court order. But in *Major General B.M. Bhattacharjee* v. *Russel Estate Corporation*,[16] Supreme Court took a different view on wilful disobedience. The respondent in violation of the court order had allotted and delivered flats, to third parties. The court considered the action as wilful disobedience amounting to contempt.

So also when the respondent constructed a building and opened a guest house, during the existence of interim stay order made by the Supreme Court not to start running guest

---

allowed the appeal. Defendant appealed to the High Court. Appeal was allowed partially. On 31st July, 1974, the plaintiff applicant sent telegram to the opposite parties asking them to hand over to the plaintiff the key records etc. It was followed by return telegram refusing the request. On 5th August, 1974 the defendant went to the Supreme Court and on 26-08-1974 got a stay of operation of the order of the High Court. It was alleged that the defendant committed contempt of court in between the order of the High Court and the stay order of the Supreme Court by not allowing the plaintiff to function as Principal. Court observed: "Wilful disobedience of an order of injunction cannot be inferred from the inaction of the institution to invite the decree holder to come and take charge of the office. The circumstances established in the case are not sufficient for drawing the conclusion that the opposite parties had either intended or actually disobeyed the decree of this Court" (*Id.* at 214). The same view was followed by the Patna High Court in *Nawalkishore Prasad Sinha* v. *State of Bihar* (AIR 1983 Pat. 8) wherein Annual General Meeting was held after the stay order.

15. AIR 1992 Guj. 155.
16. AIR 1993 S.C. 1632. In this case different petitions were filed against Russel Estate Corporation for getting a direction that the respondent should not allot the flats to persons other than the petitioners. The matter was taken in appeal to the Supreme Court by special leave. Supreme Court passed the following order. "...the respondents (1) and (2) should not make any further allotment of any other flats in the building in dispute with effect from today...." Contempt petition arose when flats were allotted to third parties in violation of the said order.

house without first obtaining a valid licence from the Municipal Corporation of Delhi was held to be a deliberate flouting of the orders of the Supreme Court and amounted to contempt of court and the contemner was punished.[17]

Since contempt jurisdiction is an extraordinary one for maintaining the dignity of the court, it will not use it whenever an alternative remedy is available[18] or when there is substantial compliance[19] of its orders. But the plea of inability to comply with the order[20] had not been accepted by the court especially when the party had the means to comply with the order. In case of inability the duty of the party is to bring the matter to the notice of the court in advance, and not to plead inability when extraordinary jurisdiction is exercised.

---

17. *Rajiv Choudhary* v. *Jagadish Narain Khanna* [(1996) 1 S.C.C. 508]. See also *Suresh* v. *Imran Khan* (1995 Cri. L.J. 3652) (Supreme Court).
18. *Shaik Mohiddin* v. *Section Officer Karnataka Electricity Board* 1994 Cri. L.J. (Karnataka High Court) 3639. When the respondent was likely to disconnect the power supply, the petitioner filed a civil suit and got an injunction. Contempt petition arose because even after the injunction and direction by the court the respondent disconnected the electricity supply. In case of breach of injunction, action can be taken under Rule 2A of Order 39 of Civil Procedure Code. Since alternative remedy was available contempt petition was not entertained.
19. *Sukumar Mukhopadhyay* v. *T.D. Karam Chandani* 1995 Cri. L.J. (Calcutta High Court) 1610. T.D. Karam Chandani was the superintendent of customs at the material time. He moved a writ petition in the Calcutta High Court challenging initiation of departmental proceedings against him. He wanted to have a perusal of certain documents which was also permitted. Contempt petition arose because though all available documents had been given for perusal one document which was not available was not given. Court held that there was substantial compliance with the order and if the appellant intended to disobey the order he would have not even permitted inspection.
20. *G.G. Suryakant* v. *M/s. Leema Resorts (Pvt.) Ltd.* 1995 Cri. L.J. (Madras High Court) 724. Contempt petition arose in this case because of the disobedience of the order of the court directing to deposit arrears of rent due in a rent suit. In this case though it was claimed that the non deposit of arrears was not wilful but inability to pay, court observed that the person had the means to deposit the amount as ordered but failed to deposit and the failure to deposit the amount was nothing but a wilful and deliberate act.

The question whether the Speaker of a Legislative Assembly can claim any immunity from contempt proceedings arose in *I. Manilal Singh* v. *Dr. H. Boro Singh*.[21] In this case the court made a distinction between two different capacities and functions of the speaker. As a presiding officer of the Legislative Assembly he can claim the immunities. But when he is performing administrative functions such immunities cannot be claimed. Thus when the speaker is assigning work to the Secretary or compulsorily retiring him or refusing to pay his salary, he is performing an administrative function[22] and in such circumstances if he refuses to comply with the court's order he is liable for civil contempt.

(i) Personal knowledge

A person who is alleged to have disobeyed the order should be proved to have knowledge of the order which is a pre-condition for constituting wilful disobedience. The Supreme Court considered the question of knowledge in *Bunna Prasad* v. *State of U.P.*[23] and held:

> It is also clear that in such matters those who assert that a person had knowledge of the order must prove this fact beyond all reasonable doubt. If there is any doubt, the benefit ought to be given to the person charged with contempt of court. If a person *bona fide* comes to the conclusion on the material placed before him that the source of information is not authentic, he cannot

21. AIR 1994 S.C. 505. In this case contempt arose because of the disobedience of the order of the Supreme Court to give the salary and assign work to I. Manilal Singh, Secretary of the Legislative Assembly. In spite of repeated orders he refused to appear in person.

22. *Id.* at 509.

23. AIR 1963 S.C. 1348. In this case one Yashode filed a complaint before the Nyaya Panchayat and the proceedings were going on. While so the accused (Mahabir) filed an application before S.D.M. Deoria for transfer of the case, but the S.D.M. rejected the application. On Dec. 20, 1963 Mahabir moved an application under Art. 227 of the Constitution before the High Court and got a stay of proceedings pending before the Nyaya Panchayat on Nov. 28, 1963. The same fact was informed to the Nyaya Panchayat. But on Dec. 25, 1963 the Nyaya Panchayat met and proceeded to hear the case. Hence the contempt petition.

be held guilty of contempt of court for disobeying the order.[24]

(ii) Validity of the order

The order which is claimed to be disobeyed should be valid and the court should have jurisdiction and authority to issue the same.

But the Madras High Court in *Nalla Senapathi Sarkarai Manradiar, Palayamkottai, Dharapuram Taluk* v. *Sri Ambal Mills (P) Ltd.*,[25] expressed the view that an order even if issued without territorial jurisdiction should be obeyed, the disobedience of which amounts to contempt of court.

The court observed:

> ...even on the assumption that territorial jurisdiction was *ex facie* lacking, the interim order of injunction could by no means be flouted with impunity, by a party thereto having knowledge of that order. On the contrary, such conduct would amount to deliberate contempt of court, and render that party liable for a contempt which affects the administration of justice.[26] The court did not make any observation on other cases, where inherent jurisdiction was absent. The court did not reject the argument that when inherent jurisdiction itself is lacking, the order of the court is a nullity, and hence contempt can be committed by disregard or disobedience of such an order.[27]

Thus the court made a distinction between irregular orders and orders without inherent jurisdiction. Regarding the former, the disobedience will result in punishment for contempt[28] because such an order cannot be a void one. But in the case of the latter, the court had not given any

24. *Id.* at 1351.
25. AIR 1966 Mad. 53.
26. *Id.* at 56.
27. *Ibid.*
28. The same view was also expressed by Oswald. "An order irregularly obtained cannot be treated as a nullity, but must be implicitly obeyed, until by a proper application, it is discharged." Oswald, *Contempt of Court*, 107 (1910).

definite answer. Allahabad[29] and Bombay[30] High Courts and the Supreme Court[31] also made a distinction between lack of pecuniary or territorial jurisdiction and lack of inherent jurisdiction, but had not made any finding regarding disobedience of orders made without inherent jurisdiction.

Disobedience of an order irregularly made or without pecuniary or territorial jurisdiction will amount to contempt of court because such defects can be rectified.

The Delhi High Court considered the scope of orders issued by a court which lacked inherent jurisdiction in *Amarnath* v. *Municipal Corporation of Delhi*.[32] In this case the question

---

29. *State of Uttar Pradesh* v. *Ratan Shukla* AIR 1956 All. 258. "It is not the law that a court dealing with a matter which is beyond its jurisdiction can be contemned with impunity or that the liability of a person to be punished for contempt of court depends upon whether the court was acting within its jurisdiction at the time when it is alleged to have contemned."
30. *Naranbhai* v. *Nandlal* AIR 1956 Bom. 476. There is a distinction between want of inherent jurisdiction and irregular exercise or assumption of jurisdiction. In the former case, the decree is a nullity, in the latter the proceedings cannot be impugned in a collateral action, but the error can be remedied only by a proceeding in the nature of an appeal and where there is no such remedy, it concludes forever.
31. *Padam Sen* v. *State of Uttar Pradesh* AIR 1961 S.C. 218. Supreme Court pointed out that the trial court has no such inherent power (to appoint a commissioner under Sec. 151 Civil Procedure Code to seize account books) at all and such a commissioner appointed without jurisdiction was not a public servant under Sec. 21 of the Indian Penal Code.

    Obviously this is an instance of an inherent lack of jurisdiction and it has to be safeguarded from the quite different case of mere lack of pecuniary or territorial jurisdiction which does not proceed to the root of the power of the court.

    So also in *Hira Lal Palai* v. *Sri Kalinath* AIR 1962 S.C. 199. "It is well settled that the objection as to local jurisdiction of a court does not stand on the same footing as an objection to the competence of a court to try a case. Competence of a court to try a case goes to the very root of the jurisdiction and where it is lacking, it is a case of inherent lack of jurisdiction. On the other hand an objection as to the local jurisdiction of a court can be waived and this principle has been given statutory recognition by enactments like Sec. 21 of the Code of Civil Procedure" (*Id.* at 201).
32. 1981 Cri. L.J. (Delhi High Court) 1880. In this case, a suit had been

considered was whether an order passed by a court which had no inherent jurisdiction to deal with the matter was valid. The court which issued the order itself stated that it lacked inherent jurisdiction to deal with the matter.

The High Court held that disobedience of a void order (void due to lack of inherent jurisdiction) will not amount to contempt of court. The court observed:

> If the order by which the respondents were required to stay the proceedings before them was without jurisdiction, they would commit no contempt for having disregarded it because the order being a nullity, they were not bound by it. An order without jurisdiction is void and a void order binds nobody.[33]

Thus the point left unanswered by the Madras High Court in *Nallasenapathi Sarkarai Manradiar, Palayamkottai* v. *Sri Ambal Mills (P) Ltd.*[34] was answered by the Delhi High Court, which cannot also said to be conclusive. Because in *Amar Nath* v. *Municipal Corporation of Delhi*,[35] the court which issued the order stated that it lacked inherent jurisdiction. Circumstances may arise where a court with no inherent jurisdiction may issue an order as if it had jurisdiction. In such cases unless it is nullified by the superior court it continues to be a valid order. Though a decree given by a court with no inherent jurisdiction is null and void, when it is sought to be set aside in revision, the High Court may refuse to set aside the order

---

filed by one Amarnath for getting a permanent injunction from the court of the Subordinate Judge restraining the Corporation from demolishing a structure put up by him without proper approval. Though the court dismissed the suit because of lack of jurisdiction and also because it was premature, the judge ordered that the Municipal Corporation shall not take demolition action against the property of the petitioners unless and until the Municipal Corporation served fresh demolition notice in accordance with the provisions of law. Thinking that the suit had been dismissed without noticing the observation of the court, the Corporation authorities demolished the structure. Hence the contempt petition.

33. *Id.* at 1884.
34. *Supra* n. 25.
35. *Supra* n. 32.

if greater evil will result from setting aside the order.[36] So disobedience of an order of a court which lacks inherent jurisdiction has also to be treated as contempt of court. If the court lacks inherent jurisdiction it is the duty of the aggrieved party to question it.

An order, which is claimed to be disobeyed should be clear and specific. When the order itself is missing in material terms, there cannot be disobedience of terms missing. Thus when there was no specific direction to the appellant to hand over possession of the property to the receiver, although implied, this was meant to be done, because the order was passed with the consent of parties, the disobedience of which was held not contempt of court.[37]

In the absence of any express undertaking given by the appellant or any undertaking incorporated in the order impugned, it will be difficult to hold that the appellant wilfully disobeyed or committed breach of such an undertaking.[38]

The charge against the accused was that he committed contempt of court by not handing over the possession to the receiver which he undertook. The High Court accepted the contention and found him guilty of contempt.

But the Supreme Court found that the order of the High Court does not contain anything as to transfer of possession.

36. *Dayaram* v. *Goverdhan* ILR 28 Bom. 458, 460 also *Insurance Co. Ltd.* v. *Kamini Kumar* 44 IC 694.

37. *Babu Ram Gupta* v. *Sudhir Bhasin* AIR 1979 S.C. 1528, 1529. In this case a partnership firm was running a cinema theatre. Dispute arose between the partners and the matter was referred to an arbitrator and the respondent got himself appointed through the High Court as receiver. Being aggrieved, the petitioner moved the Division Bench of the Court. At this stage a consent order was passed with the agreement of parties by which Mahabir Prasad, Advocate was appointed as receiver. The order read as follows: "...with the consent of the learned counsel of the parties, we therefore appoint Shri Mahabir Prasad Advocate and Secretary of the Bar Association, Sitapur, to be the receiver of Laxmi Talkies pending decision of the disputes between the parties which have been referred to the arbitration. "The receiver will submit quarterly reports to the court....". "The appellant is directed not to interfere with the receiver appointed or with the business of the running of the Laxmi Talkies."

38. *Id.* at 1531.

In the absence of any express undertaking or order, there cannot be any breach of such order and the appellant was held not guilty of contempt.

So also simply filing an appeal to the Supreme Court is no defence in contempt proceedings. But the position would be different if the Supreme Court takes cognizance of the appeal and passes any positive order of stay.[39]

Argument based on legal opinion has also not been accepted by the court.[40] So also incapacity to comply with the order may not be a proper justification for disobedience of the order. If there is any proper justification the appellant should have brought the matter to the court and got a direction from the court. The Supreme Court came to the conclusion that the High Court was right in its opinion that the appellant had committed acts which amounted to contempt of court in *Hoshie Shavaksha Dolikuka* v. *Thirty Hoshie Dolikuka*[41] wherein the father had not handed over the child to the mother, though the court ordered him to hand over. Deliberate disobedience is contempt of court[42] and the concern of the court in such disobedience is expressed in the following words:

---

39. *S.P. Agarwal* v. *R.R. Upadhya* 1978 Cri. L.J. (Allahabad High Court) 789, 794. In this case S.P. Agarwal, applicant serving as Secretary, in the District Co-operative Bank, Bijnor, was dismissed from service. He questioned the validity of his dismissal by writ petition and the High Court stayed the order and directed the bank to pay the salary. Since it was not complied with, the present contempt petition was filed. Contention of the respondent was that the matter was taken in appeal to the Supreme Court by special leave.
40. *Id.* at 795.
41. 1982 Cri. L.J. (Supreme Court) 1937. In this case wife of the appellant filed the contempt petition for disobedience of the orders of Bombay High Court. As per the order the appellant had to return the child to the petitioner after the completion of one half of the vacation. The appellant contended that he could not comply with the order because the child was unwilling to go to mother's place and taking into account the health and welfare of the child he was prevented from taking the child to her mother's place. High Court negatived the contention and found him guilty of contempt.
42. *Lakshmi Narayan Dutta* v. *Smt. Mira Rani Dey*. 1984 Cri. L.J. (Calcutta High Court) 1033. In this case in contravention of the injunction order restraining the parties from carrying out the construction work, the respondent carried out the work.

> It seems that the trend of today is more to disregard the orders of court than to comply with the same with the belief that apologies tendered at the time of hearing will condone all acts of the contemner. The time has come when it must be made clear to the litigant public and all, that when a direction is given and orders are made, the court's orders are required to be carried out to their fullest extent and any wilful disregard to the same will not be tolerated by a court of law and severe consequences will follow if orders are found to have been violated.[43]

Indirect method of disobeying the orders of court was adopted in *M/s. Jyoti Limited* v. *Smt. Kanwaljit Kaur Bhasin*[44] by trying to get the benefits of being an incorporated company. But the corporate veil can be lifted on certain grounds and one among them is where the corporate personality is being blatantly used as a cloak for fraud or improper conduct.[45] In such a situation public interest requires that the corporate veil must be lifted to find out the person who disobeyed the order of the court.[46]

In case the alleged contemner had no authority to act in accordance with the order of the court, in case of disobedience of the order the contemner could not be held guilty of contempt. In *Ku Meena* v. *S.D. Chacharkar,*[47] the headmaster along with

43. *Id.* at 1035.
44. 1987 Cri. L.J. (Delhi High Court) 1281. In this case there was an agreement to sell certain flats by the respondents to the petitioner. Since the money had not been paid in terms of the agreement the respondents unilaterally cancelled the agreement. After the agreement, respondents as Chairman and Managing Director formed a company. Since there was a breach of contract, the petitioner filed a suit for specific performance and got an injunction restraining the respondents from disposing of the flats. But, in disobeyance of the injunction the respondents sold the flats. Hence the contempt petition. Respondents contended that the disposal was made not in their personal capacity but as Chairman and Director of the Company.
45. L.C.B. Gower, *The Principles of Modern Company Law*, 210 (3rd edn.).
46. *Supra* n. 44 p. 1286.
47. 1994 Cri. L.J. (Bombay High Court) 2647. Contempt petition arose in this case because of non-compliance of the judgment and order of the School Tribunal. The petitioner who was serving as a teacher was terminated from service on the ground of reduction in division. The School Tribunal directed the respondents to reinstate the teacher with

the President and Secretary of the society which runs the school, were charged for contempt for disobeying the order of the school tribunal to reinstate the terminated teacher. The power of appointment and termination rests with the management and not with the headmaster. Though the headmaster was also charged for contempt, he was held not guilty of contempt because there was no wilful disobedience on his part. But other respondents were held guilty of contempt because there was wilful disobedience on their part.

(iii) Third party liability

According to the Madras High Court[48] only the alleged contemner is liable and not a third party to the charge. A stranger to the proceedings cannot be held liable. But a peculiar situation was considered by the Calcutta High Court in *P.K. Kripalani* v. *Mahabir Ram.*[49] In this case soon after the delivery of possession was given to the landlord by the bailiff, the sub-tenant who was not a party to the proceedings took possession of it. The sub-tenant was held liable for contempt. The court observed:

> It makes no difference that he was no party to the action for a stranger has no more right than a party, wilfully and wrongfully to oust the court's officer from possession or prevent him from carrying out the court's order.[50]

This decision does not lay down any general rule that a third party can also be held liable for contempt for disobeying the orders of the court to which he is not a party. However, the sub-tenant was held liable for interfering with the administration of justice by preventing the bailiff from carrying out his duty.

---

continuity of service and also to pay arrears of salary within sixty days. Even after repeated demand the request was not complied with.

48. *Sadhu Venkayya* v. *Colla Meenakshamma. Supra* n. 7.

49. AIR 1952 Cal. 452. In this case the applicant filed an ejectment suit in the court of small causes and the same was brought to the High Court on revision. High Court made the following order: "The bailiff of the court to give possession of the property to the applicant on July 2, 1951."

50. *Id.* at 454.

If a person is doing an act which is prohibited by the court, he is liable for contempt though not a party to the proceedings. This view was expressed by the Madras High Court in *Nalla Senapathi Sarkarai Manradiar, Palayamkottai, Dharapuram Dt.* v. *Sri Ambal Mills (P) Ltd.*[51]

In such cases, the concerned person is liable for contempt, not for disobeying the orders of the court to which he is not a party, but for interfering with the course of justice which is a case of criminal contempt. Civil contempt is based on the disobedience of the orders of the court and the disobedience can be committed only by a party to the proceedings.

The same view was followed by the Madras High Court in *Vidhyacharan Shukla* v. *Tamil Nadu Olympic Association*:[52]

> A stranger or a third party may be involved in contempt only if he is found aiding or abetting or otherwise obstructing the enforcement of the court's order. There is and there can be no dispute to the rule that a person cannot be held guilty of contempt in infringing the order of the court he knows not.[53]

Court further observed:

> We can see thus clearly that the courts in India invariably accepted the law applied in England and found: (1) a

---

51. *Supra* n. 25. The same position is also obtained in England; A stranger to an action who aids and abets the breach of a prohibitory order, obstructs the course of justice and this contempt is punishable by committal or attachment: 8 *Halsbury's Laws of England* 21 (3rd Edn.).
52. AIR 1991 Mad. 323. The question of contempt arose in this case because of the alleged disobedience of the order passed by the trial judge. In the election held on 27-11-1988 at Madras the first defendant was elected as the President and second defendant was elected as the Secretary General of Indian Olympic Association. However on 16-5-1990 a notice was served in the office of the President expressing the loss of confidence in the Executive council and demanding a meeting for fresh election. This lead to filing of suit and counter suit by the parties concerned. The court appointed an observer and ordered him to conduct the meeting and hold the election on 15-6-1990. As the meeting was about to be organised V.C. Shukla and others who were third parties interfered in the proceeding making it difficult for carrying out the court's order.
53. *Id.* at 342.

party to the suit if he had notice or knowledge of the order of the court and (2) a third party or a stranger if he had aided or abetted the violation with notice or knowledge of the order of injunction, guilty of civil contempt and otherwise found a third party guilty of criminal contempt if he has been found knowingly obstructing implementation of its order or direction.[54]

By performing a prohibitory act of which the concerned person had knowledge, but not a party to the proceedings, one is not committing civil contempt by disobedience of the order, but is committing criminal contempt by interfering with the course of justice.

It was held by the Supreme Court in *Satyabrata Biswas* v. *Kalyan Kumar Kisku*[55] that in any event, in a contempt proceedings no order can be passed against a person who is not a party thereto and without giving any notice to him and affording an opportunity of hearing to such person.

The principles laid down by the Madras High Court[56] were invariably followed even after the enactment of the Contempt of Courts Act, 1971. But a perusal of decisions shows that disobedience of the orders of the court would result in punitive action. This trend has to be followed and accepted because the judiciary which has the powers of neither the purse nor the sword, has to extract due compliance of its orders through this jurisdiction.

3. BREACH OF UNDERTAKING

An undertaking given to the court is a solemn promise made to the court and it is to be respected. Any breach

54. *Id.* at 358.

55. AIR 1994 S.C. 1837. During the pendency of a title suit, *status quo* order was obtained. Contrary to this order a padlock was put in the main entrance, discontinued the water supply etc. While so A.K. Ghosh who was neither a tenant nor a person with any authority created a sub tenancy over that property in favour of one Sumani Builders. It was claimed that the creation of sub tenancy was in violation of *status quo* order. Supreme Court set aside the order of the Division Bench of Calcutta High Court and directed the Single Judge to dispose of the application for contempt in its proper perspective confining himself to contempt jurisdiction.

56. *Supra* n. 7.

of such an undertaking is treated as contempt of court in England.[57]

During pre-independence period the same common law principle was followed. In order to constitute a breach of an undertaking to be contempt of court, the undertaking must be given to the court.[58]

After independence, the Bombay High Court considered the consequences of breach of undertaking in *Bajranglal Gangadhar Khemka* v. *Kapurchand Ltd.*[59] In this case the Bombay High Court laid down two important conditions to be satisfied for attracting the contempt jurisdiction, *viz.* (i) In order to constitute the breach of an undertaking to be liable for contempt, the undertaking must be given to the court, and (ii) the breach of the undertaking should be wilful.

(i) The undertaking to the court

In *Bajranglal Gangadhar Khemka* v. *Kapurchand Ltd.*[60] the Bombay High Court negatived the argument that the undertaking referred to is not an undertaking to the court but a promise made to the other party. The court held:

> There is no reason why even in a consent decree a party may not give an undertaking to the court. Although the court may be bound to record a compromise, still, when

---

57. The breach of an undertaking given to the court by a person or corporation in pending proceedings on the faith of which the court sanctions a particular course of action or inaction is misconduct amounting to contempt. 8 *Halsbury's Laws of England* 29 (3rd Edn.). *See* also *Cotton* v. *Hayl* 1910 I Ch.D. 610.
58. *Nisha Kanto* v. *Saroj Bashmi* AIR 1948 Cal. 294, 296. The same view was expressed by the Calcutta High Court in *Prokash Chandra* v. *Minidranath*, ILR (1946) 2 Cal. 499.
59. AIR 1950 Bom. 336. The plaintiff in this case was the lessee of a cinema theatre known as Paradise Cinema and in the lease deed there was a clause which gave the plaintiff an option to purchase the property. When the defendant agreed to sell the cinema theatre to third party, plaintiff filed a suit to enforce the condition in the lease deed. The suit was compromised. One of the conditions for compromise was that the defendant should execute a lease deed within two months in favour of the plaintiff. Non-compliance of this undertaking was the subject matter of the present contempt petition.
60. *Ibid.*

> the court passes a decree, it puts its imprematture upon those terms and makes the terms a rule of the court; and it would be open to the court, before it did so to accept an undertaking given by a party to the court. Therefore, there is nothing contrary to any provision of the law whereby an undertaking cannot be given by a party to the court in the consent decree, which undertaking can be enforced by proper committal proceedings.[61]

The court further observed:

> In a contempt matter, unless the court is clearly satisfied that the undertaking was given to the court, the court would not proceed to commit the person in default to jail. But in our opinion, the expression 'undertake' has come to acquire through long practice, a technical meaning. In all orders and decrees of the court, whenever the expression a party undertakes has been used, it has always borne the meaning that the undertaking has been to the court.[62]

In *Lala Baijnath Prasad* v. *Lala Shyam Sunder*[63] also Calcutta High Court refused to accept the contention that the undertaking mentioned in the order was not undertaking given to the court

61. *Id.* at 337. Calcutta High Court also accepted the view that breach of an undertaking is liable for punishment under contempt in *Smt. Lajuklata* v. *Nrishingha Prasad* (AIR 1952 Cal. 669) (Undertaking to vacate certain premises on a certain day). The court observed : "The court, it is true, ought not to be vindictive in matters of this kind. At the same time, the court cannot itself be trifled with. Litigants before this court ought to understand that they will not be permitted to give undertakings to this court and then break them with impunity, farless will they be permitted to have recourse to such dubious means as arming themselves with the orders of a subordinate court in prosecution of a scheme, to flout the orders of this court (at 670).
62. *Id.* at 338.
63. 1961 (2) Cri. L.J. (Calcutta High Court) 222. In a partition suit certain properties had to be delivered by one party to the other. When the Sherriff went to deliver possession of properties the respondent resisted him. Subsequently the advocate for the respondent gave an undertaking to the court, whereby the respondent was to vacate the premises and to pay a sum of Rs. 500/- per month as mesne profits. It was claimed that there was a breach of this undertaking.

but merely amounted to a promise made by one party to the other.

Thus the Calcutta High Court further liberalised the principle laid down by Das, J. in *Sukumar Mitra* v. *Tarasankar Ghosh*,[64] and held that even if the undertaking does not contain the word 'to the court' it has to be viewed as if it has been made to the court.[65]

Even after the passing of the Contempt of Courts Act, 1971, the same position continues. When the respondent did not comply with the undertaking to vacate the premises on a particular date, but made an application to the department of rehabilitation, claiming ownership it was held that there was wilful breach of undertaking amounting to contempt of court.[66] So also forceful possession of the premises after giving an undertaking that he would not dispossess the petitioner except through due process of law would amount to breach of undertaking even if the possession of the petitioner was not legal.[67] Whether the possession is lawful or unlawful is a different thing but once the party has given an undertaking to the court it has to abide by it, and if there is wilful breach it will amount to contempt of court:[68]

64. AIR 1952 Cal. 591. It is well settled that a breach of an undertaking given to the court by a person in pending proceedings on the faith of which the court sanctions a particular course of action is misconduct amounting to contempt (*Id.* at 593).
65. *Supra* n. 63 p. 225.
66. *Virochan* v. *Ram Saran Das* 1982 Cri. L.J. (P. and H. High Court) 1219. In this case the question for consideration was whether the breach of undertaking to hand over possession of the property to the petitioner would amount to contempt in case he did not comply with it. Not only that, the alleged contemner made an application to the Rehabilitation Department stating that the property belonged to it.
67. *Nand Gopal* v. *Kartar Singh* 1984 Cri. L.J. (Delhi High Court) 213. In this case, the petitioner was in occupation of a certain premises under an agreement with the respondent. When the respondent interfered with the possession, petitioner filed a suit and in the suit respondent gave the following undertaking: "I shall not dispossess the plaintiff except by due process of law." In spite of the undertaking, the respondent forcibly occupied the premises.
68. The same view was expressed by the Supreme Court in *Balaram Singh* v. *Bhikam Chand Jain* AIR 1985 S.C. 1726. In this case in flagrant

> The undertaking is always understood to be an undertaking to the court. An undertaking is a promise given to the court by a party to a proceeding to do or not to do a particular thing which is enforceable as an injunction because when the court accepts an undertaking given by the party its order amounts in substance to an injunction. Breach of the undertaking is misconduct amounting to contempt.[69]

Hence the respondents were punished.

An argument based on incapacity to comply with the undertaking also was not accepted by the Bombay High Court in *Venubhai Savleram Sangaonkar* v. *Gajanan Savleram* alias *Sawalaram Sangaonkar*.[70] Similarly, the court negatived the

---

disregard of the assurance given to the court the contemners made certain advertisements. The court held: "we must take serious view of the conduct of the contemners in committing a breach of the undertaking in view of the growing tendency to trifle with the court's orders based on undertaking with impunity" (*Id.* at 1728.). The same view was followed in *Jahurul Islam* v. *Abdulkalam* AIR 1994 S.C.1403. The respondent tenant gave an undertaking to hand over peaceful possession of certain shops. Not only that he had not complied with the undertaking but also made up certain persons to file a suit and claim title over the property. So also Allahabad High Court in *Gyan Chand* v. *Ramesh Chand* 1985 Cri. L.J. (Allahabad High Court) 1907. The tenant refused to hand over possession of the property even after giving such an undertaking. It was held: "I have every reason to hold that the respondent had deliberately and wilfully committed breach of the undertaking given by him to this court" (at 1908).

Same view was followed by the Supreme Court in *Devi Lal and another* v. *Mohan Prasad and another* [(1996) 5 S.C.C. 378].

69. *Tukaram S/o Khanduji Gaikward* v. *Santhosh Mahadeorao Sayam.* 1995 Cri. L.J. (Bombay High Court) 577. The petitioners who were working as Jr. clerk and teacher in the school run by the respondents had been terminated and the School Tribunal, Nagpur, on petition and on undertaking by the respondents disposed off the matter. The respondents did not comply with the undertaking and wilfully disobeyed the common order passed by the learned School Tribunal.

70. 1992 Cri. L.J. (Bombay High Court) 1160. In this case rival members of the family claimed right over certain properties. In the suit Gajanan Savleram gave the following undertaking: "I say that I am staying in Bungalow at... I hereby give an undertaking to the Hon'ble Court on behalf of myself and other members of family, that I will vacate the said premises and hand over the peaceful possession of the said

contention that legal heirs are not liable for the contempt committed by a person.

(ii) Breach of undertaking distinguished from consent decrees and compromise decrees

The Bombay High Court in *Bajranglal Gangadhar Khemka* v. *Kapurchand Ltd.*[71] laid down that an undertaking of the party, once it is incorporated in the order of the court, it is an undertaking to the court and the breach of it will result in contempt proceedings. Also, before the Calcutta High Court in *Sukumar Mitra* v. *Tarasankar Ghosh*,[72] it was argued that an undertaking contained in a joint compromise petition is a qualified one and should be taken as one between the parties. But the court has not made any finding and concluded that it is not a fit case for contempt jurisdiction.

---

premises to Smt. Venubai Savleram Sangaonkar on or before 8th Oct., 1983. I say that I will not obstruct Smt. Venubai if she visits the premises during this period for watering the plants." Breach of this undertaking is the cause of the contempt petition.

71. AIR 1950 Bom. 336.

72. AIR 1952 Cal. 591. The petitioner in this case was the landlord and he filed an eviction suit which was decreed in his favour. The tenant preferred an appeal. Finally they filed a joint compromise petition. The relevant portion reads as follows:

"The appellant Tarasankar Ghosh, opposite party undertakes to court to vacate and make over peaceful and vacant possession of the upper flat in the premises No. 98-A, Bakul Bagan Road...." In case the appellant fails to vacate the flat, the respondent shall execute the deed. On the basis of the compromise petition court ordered: "It is hereby ordered and decreed by and with consent of the appellant and the plaintiff respondent, that the appeal as between them be and the same is hereby disposed of in accordance with the terms of the said joint petition of compromise...." The same High Court in *Suretennessa Bibi* v. *Chintaharan Das* 1955 Cri. L.J. (Calcutta High Court) 654, considered similar situation and held the breach of such an undertaking amounts to contempt of court. In this case, the petitioner filed an ejectment suit and succeeded. The second appeal filed by the respondent was disposed of in terms of the joint petition of compromise. The second paragraph of the petition read as follows: The aforesaid appellant gives a personal undertaking to the Hon'ble Court that he will give quite and vacant possession of the premises to the above said respondent by 25-02-1954. Since he failed to give possession, contempt petition was filed for breach of personal undertaking to the court.

But taking into account the opinion given by the Bombay High Court and also the wording in the order—"It is hereby ordered and decreed..." indicates that the breach of such an order should have been a breach of an undertaking given to the court.

But the Punjab High Court in *Badri Das* v. *Labhumal*[73] adopted a mistaken view that breach of an undertaking in a decree which incorporated the private compromise between the parties will not amount to contempt of court.

The above view does not appear to be correct, because once an undertaking is incorporated in the decree, it becomes an undertaking given to the court.

The uncertainty in law due to the decisions of different High Courts was settled by the Supreme Court in *Chaganbhai Norsinbhai* v. *Soni Chandubhai Gordhanbhai.*[74] The Supreme Court negatived the argument that the order is not an undertaking to the court but a consent decree. Because;

> The order incorporated express undertakings to the court although these may have induced the plaintiff to agree to the passing of the order in the form in which it was passed instead of pressing for an order of dismissal of the revision application before the High Court after which he could have executed his decree immediately. This feature in itself could not convert the order actually passed upon the undertakings given into a mere consent

---

73. AIR 1959 Punj. 322. In a money suit, the defendant agreed to pay the money in instalments. He also made an undertaking not to dispose of his immovable property. But subsequently before the payment of money he disposed of the property which gave way for this contempt petition.
74. AIR 1976 S.C. 1909: In this case Division Bench of the Gujarat High Court punished the contemner for breach of an undertaking which contained the following: "The defendant gives solemn undertaking to this Hon'ble High Court that he will vacate the suit premises by handing over the key of the premises to the court of the Civil Judge, Junior Division, Anand in pursuance of the decree within one and a half months after receipt of notice from the plaintiffs that the plaintiff Dr. I.G. Soni has returned from abroad and intends to start medical practice in the suit premises." Hence the appeal.

> order. It was clearly a case of express undertakings to the court incorporated in the order.[75]

The same view was upheld in the subsequent decision of the Supreme Court[76] and also by the Calcutta High Court.[77] The following observation of the Calcutta High Court in *Gour Gopal Dutt* v. *Smt. Shantilata Mitra*[78] is pertinent:

> Now the execution of a decree is between the parties, that is between the judgment creditor and the judgment debtor. But an undertaking to the court is a matter between the court and the person who gives the undertaking to court and they are entirely different and separate.[79]

Further if anyone is allowed to get away so easily from solemn undertaking then undertaking to court loses all significance.[80] Regarding the effect of undertaking, the court rightly pointed out that when an undertaking given to the court is incorporated in the order of the court it becomes part of the order of the court.[81]

But the Himachal Pradesh High Court, without affecting the principle laid down by the Supreme Court and Calcutta High Court, in *B. Himmat Sinka* v. *M/s. Kuldip Industrial Corporation*[82] held the appellants not guilty of contempt, since

---

75. *Id.* at 1909.
76. *Smt. Pushpaben* v. *Narandas* v. *Badiani* AIR 1979 S.C. 1536. In this case Supreme Court considered the breach of an undertaking contained in a compromise decree and held that breach of an undertaking in the compromise decree will have the same effect as breach of an undertaking given to the court.
77. *Gour Gopal Dutt* v. *Smt. Shantilata Mitra* AIR 1976 Cal. 475. This case also involves a suit for ejection and passing of the consent decree.
78. *Ibid.*
79. *Id.* at 476.
80. *Id.* at 477.
81. *Ibid.*
82. 1981 Cri. L.J. (Himachal Pradesh) 1414. In this case the appellant along with others were serving as directors of the company called, Hypine Carbours Ltd. A petition for winding up of the company was filed and the same was allowed by the lower court. Sri Ahuja appearing for the appellant gave an undertaking and based on the undertaking court passed the following order: "Sri Ahuja undertakes on behalf of his clients to produce all the other account books, pass book.... These

the undertaking was not express or specific, but vague and that too not accepted in clear words by the court.[83]

The reasons given by the court are:

(i) It is not indicated in the order that the undertaking given by the counsel of the appellants was accepted by the court, and

(ii) It is not clarified that in case arrears of salary is not paid or settlement is not reached within a month, the appellants would be liable for contempt of court.

The reasoning and the conclusion cannot be said to be correct because once the undertaking is incorporated in the order of the court, it becomes an undertaking to the court[84] and if there is any breach, it will amount to contempt of court. Similarly, liability for contempt is not dependent on the specific mention of liability. It depends upon the breach of undertaking given to the court.

So, disobedience of the orders of the court, and the breach of undertaking given to the court should be treated as contempt of court. The same principle should be applied even if it is contained in the consent decree or compromise decree. The undertaking should be incorporated in the court's order and it should be definite and clear.

In *Sardari Lal* v. *Ram Rakha*[85] the Delhi High Court considered two important questions:

---

materials should be handed over to the official liquidator within a week now.... So far as the wages of the labourers are concerned, Shri Ahuja states that about Rs. 20,000/- would be deposited by his clients on 26-08-1978 with the court of the Judicial Magistrate, Nalagarh for payment to the workers." No steps were taken to honour the undertaking. So the application was filed by the official liquidator for contempt of court. Learned Single Judge found the appellants guilty of contempt. Hence the appeal.

83. *Id.* at 1420.

84. See *Chhagan Bhai Norsinbhai* v. *Soni Chandubhai Gordhan Bhai. Supra*, n. 74.

85. 1984 Cri. L.J. (Delhi High Court) 1098. In this case the respondent gave an undertaking to the Rent Control Tribunal to deliver peaceful possession of the premises within 15 days. But he did not do so. Hence, contempt petition for breach of undertaking given to the Tribunal.

(i) Whether the undertaking, if any, given by a party in the court is the same thing as an undertaking given by the party to the court.

(ii) Whether as a consequence of the undertaking given, on the basis of which the court's order is made, the incorporation of the terms on which the matter is disposed of, would convert the terms into an undertaking to the court.

Both the questions were answered in the affirmative.

> When the tribunal is bound to decide judicially any agreement, the recording of the promise and the passing of the decree cannot be said as nothing more than an agreement of the parties with the sanction of the court superadded. The court was an active participant to the terms of the compromise and its validity in a case for eviction on permissible grounds and material.[86]

After perusing the facts the court concluded:

> A cumulative effect of all these particular facts and the terms of the statements persuade us to hold that the respondent did give an undertaking to the court.... The fact that the undertaking does not expressly mention that it was given to court is a matter of no consequences as on the interpretation of the terms of the statement and a long practice understood by the counsel and judges of this court and the courts subordinate to it, it is clear to us that the undertaking must have been given to the court.[87]

Thus the expression, "a party undertakes" or "gives a solemn promise" used in the statements of the parties or their counsel or in the orders and decrees of the court, unless the context otherwise suggests, means an implied undertaking to the court. The undertaking is always an undertaking to the court, which could be enforced by committal proceedings.[88] If

86. *Id.* at 1104.

87. *Id.* at 1105.

88. *Id.* at 1107. Similar question was again considered by the Delhi High Court in *M/s. Indo-Keniyan Industrial Enterprises* v. *M/s. Metal Forgings (P) Ltd.* 1986 Cri. L.J. (Delhi High Court) 1592. The Delhi High Court negatived the contention that there was no undertaking given to the court but a compromise was arrived at by the parties and as per

a party gives an undertaking which is misleading, misguiding and is made without any intention of performing it, it will amount to contempt of court.[89]

But the Supreme Court in *Rita Markanday* v. *Surjit Singh Arora*[90] held; "However the respondent herein cannot be held liable for contempt on this score also for the order in question clearly indicates that it was passed on the basis of the agreement between the parties and not on the representation of the respondent made before the court. It was the petitioner who agreed to the unconditional extension of time by four weeks for the respondent to vacate and subsequent extension of time on his giving an undertaking and this court only embodied the terms of the agreement so arrived at in the order. We are, therefore, of the opinion that the respondent cannot in anyway be held liable for contempt for alleged breach of the order."[91] But it is submitted that once the agreement is incorporated in the order of the court, it becomes an undertaking to the court and the breach of it should be held to be a breach of undertaking.

4. CONCLUSION

Disobedience as contempt. The creation of different courts of record by different Charters gave such courts the right to punish the disobedience of their orders as contempt of court. What constitutes disobedience or when can there be

---

the compromise, the respondent had to use the front portion of the disputed land and to hand over the peaceful possession to the petitioner later. But the respondent had not surrendered possession as per the terms of the agreement. Hence the contempt petition. The joint compromise petition was recorded by the court.

89. *Dr. (Mrs.) Roshan Sam Joyce* v. *S.R. Cotton Mills Ltd.* AIR 1990 S.C. 1881. Respondent No. 1 was the company and respondent No. 2 was the Managing Director of the company. In the eviction suit filed by the petitioner, court gave a decree but the respondent wanted 8 weeks time to vacate. This was granted on giving an undertaking that the respondents will not part with the possession of the suit premises or create any third party interest in the suit premises in any manner whatsoever. But even after giving the undertaking the respondent No. 1 filed special leave petition and respondent No. 2 filed a suit claiming sub tenancy right etc. Hence the contempt petition.

90. AIR 1997 S.C. 2174.

91. *Id.* at 2178.

disobedience was answered by the Madras High Court in *Sadhu Venkayya* v. *Colla Meenakshamma.*[92] Accordingly the following tests are applied to ascertain whether there is disobedience or not: (1) There should be personal service of the order; (2) the order alleged to be disobeyed should be a valid order; (3) the liability should be vested on the person charged and not on third party; (4) the disobedience should be wilful. These tests are applied by the judiciary with minor changes. Even after the passing of the Contempt of Courts Act, 1971 these tests continue to be good because the definition of civil contempt includes wilful disobedience of judgment, decree and the like. By subsequent judicial decisions the above conditions have been modified and the conditions to be satisfied before holding a person guilty of contempt of court, are:

(i) There should be knowledge of the court's order either mandatory or prohibitory.

(ii) Any order passed by a court has to be obeyed.

(iii) Though third party has no liability, if his act is in violation of the court's order, he should be made liable, and

(iv) The disobedience must be wilful.

Breach of Undertaking. An undertaking is a solemn promise made to the court. Before enacting the Contempt of Courts Act, 1971, the principle laid down by the Bombay High Court in *Bajranglal Gangadhar Khemka* v. *Kapur Chand Ltd.*,[93] was that the undertaking must be to the court and the breach of it should be wilful. Difficulty arose in the case of the breach of compromise decrees and consent decrees. The Supreme Court laid down that when such a decree is incorporated in the order, and is issued under the seal of the court, it is an undertaking to the court and hence it has to be obeyed. So once the undertaking is contained in the order of the court, the disobedience of that undertaking should be dealt with under the contempt jurisdiction.

92. *Supra* n. 7.

93. *Supra* n. 59.

10

Contempt of Court—By Subordinate Judiciary

1. INTRODUCTION

Lord Hardwicke L.C.'s statement that contempt of court may be said to be constituted by any conduct that tends to bring the authority and administration of law into disrespect or disregard[1] led to certain conduct of judicial officers being treated as contempt. Disobedience of the court's orders is one which brings the authority of the administration of justice into disrespect. This disrespect can be shown even by a judicial officer. In *Ex parte Langley, Ex parte Smith, In re Bishop*[2] a Sherriff's officer was charged for contempt for conducting an auction sale in spite of an injunction from the Court of Bankruptcy. But it was held that lack of knowledge was a good defence.

In India the contempt jurisdiction was applied by the Lahore High Court against a subordinate judicial officer in *Muhammad Ali* v. *Qadir Bakhsh*[3] and a first class Magistrate

1. *St. James Evening Post* case (1742) 2 Atk. 469.
2. (1879) XIII Ch. D. 110.
3. AIR 1949 Lah. 270. In this case, First Class Magistrate, Lahore, passed an order of attachment under Sec. 145 Criminal Procedure Code. But one of the parties filed a suit in the Subordinate Judges Court and obtained a stay order against the opposite parties restraining them from proceeding under Sec. 145 Criminal Procedure Code. Next day when the matter was informed to the Magistrate, he lost temper and used abusive words against the Subordinate Judge. He said: "This is a foolish order, passed by a foolish judge and secured by a foolish lawyer. I am not going to take notice of it. From where have you come ? What is your standing? ..."

was punished for disobeying the orders of the Subordinate Judge. In this case it was observed:

> It is of greatest importance that the prestige and dignity of the courts of law should be preserved at all costs. There cannot be anything of greater consequence than to keep the streams of justice clear and pure so that the litigants may have the utmost confidence that they would be treated in a considerate manner by courts of law. If parties to a litigation feel that they are likely to be subjected to insulting behaviour at the hands of the presiding officers of the courts it would shake all confidence in the administration of justice and would thus pollute the stream of justice.[4]

Judicial officers can bring the administration of justice into disrespect by disobeying the orders of the superior court, by interfering with the functioning of other officers, by misuse of their own office or by not following a well-settled precedent. These different modes of interferences are discussed in this chapter.

2. DISOBEDIENCE OF ORDERS

In case of disobedience by judicial officers also, the four indispensable pre-requisites[5] and the wilful disobedience has to be established. Patna High Court in *Harkishun Singh* v. *Chhotan Mahtan*[6] considered the question of disobedience of

---

4. *Id.* at 273.
5. The four indispensable pre-requisites as laid down in *Tarafatulah Mandel* v. *S.N. Maitra* (AIR 1952 Cal. 919) are personal service, precise act of contempt, precise responsibility to obey and the alleged contempt being subsequent to the service of the order said to have been disobeyed.
6. AIR 1951 Pat. 494. In this case there was a dispute relating to the use of a stream between persons belonging to two villages. An order had been passed by the Sub Divisional Magistrate. But the matter had been taken to the High Court by revision and the High Court stayed any kind of deviation of stream by putting bandh. While so Sub Divisional Magistrate visited the area in connection with the other function and one person approached the Magistrate got permission and deviated the stream. Though the other party informed the Magistrate of the stay order and showed the letter from the advocate, he refused to act on the stay order and hence the contempt petition.

the stay order of the High Court by the subordinate court. The order was prohibitory one and the Sub Divisional Magistrate was informed of it. But, as there was no deliberate or wilful disobedience, it was held that there was no contempt, and the Sub Divisional Magistrate was discharged.

But the court made the following observation:

> When an order of stay or other such prohibitory order has been made by this court and when the Subordinate Judge or Magistrate is informed of the order by the advocate or pleader he ought ordinarily to accept what is stated by the advocate or pleader and stay further proceedings...when a Subordinate Judge or Magistrate disregards a prohibitory order of which he has been given a notice in this way (informed by the advocate) it amounts to contempt of court.[7]

The Orissa High Court in *Chintamoni Palai* v. *State,*[8] followed the observation of Patna High Court and held the Sub Magistrate guilty of contempt for disobeying the stay order of the High Court, even after being informed of the stay order by the concerned advocate.

So also when the High Court on revision directed the Magistrate to consider the matter and dispose of the matter in accordance with law and evidence and if the Magistrate once again passed the same order of discharge without looking into the evidence, the Magistrate is guilty of contempt.[9]

But simple delay in executing an order especially when there were reasonable grounds for the delay, will not amount to disobedience and will not result in contempt,[10] because

---

7. *Id.* at 497.
8. AIR 1952 Ori. 167. In this case, the accused person filed a transfer application and the government advocate requested for time to get instructions. In the meantime further proceedings in the Magistrate Court was stayed. It was informed to the Magistrate by the advocate of the accused. Disbelieving the whole thing, the Magistrate took an unusual step and forfeited the bond and taxed the accused persons each with penalty of Rs. 10.
9. *S. Venkataraman* v. *P.V. Singvi* (1997 Cri. L.J. 1840) (Karnataka High Court).
10. *H.P. Singh* v. *Thakur Prasad Tewari* AIR 1953 S.C. 436. In this case one Ramrajib Singh was detained under Bihar Maintenance of Public

there was no deliberate disobedience. There was only gross negligence on the part of those whose duty it was to carryout the orders of the High Court[11] and that is not the test of contempt. The same view was followed by the Calcutta High Court in *State* v. *D. Rudra, Additional District Magistrate.*[12] In this case, the contemner, Additional District Magistrate, Alipore did not carry out the order of the High Court, that the appellants should surrender the bail and serve the rest of the period in jail. The court held:

> We are prepared to accept that these officers did not wilfully override any order of this court. But the entire trouble was due to the fact that it was not a case of the Additional District Magistrate controlling the Judicial Peshkar but the latter controlling the Magistrate.[13]

The Supreme Court in *Debabrata Bandopadhyay* v. *State of West Bengal,*[14] cautioned all concerned that orders of stay, bail, injunctions received from superior courts must receive

---

Order Act, 1947. But he got a release order from the High Court and the High Court's order was forwarded to the Magistrate. Since the Magistrate happened to be out of station there was some delay in releasing the petitioner. Hence he filed a contempt petition before the High Court and the High Court found the Magistrate guilty of contempt. Because the disobedience being the result of gross negligence was not merely accidental eventhough there was no intention to flout or disobey the order of this court. But intention in that sense is not the sole test in a case of contempt though it may be taken into consideration on the question of punishment. But the court accepted his apology. Hence the appeal to the Supreme Court.

11. *Id.* at 437.
12. AIR 1969 Cal. 602. In this case, High Court dismissed an appeal against conviction under Sec. 414 of the Indian Penal Code, and made an order directing the accused appellants, to surrender forthwith their bail and to serve out the remainder of the sentence imposed upon them. This order was not however carried out by the contemner who functioned as Additional District Magistrate, Alipore, at the relevant period.
13. *Id.* at 603.
14. AIR 1969 S.C. 189. In this case one Birendra Kumar Sarkar, Sub-agent of Phosphate Co. Ltd., Krishnagar District, Nadia, was prosecuted for contravention of Fertilizer Control Order. Fertilizer seized was sold and the sale proceeds was held in deposit in court. Sessions Judge on appeal directed the Magistrate to deliver the amount to

close and prompt attention and unnecessary delay in despatching or dealing with them may well furnish grounds for an inference that it was due to indifference and sometimes even of contumaciousness.[15]

The Court further observed:

> Punishment under the law of contempt is called for when the lapse is deliberate and in disregard of one's duty and in defiance of authority. To take action in an unclear case is to make the law of contempt do duty for other measures and is not to be encouraged.[16]

So it was held that there was no disobedience neither of High Court nor of Sessions Court.

In *B.K. Kar* v. *Hon'ble Chief Justice and his companion Justices of the Orissa High Court*[17] also the Supreme Court maintained that only intentional disobedience is to be held as contempt of court and not simple ignorance or mistaken view of law.

Sarkar on furnishing proper security, and he got the amount deposited in the bank on 13th January, 1964.

The company in the meantime moved the High Court for stay of operation of the order of the Sessions Judge and got the stay on 13th January, 1964. It was communicated to the Magistrate on 16th January, 1964. In these circumstances court has to consider whether there was any disobedience of the order of Sessions Judge or that of the High Court.

15. *Id.* at 193.
16. *Ibid.* Allahabad High Court also followed the same view in *Pannalal* v. *R.K. Sinha* 1977 Cri. L.J. (Allahabad High Court) 980. It was alleged that the Sessions Judge intentionally disobeyed the order of the High Court by taking the applicant into custody in spite of the stay order issued by the High Court. But the appellant was taken into custody in utter ignorance of the stay order and accordingly the opposite party did not intentionally flout the stay order issued by the High Court and as such it will not amount to contempt of court.
17. AIR 1961 S.C. 1367. In this case a petition for delivery and redelivery was made before the Sub Divisional Magistrate. While so a review petition filed by one of the parties was admitted by the High Court and the High Court granted interim stay of proceeding before the Sub Divisional Magistrate. The matter was informed to the Magistrate by telegram. But the Sub Divisional Magistrate refused to act on this telegram. Hence the contempt petition. High Court found the Sub Divisional Magistrate guilty of contempt.

The court observed:

> Before a subordinate court can be found guilty of disobeying the order of superior court and thus to have committed contempt of court, it is necessary to show that disobedience was intentional. There is no room for inferring an intention to disobey an order unless the person charged had knowledge of the order. If what a Subordinate court has done is in utter ignorance of an order of a superior court, it would clearly not amount to intentional disobedience of that court's order and would therefore not amount to a contempt of court at all.... The knowledge must however be obtained from a source which is either authorised or otherwise authentic.[18]

Lack of knowledge can be claimed as a defence for an action for civil contempt by judicial officers. But in case the alleged contemner purposely evades knowledge, the lack of it cannot be taken as a defence.

In *Superintendent of Central Excise* v. *Somabhai Ranchhodhbhai Patel*[19] in the execution of a decree High Court ordered to withdraw the fifty per cent decretal amount on security and fifty per cent without security. Supreme Court on appeal permitted to withdraw the whole amount only on security. But the civil judge, Senior Division, on application of the party permitted withdrawal of fifty per cent without security. Since there is no extraneous consideration or dishonest motive for violation of the order court accepted the unconditional apology of the judge and dropped the proceedings.

Thus in *M/s. Kalloo Mal Visheshwar Prasad* v. *Secretary to Government of U.P. Lucknow*[20] it was held that the District Magistrate deliberately evaded the service of the order and he

18. *Id.* at 1370.
19. AIR 2001 S.C. 1975.
20. 1974 Cri. L.J. (Allahabad High Court) 529. In this case a house was owned by Messers Kalloo Mal Visheshwar Prasad and acquisition proceedings were taken up by the Magistrate to acquire the house under U.P. Temporary Accomodation Requisition Act, 1974. Notice was issued. The owner filed a writ under Art. 226 and got a stay. The District Magistrate not only refused to accept the stay order, but passed an acquisition order and served the same on the house owner. Hence the contempt petition.

was not acting *bona fide*. The court found "legally not sound" the plea that the District Magistrate was not under any duty to comply with the orders of this court unless certified copy of the order was served on him.[21]

It is clear that simple non-compliance of the order of the superior court by the inferior court will not constitute contempt because there was no wilful disobedience. For such non-compliance departmental proceedings have to be resorted to. But if the disobedience is wilful or if it is intentional, the authority can be held liable for contempt.

High Court of Sikkim accepted the same view in *A.K. Jain* v. *State of Sikkim*.[22] In this case the High Court followed the opinion of the Supreme Court in *Baradakanta Misra* v. *Bhimsen Dixit*,[23] but modified the decision because of lack of knowledge of the decision of the High Court, and observed:

---

21. *Id.* at 535. It was further held:

> A prohibitory order actually need not be served upon the person who is prosecuted for breach of that order. If it is proved that the person alleged to have committed breach of the prohibitory order had knowledge from some other source, he would be guilty for breach of that order and it would be no valid defence for him that the certified copy of the order or official communication had not been received by him, provided he had no reason to doubt the authenticity of the order conveyed to him (*Id.* at 536).

In this case even after getting knowledge which is authentic the District Magistrate had not complied with the order. So the District Magistrate was held guilty of disobedience of the order (*Id.* at 539).

22. AIR 1992 Sikkim 20. In this case certain defamatory allegations were published in the "Nav Bharat Times", against which criminal complaint was made before the court of the Judicial Magistrate, East and North Sikkim. The Magistrate after recording evidence passed an order directing the respondents to appear in person and face the charge under Sec. 500 and 501 of I.P.C. High Court on revision modified the order of the Magistrate and held, the parties need not appear in person on 5-8-91. On the very same day a similar petition was filed before the same Magistrate and the court on 9-8-91 passed similar order summoning the accused persons. This is the cause of contempt petition.

23. AIR 1972 S.C. 2466. In this case it was laid down that disobedience on the part of a judicial officer to specific order of the High Court or deliberate conduct of not following the law laid down in a previous decision of the High Court amounts to contempt of court.

> Undoubtedly allowance must be given for erroneous construction of law and unless the disobedience to the decision of the High Court is intentional no case of contempt may be said to be made out, but in the present case, the previous judgment was not even referred to and even no attempt was made to show why notwithstanding the previous judgment the issue of process in the subsequent complaint was considered justified. This makes out a *prima facie* case against him for contempt of this court.[24]

Though lack of knowledge can be an excuse in cases of contempt by judicial officers, it is not always so when there could be an opportunity for the officer concerned to know about the High Court's order.

When an advocate was punished for contempt of court, can he appear thereafter as a counsel in the courts, unless he purges himself of such contempt? If he cannot, then what is the way by which he can purge himself of such contempt? these are the important questions considered by the Supreme Court in *Pravin C. Shah* v. *K.A. Mohd. Ali*.[25] In this case an advocate who has been twice charged for contempt of court and punished by imposition of fine simply paid the fine and went on practising in the court as usual. The matter was brought to the notice of the Bar Council of Kerala and the Bar Council debarred him from acting or pleading in any court till he gets himself purged of the contempt of court by an order of the appropriate court. This order was set aside by the Bar Council of India on appeal. That order is under consideration before the Supreme Court.

The relevant rule that is Rule 11 of the Rules framed by the High Court of Kerala reads as follows:

> No advocate who has been found guilty of contempt of court shall be permitted to appear act or plead in any court unless he has purged himself of the contempt.

This rule shows that it is not necessary for the disciplinary committee of the Bar Council to impose the said interdict as a punishment for misconduct. It is a self-operating rule for

24. *Supra* n. 22 p. 33.
25. AIR 2001 S.C. 3041.

which only one stipulation need be satisfied, that is the advocate concerned should have been found guilty of contempt of court.[26]

The court observed:

> We cannot therefore approve the view that merely undergoing the penalty imposed on a contemner is therefore not sufficient to complete the process of purging himself of the contempt, particulary in a case where the contemner is convicted of criminal contempt.... There must be something more to be done to get oneself purged of the contempt when it is a case of criminal contempt.[27]

Court further observed:

> The first thing to be done in that direction when a contemner is found guilty of a criminal contempt is to implant or infuse in his own mind real remorse about his conduct which the court found to have amounted to contempt of court. Next step is to seek pardon from the court concerned for what he did on the ground that he really and genuinely repented and that he has resolved not to commit any such act in future. It is not enough that he tenders an apology. The apology tendered should impress the court to be genuine and sincere. If the court, on being impressed of his genuiness, accepts the apology then it could be said that the contemner has purged himself of the guilt.[28]

Thus a mere statement made by a contemner before the court that he apologises is hardly enough to amount to purging himself of the contempt. The court must be satisfied of the genuiness of apology. If the court is so satisfied and on its basis accepts the apology as genuine the court has to make an order holding that the contemner has purged himself of the contempt. Till such an order is passed by the court the delinquent advocate would continue to be under the spell of the interdict contained in Rule 11 of the Rules.[29]

26. *Id.* at. 3044.
27. *Id.* at 3047.
28. *Id.* at 3048.
29. *Ibid.*

3. INTERFERENCE OF ONE OFFICER WITH THE FUNCTIONING OF ANOTHER

In such cases of interference unless there is improper or corrupt motive it cannot be said to constitute contempt of court.

In *State* v. *Sankar Charan Sahu*[30] though the High Court found the actions of the Magistrate amounting to contempt, the Supreme Court[31] held it was not. In this case the munsiff ordered the arrest of a person, in execution of a money decree. But the magistrate who took action under Sec. 144 Cr. P.C. in effect prevented the arrest of the judgment debtor.

According to the Supreme Court, for constituting contempt, there should be wilful disobedience and it should proceed from improper or corrupt motives. In the instant case though the appellant acted without proper care and caution, there is

30. AIR 1952 Ori. 215. In this case M.S. Rao obtained a decree for recovery of money and in execution he obtained an arrest warrant against one Hrudananda Sahu. A criminal case was also pending against the judgment debtor. Present contempt petition arose because of the arrest warrant issued by the munsiff for the recovery of money and the order of release issued by the Magistrate. Concerned Sub Divisional Magistrate passed the orders without proper jurisdiction. The High Court held: "In any case the power of the magistrate under Sec. 144 Cr. P.C. is meant to prevent imminent breach of peace and not for conferring immunity of a judgment debtor under Sec. 135 Cr. P.C. His order was intended to have the effect and in fact had the effect of preventing the process server of the civil court from executing the process issued to him by the munsiff and as such amounts to contempt of court (*Id.* at 217).

31. *S.S. Roy* v. *State of Orissa.* AIR 1960 S.C. 190. The court observed: As has been said by the Privy Council in *Borton* v. *Field* (1843) 4 Moo. P.C.C. 273, it is not sufficient in such cases for the purpose of visiting a judicial officer with the penal consequences of proceeding in contempt simply because he committed an error of judgment or the order passed by him is in excess of authority vested in him. The error must be wilful error proceeding from improper or corrupt motives in order that he may be punished for contempt of court (*Id.* at 190). So also in *Arun Kshetrapal* v. *Registrar High Court, Orissa,* AIR 1976 S.C. 1967, though the High Court found the District Magistrate, who sent a message to the Advocate General requesting him to request the High Court not to insist on the production of detenue in connection with a writ of *habeas corpus*, guilty of contempt, Supreme Court held that he was not guilty of contempt.

nothing on record to suggest any wilful culpability on his part and it has been expressly held by the High Court that he was not actuated by corrupt or dishonest motive. In these circumstances the order passed by the High Court was reversed.[32]

An important legal situation arose in *State of Rajasthan* v. *Prakash Chand*.[33] In this case, Chief Justice of Rajasthan High Court in exercise of his powers transferred a part heard matter from the Single Judge to Division Bench. Aggrieved by the action of the Chief Justice, the judge who was hearing the matter, issued show cause notice to the Chief Justice as to why proceedings under Contempt of Court Act, be not taken against him for transferring the part heard writ petition to the Division Bench for hearing. Supreme Court after referring the relevant provisions of law held that the action of the judge is not only subversive of judicial discipline and illegal but is also without jurisdiction.[34]

The Court observed:

> No such notice could be issued to the Chief Justice since the order referring the case to the Division Bench was an order legally made by the Chief Justice in exercise of his statutory powers. Such an order can never invite initiation of contempt proceeding against him. The issuance of notice smacks of judicial authoritarianism and not permissible in law.
>
> Even otherwise it is a fundamental principle of our jurisprudence and it is in public interest also that no action can lie against a judge of a court of Record for a judicial act done by the judge. The remedy of the aggrieved party against such an order is to approach the higher forum through appropriate proceedings.[35]

4. NON-COMPLIANCE OF THE ORDERS

Non-compliance of the order may give way for departmental proceedings. But for constituting contempt deliberate breach of the order or wilful disobedience should be established.

32. *Ibid.*
33. 1998 Cri. L.J 2012 (Supreme Court).
34. *Id.* at 2025.
35. *Id.* at 2025.

Allahabad High Court in *Brijkishore Mehrotra* v. *G.P. Shrivastava*[36] made a distinction between non-compliance of the order and disobedience of the order. It was alleged that the First class Magistrate had committed contempt of court of the Sessions Judge by refusing to accept the copy of the order of the Sessions Judge which directed the Magistrate to accept the cash security and release the applicants on bail. The copy of the order was given to the magistrate at his residence though during working hours and the magistrate refused to act upon it. The magistrate, by leaving the court earlier than 5 P.M. committed breach of departmental rules but there was no disobedience of any order.[37]

But, it is a case of delay defeating justice. By refusing to accept the order of the Session's Court, the magistrate made the accused person to continue in jail which in turn restricted his personal liberty. Magistrate is a 24 hours duty officer and he was bound to act on the order of the Sessions Judge immediately. By non-compliance he has committed disobedience. Such non-compliance is said to be not constituting contempt because there is no wilful or deliberate disobedience. For constituting contempt, deliberate disobedience should be established.

5. MISUSE OF OFFICIAL POSITION

Sometimes when the presiding officers misuse their official position there is enough scope for contempt. In *M.K. Prakash* v. *A.P. Parukutty Moopilamma*[38] the court observed that having

36. AIR 1956 All. 417. In this case a complaint was pending before the court of the First Class Magistrate, the respondent. On refusal to accept the bond and cash security by the respondent, the accused persons moved Sessions Judge and Sessions Judge directed the Magistrate to accept the cash security and release the accused. Advocate of the accused met the magistrate at his residence. But the magistrate refused to act in accordance with the order of the Sessions Judge. Hence the, contempt petition.
37. *Id.* at 421.
38. AIR 1971 Ker. 248. In this case, there was a long pending litigation relating to some private forest. One of the parties after obtaining permit under the Madras Preservation of Private Forest Act, 1949, cut and removed some timbers. But because of a complaint from third person it was seized and kept under the control of the Forest Range Officer. While so an application was moved before the third

known the existence of different petitions, the munsiff misused his powers and functions as a judicial officer and had deliberately acted not only in an illegal manner but in a most non-judicial manner, making administration of justice a mockery.[39]

6. NON-OBSERVANCE OF WELL SETTLED PRECEDENT

The doctrine of Stare decisis[40] which obliges the judiciary to follow its earlier decisions gave way for the well settled principle of precedent. The principle of law laid down by higher judiciary has a binding authority on the lower judiciary.[41] When a well settled precedent was not followed by a judicial officer it would amount to contempt of court.[42] Because non

---

respondent (Munshiff) by respondents one and two to release the wood and it was alleged that respondent three misused his office in releasing the logs of wood. The respondent knew that criminal revision petition was pending before the High Court relating to the custody of logs of wood.

39. *Id.* at 256.

40. In general it means stick on to the decision. Rupert Cross states: The general orthodox interpretation of stare decisis and that which is in general indicates stare rationibus decidendis. But a narrower and more literal interpretation is sometimes employed. Rupert Cross, *Precedent in English Law* 105 (1977). For further discussion of stare decisis *see* Ch. III and VI *Ibid.*

41. A court is bound to follow any case decided by a court above it, and appellate courts (other than House of Lords) are bound by their previous decisions. (Rupert Cross *Precedent in English Law* 102, 103 (1991). "I think adherence to precedent should be the rule and not the exception". Justice Benjamin N. Cardozo *The Nature of Judicial Process* 149 (1957). But he claimed that the rule should be relaxed.

    Indian Constitution also provides for the observance of the law laid down by the Supreme Court by the lower court. "The law declared by the Supreme Court shall be binding on all courts within the territory of India" (Art. 141).

    Faced with the freedom of choice between traditional doctrine of stare decisis and the American doctrine of review of precedents the Supreme Court of India inevitably lent its preference to a flexible use of the doctrine of precedent without imposing the fetters of stare decisis on itself. Lakshminath, *Precedent in the Indian Legal System* 17 (1990) (For further details *see* Ch. II).

42. *Shri Baradakanta Mishra* v. *Shri Bhimsen Dixit* 1973 Cri. L.J. (Supreme Court) 19. The appellant was a member of the subordinate judicial service of the State of Orissa. At the relevant time he was serving as Commissioner of Hindu Religious Endowments. In the village

observance of the principle of law laid down by the higher judiciary would undermine the respect for the higher judiciary and its constitutional authority.[43]

But strict adherence to the precedent will destroy judicial creativity. So the question is how to reconcile the concept of stability and continuity and yet permit constant change.[44] As suggested by Julius Stone, by means of creation of new law under old formulae which he termed of "fertilising the organism of law,"[45] it can be achieved. Further method suggested is that the search for understanding may well have to begin with the inbuilt dualism between leeways of choice and checks of arbitrary choice, within the very materials and methods with which the judges have to work.[46]

It is therefore clear that law can be adopted to the changing conditions and an innovative judge can create new principles, without deviating from the doctrine of precedent.

Sometimes it may so happen that the decision of the

Sanabalpur, there was a dispute as to the hereditary trusteeship of a temple and Addl. Asst. Commissioner before whom the matter was pending, appointed an interim trustee pending disposal of the case. This appointment was questioned before the Commissioner by the aggrieved party. In the meantime Orissa High Court in *Bhramerbar Sar Sanmatra* v. *State of Orissa* AIR 1970 Ori. 141 laid down a principle and that was brought to the notice of the Commissioner (Appellant). But he refused to follow the decision under the guise that the matter was taken in appeal to the Supreme Court. Hence the contempt petition. High Court found the appellant guilty of contempt of court.

43. *Id.* at 22, 23.

44. To this question posed by Justice Stone, the answer is also given by him. For further discussion *see* Julius Stone, *Legal System and Lawyers Reasoning,* Ch. 6§13 and Ch. 7§1 (1968). The same question was considered and answered by Justice Cardozo also. Justice Benjamin N. Cardozo, *The Nature of the Judicial Process,* 160 (1957).

45. Julius Stone, *Legal System and Lawyers Reasoning,* 215 (1968).

46. *Id.* at 234. Justice Cardozo suggested alternative approach through logic, philosophy, history, traditions, sociology, prevailing community standards or even expediency.

Lakshminath also suggested to maintain a minimum harmony and balance between activist orientations, and doctrine of binding precedent. Lakshminath *Precedent in the Indian Legal System,* 25 (1990).

higher court itself is *per incuriam.*[47] *Per incuriam* decision will also have the binding authority on the lower court and the lower court is bound to follow.[48] But here also the lower court judge can apply the principle of distinguishing and avoid the application of a wrong principle.

By refusing to follow a well settled precedent, the lower court not only commits contempt of court but also refuses to perform a constitutional obligation.

A question may arise whether disobedience of a precedent even if it is *per incuriam* will amount to contempt of court.

Though a court has a duty to follow the precedents it may not be possible in the interest of justice to follow the precedent verbatim in cases which may have to be viewed differently. Also in *per incuriam* decisions there is no binding precedent because the court arrived at the conclusion without analysing proper earlier decisions.[49] The court should have in such context the privilege of distinguishing, which cannot be viewed as disobedience. The act of distinguishing is a significant right of a judge whose prime consideration should be to uphold justice in the light of law. Therefore, a judge may feel a compulsion to refuse to follow a precedent which may be *per incuriam.* This act of distinguishing may save the judge from contempt proceedings. But express refusal to follow well settled precedent will attract contempt jurisdiction.

---

47. A decision of the court which is mistaken. A decision of the court is not a binding precedent if given per incuriam; *i.e.* without the court's attention having been drawn to the relevant authorities or statutes. Osborn's *Concise Law Dictionary* 249 (7th Edn.).
48. Rupert Cross and J.W. Harris, *Precedent in English Law,* 158, 159 (Fourth edition). But the Privy Council in *Baker* v. *Queen* (1975 A.C. 774) expressed the view that although inferior courts were bound to follow the decisions of the Higher Court even if they were *per incuriam,* they were not bound by the proposition of law incorporated into the ratio decidendi, because it does not create a precedent for use in the decision of other cases (at p. 788). The same view was followed in *National Enterprises Ltd.* v. *Racal Communications Ltd.* (1975) Ch. 397. So also in *Baros* v. *Bethal* (1982) 1 All. E.R. 106.
49. *Ibid.*

7. CONCLUSION

Judicial officers are not an exception to the contempt jurisdiction of the judiciary, as the contempt power is resorted to not for the personal protection of individual judges but for the protection of the administration of justice and also for the maintenance of the dignity of the judiciary.

So far as judicial officers are concerned as stated by the Supreme Court in *B.K. Kar* v. *Hon'ble Chief Justice and companion justices of the High Court of Orissa,*[50] the disobedience should be intentional, that is disobedience should be with the knowledge of the order. An accidental disobedience or disobedience in ignorance of the order will not constitute contempt. So also mistakes arising due to interpretation of law or simple interference cannot give way for contempt proceedings.

But so far as disobedience of precedent is concerned the Supreme Court has taken a serious view because such disobedience will affect the constitutional authority of the higher judiciary.

But in case the decision disobeyed is *per incuriam,* the judge can by the method of distinguishing make a leeway and avoid contempt proceeding. Also *per incuriam* decisions will not have any binding authority because the court reached the conclusion without analysing concerned case laws.

50. *Supra* n. 17.

PART 4

11

Conclusion

The common law concept of contempt of court was brought to India along with the introduction of the British system of administration of justice in India.

Administration of justice was the paramount function of early kings and any disobedience of their orders or interference to this function was dealt with summarily. When they created the courts and delegated the function of administration of justice to them, they also assumed this summary jurisdiction to punish for contempt. The courts, the judgments of which were kept in perpetual memory and which had the right to punish for contempt were called as courts of record. In the early period only direct interferences were treated as contempt. Later on, indirect interference was also treated as contempt. Judicial recognition of indirect interference as contempt goes back to the opinion of Lord Hardwicke L.C. in *St. James Evening Post*[1] case. This decision recognized scandalising the court and prejudicing fair trail as contempt of court.

Wilmot J. in *Almon's*[2] case further extended contempt jurisdiction by applying it to publications, and also by applying summary jurisdiction to punish indirect contempt. By creating different courts of records by different Charters for India contempt jurisdiction was also transferred. Interference with the administration of justice either by scandalising the court or prejudicing fair trial constituted criminal contempt and disobedience of the orders of the court constituted civil contempt.

Though court of record has the power to punish contempt of itself doubt arose as to its jurisdiction to punish contempt

1. (1742) 2 Atk. 469.
2. 97 E R 94.

of subordinate courts. For removing that doubt Contempt of Courts Act, 1926 was passed which was subsequently re-enacted by the 1952 Act. Parliament enacted a comprehensive legislation, namely Contempt of Courts Act, 1971 to regulate contempt proceedings and repealed the 1952 Act. Though Art. 19(1) (a) of the Constitution guarantees freedom of speech and expression it can be restricted on the ground of contempt of court by virtue of Art. 19(2). But the Supreme Court nullified the application of 1971 Act so far as exercise of contempt jurisdiction by the Supreme Court and High Courts are concerned in *Vinay Chandra Mishra's*[3] case because these courts are courts of record, a creation of the Constitution.

Contempt jurisdiction is applied for maintaining the majesty of law and also to assert impartial and uninterrupted administration of justice. So it is essential that, for constituting contempt by prejudicing fair trial the proceedings should be pending and the alleged contemner should have knowledge of the pending proceedings.

Before the passing of the Contempt of Courts Act, 1971, there was no uniformity of opinion among the various High Courts as to when the proceedings can be said to be pending. But a clear explanation of pendency of proceedings was given by the Madhya Pradesh High Court.[4] Accordingly, when a suitor takes any effective step in the prosecution of his case, the law protects him. But the difficulty in ascertaining the pendency of proceedings was settled by the Contempt of Courts Act, 1971, by providing an explanation to Sec. 3. It clearly states the circumstances in which proceedings are pending. In certain cases proceedings for contempt had been initiated where they were not actually pending, but are only imminent. The Allahabad High Court[5] held that extending the rule for the punishment of contempt of court to cases which are imminent would unduly hamper the freedom of speech of the citizen. So contempt proceedings should be initiated only when the proceedings are pending and not when they are imminent. The Contempt of Courts Act, 1971, is also silent

3. (1995) 2 SCC 584.
4. *Smt. Padmavathi Devi Bhargava* v. *R.K. Karanjia* AIR 1963 M.P. 61.
5. *Dwarka Prasad Agarwal* v. *Krishna Chandra* AIR 1963 All. 600.

about imminence of proceedings. Contempt proceedings should be initiated only when the proceedings are pending as explained in the explanation to Sec. 3 of the Act.

A question arises as to whether knowledge of pendency of proceedings is a *sine qua non* for liability for contempt. Earlier decisions stressed that knowledge of pending proceedings was essential for vesting liability. But the Madhya Pradesh High Court[6] held that knowledge of pending proceedings is not a *sine qua non* for contempt proceedings.

This opinion though followed in subsequent decisions unreasonably restricts the constitutional guarantee of freedom of speech and expression. So with a view to safeguard the freedom and to protect innocent editors and publishers, section 3 of the Contempt of Courts Act, 1971 provided that innocent publication and distribution of matters is not contempt.

Freedom of expression has its value only if the press is allowed to publish true reports. But judiciary interferes if the true reports interfered with the administration of justice or scandalised the judiciary. Judiciary has distinguished between true reporting of judicial proceedings and true reporting of matters during the pendency of judicial proceedings. Judiciary has accepted the right to give fair and accurate report of its proceedings provided it is faithful and without malice. Sec. 4 of the Contempt of Courts Act, 1971 also accepted the defence of fair and accurate report of judicial proceedings. In case of true reporting of matters during the pendency of proceedings, judiciary held the view that true reporting is not a defence, if it is likely to prejudice fair trial or scandalise the court. The reason given by the Bombay High Court[7] was that if truth is allowed to be pleaded and examined as a defence it would seriously affect the independence and integrity of the judiciary.

But it is suggested that truth should always be permitted as a good defence. On an analogy of fair and accurate reporting of judicial proceedings *bona fide* and faithful reporting of true matters should also be permitted.

---

6. *Padmavathi Devi Bhargava* v. *R.K. Karanjia* AIR 1963 M.P. 61.
7. *V.M. Kanade* v. *Madhav Gadkari* 1990 Cri. L.J. (Bombay High Court) 190.

Repeated attempts to induct public interest as a defence for contempt proceedings had not been accepted by the judiciary. Public interest, public welfare and good intention are not good defences for contempt proceedings.

Prejudicing fair trial and scandalising the court as the tests of criminal contempt as laid down by Lord Hardwicke L.C.[8] were adopted by the Indian judiciary in various decisions.

Because of the strict attitude of the judiciary as seen in the majority of decisions of the Supreme Court and High Courts the valuable rights of the citizens and the press had been restricted. Thus, the Patna[9] and Orissa[10] High Courts held the alleged contemner liable for contempt because the respective statements had the tendency to prejudice fair trial.

Advocates, officials and ministers were held liable for contempt because the statements in notices, *demi-official* letters and speeches had the tendency to prejudice fair trial.[11] In exceptional cases the contemners were held not liable.[12]

Only in exceptional cases the tests of real prejudice and substantial interference were applied.[13]

The test of prejudicing fair trial came to be understood as 'likely to prejudice', 'tendency to prejudice', 'tend to prejudice', 'calculated to produce an atmosphere of prejudice', 'tendency to influence or tendency to interfere', 'real prejudice' or 'actual prejudice' and 'substantial interference'.

Hence, the judiciary was very jealous in maintaining its dignity and even minor interference could not be borne by it. This in turn affected the constitutional guarantee of the freedom of speech and expression which necessitated the legislative intervention.[14] But the legislature gave a wide scope for judicial

8. *St. James Evening Post* case (1742) 2 Atk. 469.
9. *State* v. *Ram Briksh Benipuri* AIR 1953 Pat. 364.
10. *Hare Krishna Mahatab* v. *Balakrishnakar* AIR 1954 Ori. 57.
11. *Supra* pp. 79, 81, 82, 85 and 86 Ch. 6.
12. *Supra* pp. 81, 82 and 83 Ch. 6.
13. *See* e.g. *State of Himachal Pradesh* v. *Sri Reghunandan Lal Gupta* AIR 1954 H.P. 70. *District Magistrate Bidar* v. *Madhava Rao* AIR 1961 Mys. 12. *State* v. *Faquirchand* AIR 1957 All. 657. *Rev. Father Sebastian* v. *K. Karunakaran* AIR 1967 Ker. 177.
14. The Contempt of Courts Act, 1971.

intervention by including the terms 'interferes' and 'tends to interfere' in the definition[15] of criminal contempt.

But the approach of the judiciary after the enactment of the Contempt of Courts Act, 1971, registers a reverse tendency.

Supreme Court[16] adopted a liberal attitude and held that the respective press reports did not interfere with the course of justice.

Regarding academic publications the approach of the judiciary had been very liberal.[17]

Only in very few cases[18] courts gave punishment on the ground of prejudicing fair trial. Organising a demonstration[19] or attacking the members of the commission[20] appointed by the court are so serious that the judiciary adopted a stringent view. The court gave punishment not on the basis of mere tendency to interfere but because there is real prejudice. Whether the statement is a press report or a public speech if there is interference, the judiciary, will intervene. The Supreme Court's extreme step of punishing the Bar Council Chairman[21] can be justified because the contemner tried to extract orders by extortion and tried to degrade the dignity of the judiciary. But it is submitted that punishing a poor constable[22] for stopping the vehicle of a judge for interrogation amounts to misuse of the power and cannot be justified.

Owing to the lack of statutory explanation of "scandalising the judiciary" it had been explained in various forms by different High Courts in the pre Contempt of Courts Act period.

---

15. Sec. 2(c) of the Contempt of Courts Act, 1971.
16. *Naraindas* v. *Government of Madhya Pradesh* 1974 Cri. L.J. (Supreme Court) 924; *Kalyana Sundaram* v. *Karunanidhi* AIR 1981 S.C. 1416.
17. *J.V. Hanumantha Rao* v. *K.R. Pattabhiraman* AIR 1975 A.P. 30.
18. *See* e.g. *Subhash Chand* v. *S.M. Aggarwal* 1984 Cri. L.J. (Delhi High Court) 481; *P.C. Sen's* case AIR 1970 S.C. 1821; *Haji Rasheed Mohamed* v. *D. Ramanujam* AIR 1986 Mad. 119.
19. *K.A. Mohammed Ali* v. *C.N. Presannan* AIR 1995 S.C. 454.
20. *Tarun Bharat Sangh, Alwar* v. *Union of India* AIR 1993 S.C. 293.
21. *In re Vinay Chandra Mishra* (1995) 2 SCC 584.
22. *Red Light on the Cars of the Hon'ble Judges of the High Court* v. *State of U.P.* AIR 1993 All. 211.

It had been construed as distorted version of judgment,[23] allegation of corruption[24] and other unfounded allegations.[25] The right of the press to criticise the judicial system was recognized by the judiciary but when it interfered with the administration of justice, or when it lowered its authority it was held as contempt.[26]

Though Lord Atkin's statement that "justice is not a cloistered virtue, she must be allowed to suffer the scrutiny and outspoken comments of ordinary men" holds good at all times, the strict attitude of the judiciary resulted in several persons being held liable for contempt. Thus a statement in the resolution of the Bar Association that the judicial officers are thoroughly incompetent in law and do not inspire the advocates in their work,[27] a statement in the article mentioning the unsatisfactory method of recruitment of judges, threat by a party to the advocate of opposite side,[28] statements in the affidavit imputing partiality and dishonesty to the judge,[29] statement in the public speech that judges are guided by class hatred, class interest and class prejudices[30] and the like were held scandalous.

Only vindictive or scurrilous attacks on a court or judge based on false allegations or made recklessly may amount to contempt by scandalising the court and not *bona fide* criticism without malice.[31] But the early decisions do not indicate such an attitude of the judiciary.

Sec. 2(c) of the Contempt of Courts Act, 1971 gave wide scope for judicial intervention by including the terms 'tends to scandalise', or 'lowers' or 'tends to lower the authority of any court' in it.

---

23. *Registrar Assam High Court* v. *Frank Morasse Resident Editor Times of India* AIR 1954 Ass. 201.
24. *Sukh Raj* v. *Hem Raj* AIR 1967 Raj. 203.
25. *In the matter of Hiran Bose, contemner* AIR 1969 Cal. 1.
26. *Perspective Publications (P) Ltd.* v. *State of Maharashtra* AIR 1971 S.C. 221.
27. *State* v. *Brahma Prakash* AIR 1950 All. 556.
28. *Damayanthi G. Chandramani* v. *Vaney* AIR 1966 Bom. 19.
29. *Advocate General A.P.* v. *Abbaraju Rama Rao* AIR 1968 A.P. 207.
30. *E.M. Sankaran Namboodiripad* v. *T.N. Nambiar* AIR 1970 S.C. 2015.
31. *Supra* pp. 122, 123 Ch. 7.

Judicial decisions since the Contempt of Courts Act, 1971, show the liberal attitude of the judiciary. Only reckless and *mala fide* allegations,[32] use of intemperate language[33] and baseless allegation of corruption[34] were considered scandalous. In such cases also court found the statement to be contempt not on the basis of mere tendency to scandalise or tendency to lower the authority of the court, but because the statements were *per se* derogatory, scandalous and contemptuous. Though an editor[35] was found guilty of contempt for scandalising the court, the Supreme Court dropped the proceedings adopting a magnanimous attitude.

In cases where the language was offensive, casting aspersions on the judges, and lowering the dignity of the court, when motives were imputed and when there was reckless allegation[37] judiciary applied the contempt jurisdiction.

A letter written by the President of the Rajasthan Judicial Service Association to the Hon'ble Union Home Minister was held not to constitute contempt because there was no improper motive or malicious intention.[38] The same liberal attitude was adopted by the Bombay High Court[39] also.

The Supreme Court modified its decision in *Sankaran Namboodiripad's*[40] case in its subsequent decisions.[41] It adopted a very liberal attitude and held the respective Ministers were not guilty of contempt and the right to criticise the judicial system was recognized. The same liberal attitude is seen in

---

32. *State of U.P.* v. *Das Vidhi* 1973 Cri. L.J. (Allahabad High Court) 1271.
33. *S.C. Tyagi* v. *N.C. Gupta* 1974 Cri. L.J. (Allahabad High Court) 428.
34. *State of U.P.* v. *Narendra Pal Singh* 1990 Cri. L.J. (Allahabad High Court) 1637.
35. *In re Mulgoakar* AIR 1978 S.C. 727.
36. *Advocate General Orissa* v. *Baradakanta Misra* 1974 Cri. L.J. (Orissa High Court) 70.
37. *State* v. *R.N. Patra* 1976 Cri. L.J. (Orissa High Court) 440.
38. *State of Rajasthan* v. *M.R. Mitruka* 1978 Cri. L.J. (Rajasthan High Court) 1440.
39. *Bhalchandar Gangadhar Ghate* v. *Prathad Sadji Raghute* 1977 Cri. L.J. (Bombay High Court) 1490.
40. AIR 1970 S.C. 2015.
41. *M.R. Pareshwar* v. *Dr. Farooq Abdullah* AIR 1984 S.C. 615. *P.N. Dude* v. *P. Shiv Shankar* AIR 1988 S.C. 1208.

subsequent decisions of various High Courts and the Supreme Court.[42]

But such liberal attitude does not extend to highly derogatory and scurrilous remarks, even if made by advocates.[43]

Courts gave more importance to the tone and tenor of the language than to the contents. Unfounded allegations of *mala fides*, bias, prejudice, ridiculing the performance of a judge, open abuse and casting aspersions on his integrity have always been considered to mean scandalising the court.

In 1950 when the Bar Association passed a resolution stating that the officers are thoroughly incompetent in law, and do not inspire them in their work, it was held as contempt of court because the language was not objective and dignified.[44] But in 1978 in the Rajasthan case the letter in question was held not scandalous since it was not actuated by any improper motive or malicious intention.[45] This shows the differences in approach and the liberal attitude of the judiciary.

Of late, the question of contempt by disobedience assumed great significance because of the questioning attitude of the authorities. In such cases irrespective of whether the disobedience was by administrative authorities, individuals or subordinate judiciary, contempt jurisdiction has been applied by the judiciary.

The Calcutta High Court[46] laid down four prerequisites for a person or authority to be held liable for contempt. They are 'personal service' of the order to the person alleged to have disobeyed, 'precise act of contempt', 'precise responsibility of the contemner' and 'the date of the alleged disobedience being subsequent to the service of the order'.

But personal service of the order, by subsequent judicial interpretation, is understood as knowledge of the order. Hence, official communication of the order is not necessary but credible

---

42. *Supra* pp. 125-129 Ch. 7.
43. *M.B. Sanghi, Advocate* v. *High Court of Punjab and Haryana* AIR 1991 S.C. 1834. *Pritam Pal* v. *High Court of Madhya Pradesh*, AIR 1992 S.C. 904; *In re Vinay Chandra Mishra* (1995) 2 SCC 584.
44. *Supra* pp. 118, 119 Ch. 7.
45. *Supra* pp. 135, 136 Ch. 7.
46. *Tarafatulah Mandal* v. *S.N. Maitra* AIR 1952 Cal. 919.

information of the order[47] is sufficient. It should be an authentic information from the advocate or from the party. The consequence is that lack of official communication is not a defence for contempt proceedings.

Further, precise act of disobedience should be established. Whether it be the administrative authority, individual or subordinate judiciary, there could be no contempt if there is no disobedience. But if the order itself is invalid because of lack of inherent jurisdiction[48] or if it is not specific and clear[49] there cannot be any contempt. So also simply filing an appeal is no excuse,[50] but if the order is stayed it is a good defence.[51] Thus lame excuses by the administrative authorities were not recognised by the judiciary, when there was a clear case of disobedience of the court order.

In case of lack of jurisdiction, courts made a distinction between lack of territorial or pecuniary jurisdiction and lack of inherent jurisdiction and held the former valid because it can be rectified.[52] But the latter void and a void order binds nobody and disobedience of such order will not constitute contempt.[53] But in case the court which issued the order lacked inherent jurisdiction but had issued the order as if it had the jurisdiction, it would continue to be good order till it is set aside by the higher court. So it is submitted that disobedience of any order should be subject to contempt jurisdiction, and if the court lacks inherent jurisdiction the aggrieved party has to make an appeal to the higher court and get it quashed or stayed failing

47. *Gurbachand Singh Lachhman Singh* v. *Hoshiar Singh* AIR 1959 Punj. 205.
48. *Union of India* v. *Maria Cabral e sa* AIR 1982 S.C. 691; *State of Jammu and Kashmir* v. *Mohd. Yaqoobkhan* (1992) 4 S.C.C. 167.
49. *Ratan Narain Mulla* v. *Chief Secretary, Government of U.P.* (1975) Cri. L.J. (Allahabad High Court) 1283.
50. *Prakash Chand* v. *S.S. Grewal* 1975 Cri. L.J. (Punjab High Court) 679.
51. *Hans Raj Dhir* v. *Himachal Pradesh* 1985 Cri. L.J. (Himachal Pradesh High Court) 1030.
52. *State of U.P.* v. *Ratan Shukla* AIR 1956 All. 258; *Hiralal Palai* v. *Sri Kalinath* AIR 1962 S.C. 199.
53. *Amarnath* v. *Municipal Corporation of Delhi* 1981 Cri. L.J. (Delhi High Court) 1880.

which it continues to be a good order and disobedience should constitute contempt.

Generally parties to the suit alone are bound by the decision of a court and a third party is under no obligation to obey the order.[54] But by subsequent decisions, a third party is also held liable if he aided or abetted the disobedience of the order.[55] Even if one is not abetting the disobedience which is a civil contempt if he interferes with the due execution of the orders, he would be interfering with the administration of justice and that would amount to criminal contempt. Thus, the law on civil contempt has been made stringent by making the third party liable for contempt.

At the time of alleged disobedience the order should be in existence. If the order had been vacated, stayed or lost its validity due to lapse of time, there can be no disobedience of the order amounting to contempt.

Thus, the law requires that the following conditions should be satisfied in order to make an authority or individual liable for contempt by disobedience:

- (i) There should be knowledge/authentic information of the order of the court.
- (ii) The order should be a valid and enforceable one.
- (iii) A third party to the proceedings can be held liable if he aids or abets disobedience.
- (iv) At the time of alleged disobedience the order should be in existence.

At times, officials may not directly disobey, but may not give effect to the orders of the court. Such acts like direction to ignore the decision of the High Court[56] making suggestions instead of carrying out the order of the court,[57] are also treated

---

54. *Narain Singh* v. *Hardayal Singh Harika, Executive Officer, Municipal Committee, Patiala*, AIR 1958 Punjab 180.
55. *Vidyacharan Shukla* v. *Tamilnadu Olympic Association* AIR 1991 Mad. 323.
56. *Dibakar Satpathy* v. *Hon'ble the Chief Justice and his companion justices of the Orissa High Court* AIR 1961 S.C. 1315.
57. *Gouri Shankar Jain* v. *The State of Bihar* 1973 Cri. L.J. (Patna High Court) 137.

by the judiciary as disobedience. Thus indirect disobedience of the orders of court is also viewed seriously by the court. This strict approach of the judiciary has to be maintained and safeguarded for the maintenance of the dignity of the court.

Genuine reasons because of which the order of the court, could not be complied with,[58] though not recognized as a defence, had been considered for mitigation of sentence. For a genuine reason due to which the order could not be complied with, the concerned authority or individual has to approach the court in advance and get necessary modification of the order.

Administrative authorities have the right to proceed against subordinates for misconduct. Sometimes actions of the authority may interfere with the administration of justice, and such acts are viewed seriously by the court and treated them as contempt of court. Thus issue of show cause notice[59] framing charges, conduct of parallel enquiry[60] were considered to interfere with the administration of justice and the court held them as contempt.

But appointment of a commission of enquiry will not attract contempt proceedings because they are performing a statutory function.[61]

Judiciary is very keen to keep the administration of justice from outside interference. Though the authorities have the right to take disciplinary proceedings against the subordinates, they have no right to interfere with the administration of justice. For avoiding conflict between the two the following suggestions are made:

(i) Once the court had taken cognizance of the matter all kinds of departmental proceedings should be stopped.

(ii) Judiciary, before taking cognizance of the matter should confirm that the departmental remedies are exhausted.

---

58. *M.L. Sachdev* v. *Union of India* AIR 1991 S.C. 311.
59. *Sankarlal Sharma* v. *M.S. Bisht* AIR 1956 All.160.
60. *D. Jones Shield* v. *N. Ramesan* 1955 Cri. L.J. (Andhra Pradesh High Court) 1028.
61. *Gokulanand* v. *Tarapada Mukerjee* AIR 1973 Cal. 233.

(iii) If the remedy is sought through the judiciary against disciplinary proceedings itself, the administrative authorities should not take any further action in the matter.

Regarding the writ of *habeas corpus*, mere failure to obey the direction of the court may not amount to contempt. But if there is wilful disobedience in carrying out the direction, that will amount to contempt of court.

Breach of an undertaking given to the court is also treated as contempt. In order to constitute the breach of an undertaking to be contempt of court the undertaking should be to the court. But the judiciary by subsequent decisions modified this principle and laid down that even if the undertaking did not contain the term 'undertake', if the undertaking is incorporated in the order of the court, it is an undertaking to the court.[62]

Further extension of this principle could be seen in applying contempt jurisdiction to consent decrees and compromise decrees.[63] Thus if the compromise or consent reached is incorporated in the order of the court, any breach of it is construed as contempt. But breach of private compromises which is not incorporated in the order of the court will not come within the purview of contempt jurisdiction. The expression "a party undertakes" or "gives a solemn promise" in the statement of the parties or their counsel, or in the orders and decrees of the court, unless otherwise suggested means an implied undertaking to the court.

Not only the administrative authorities and individuals but the subordinate judiciary is also bound by the orders of the higher court. Wilful disobedience of the superior court by the subordinate courts was treated as contempt and no leniency was shown. The only condition is that the concerned officer should be informed of the order of the superior court. No official communication is necessary,[64] but knowledge of the

62. *Lala Baijnath Prasad* v. *Lala Shyam Sunder* 1961 (2) Cri. L.J. (Calcutta High Court) 222. *Tukaram, S/o. Khanduji Gaikward* v. *Santhosh Mahodeo Sayam* 1995 Cri. L.J. (Bombay High Court) 577.

63. *Chhaganbhai Norsinbhai* v. *Soni Chandubhai Gordhan Bhai* AIR 1976 S.C. 1909. *Smt. Pushpaben* v. *Narandas* AIR 1979 S.C. 1536.

64. *Harkishun Singh* v. *Chhotan Mahtan* AIR 1951 Pat. 494; *Chintamani Palai* v. *State* AIR 1952 Ori. 167.

order of the superior court should be established. But simple delay in execution of the order is not considered to be disobedience.[65]

The doctrine of *stare decisis* imposes a duty on the judiciary to follow well settled precedent. In case the judicial officer refuses to follow a well settled precedent, he is liable for contempt.[66] This principle has to be strictly adhered to, for giving vitality to the concept of precedent. Strict adherence to precedent may affect judicial creativity. But the judges having the right to distinguish, can avoid the strict application of a previous decision and give way to new and innovative principles.

In case the precedent itself is wrong due to wrong application of law or because the decision had been arrived at without proper appraisal of the law, a question may arise whether the non-observance of such a precedent would result in contempt proceedings. Even though in England, it has been held that such a decision does not possess binding force as precedent, Indian courts are yet to make any pronouncement on this question.

The final question is: how far the Indian courts have succeeded in the delicate task of balancing the conflicting values—one, protecting the freedom of speech and expression guaranteed by the Constitution and the other upholding the honour and dignity of the court. Tolerance to criticism is a virtue and is a sign of maturity. The Indian judiciary, though hesitant and oversensitive in the early periods, now appears to have reached a level of maturity which can tolerate criticism; but which never allows irresponsible attempts to lower its dignity.

---

65. *H.P. Singh* v. *Thakur Prasad Tewari* AIR 1953 S.C. 436.
66. *Baradakanta Mishra* v. *Shri Bhimsen Dixit* 1973 Cri. L.J. (Supreme Court) 19.

APPENDICES

Appendix 1

The Contempt of Courts Act, 1971 (Act No. 70 of 1971)

ARRANGEMENT OF SECTIONS

Preamble

Sections

THE CONTEMPT OF COURTS ACT, 1971
NO. 70 OF 1971

[24*th December*, 1971]

An Act to define and limit the powers of certain courts in punishing contempts of courts and to regulate their procedure in relation thereto.

Be it enacted by Parliament in the Twenty-second Year of the Republic of India as follows:

1. Short title and extent

(1) This Act may be called the Contempt of Courts Act, 1971.

(2) It extends to the whole of India: Provided that it shall not apply to the State of Jammu and Kashmir except to the extent to which the provisions of this Act relate to contempt of the Supreme Court.

2. Definitions

In this Act, unless the context otherwise requires,—

(a) “contempt of court” means civil contempt or criminal contempt;

(b) “civil contempt” means wilful disobedience to any judgment, decree, direction, order, writ or other process of a court or wilful breach of an undertaking given to a court;

(c) “criminal contempt” means the publication (whether

by words, spoken or written, or by signs, or by visible representations, or otherwise) of any matter or the doing of any other act whatsoever which:

(i) scandalises or tends to scandalise, or lowers or tends to lower the authority of, any court; or

(ii) prejudices, or interferes or tends to interfere with, the due course of any judicial proceeding; or

(iii) interferes or tends to interfere with, or obstructs or tends to obstruct, the administration of justice in any other manner;

(d) "High Court" means the High Court for a State or a Union territory, and includes the court of the Judicial Commissioner in any Union territory.

3. Innocent publication and distribution of matter not contempt

(1) A person shall not be guilty of contempt of court on the ground that he has published (whether by words, spoken or written, or by signs, or by visible representations, or otherwise) any matter which interferes or tends to interfere with, or obstructs or tends to obstruct, the course of justice in connection with any civil or criminal proceeding pending at the time of publications, if at that time he had no reasonable grounds for believing that the proceeding was pending.

(2) Notwithstanding anything to the contrary contained in this Act or any other law for the time being in force, the publication of any such matter as is mentioned in sub-section (1) in connection with any civil or criminal proceeding which is not pending at the time of publication shall not be deemed to constitute contempt of court.

(3) A person shall not be guilty of contempt of court on the ground that he has distributed a publication containing any such matter as is mentioned in sub-section (1), if at the time of distribution he had no reasonable grounds for believing that it contained or was likely to contain any such matter as aforesaid:

Provided that this sub-section shall not apply in respect of the distribution of:

(i) any publication which is a book or paper printed or

published otherwise than in conformity with the rules contained in section 3 of the Press and Registration of Books Act, 1867;

(ii) any publication which is a newspaper published otherwise than in conformity with the rules contained in section 5 of the said Act.

Explanation. For the purposes of this section, a judicial proceeding:

(a) is said to be pending:

(A) in the case of a civil proceeding, when it is instituted by the filing of a plaint or otherwise.

(B) in the case of a criminal proceeding under the Code of Criminal Procedure, 1898, or any other law:

(i) where it relates to the commission of an offence, when the chargesheet or *challan* is filed, or when the court issues summons or warrant, as the case may be, against the accused, and

(ii) in any other case, when the court takes cognizance of the matter to which the proceeding relates, and

in the case of a civil or criminal proceeding, shall be deemed to continue to be pending until it is heard and finally decided, that is to say, in a case where an appeal or revision is competent, until the appeal or revision is heard and finally decided or, where no appeal or revision is preferred, until the period of limitation prescribed for such appeal or revision has expired;

(b) which has been heard and finally decided shall not be deemed to be pending merely by reason of the fact that proceedings for the execution of the decree, order or sentence passed therein are pending.

4. Fair and accurate report of judicial proceeding not contempt

Subject to the provisions contained in section 7, a person shall not be guilty of contempt of court for publishing a fair and accurate report of a judicial proceeding or any stage thereof.

5. Fair criticism of judicial act not contempt

A person shall not be guilty of contempt of court for publishing any fair comment on the merits of any case which has been heard and finally decided.

6. Complaint against presiding officers of subordinate courts when not contempt

A person shall not be guilty of contempt of court in respect of any statement made by him in good faith concerning the presiding officer of any subordinate court to:

(a) any other subordinate court, or

(b) the High Court,

to which it is subordinate.

Explanation. In this section, "subordinate court" means any court subordinate to a High Court.

7. Publication of information relating to proceedings in chambers or in camera not contempt in certain cases

(1) Notwithstanding anything contained in this Act, a person shall not be guilty of contempt of court for publishing a fair and accurate report of a judicial proceeding before any court sitting in chambers or *in camera* except in the following cases that is to say:

(a) where the publication is contrary to the provisions of any enactment for the time being in force;

(b) where the court, on ground of public policy or in exercise of any power vested in it, expressly prohibits the publication of all information relating to the proceeding or of information of the description which is published;

(c) where the court sits in chambers or *in camera* for reasons connected with public order or the security of the State, the publication of information relating to those proceedings;

(d) where the information relates to a secret process, discovery or invention which is an issue in the proceedings.

(2) Without prejudice to the provisions contained in sub-section (1), a person shall not be guilty of contempt of court

for publishing the text or a fair and accurate summary of the whole, or any part, of an order made by a court sitting in chambers or *in camera*, unless the court has expressly prohibited the publication thereof on grounds of public policy, or for reasons connected with public order or the security of the State, or on the ground that it contains information relating to a secret process, discovery or invention, or in exercise of any power vested in it.

8. Other defence not affected

Nothing contained in this Act shall be construed as implying that any other defence which would have been a valid defence in any proceedings for contempt of court has ceased to be available merely by reason of the provisions of this Act.

9. Act not to imply enlargement of scope of contempt

Nothing contained in this Act shall be construed as implying that any disobedience, breach, publication or other act is punishable as contempt of court which would not be so punishable apart from this Act.

10. Power of High Court to punish contempts of subordinate courts

Every High Court shall have and exercise the same jurisdiction, powers and authority, in accordance with the same procedure and practice, in respect of contempts of courts subordinate to it as it has and exercises in respect of contempts of itself:

Provided that no High Court shall take cognizance of a contempt alleged to have been committed in respect of a court subordinate to it where such contempt is an offence punishable under the Indian Penal Code.

11. Power of High Court to try offences committed or offenders found outside jurisdiction

A High Court shall have jurisdiction to inquire into or try a contempt of itself or of any court subordinate to it, whether the contempt is alleged to have been committed within or outside the local limits of its jurisdiction, and whether the person alleged to be guilty of contempt is within or outside such limits.

12. Punishment for contempt of court

(1) Save as otherwise expressly provided in this Act or in any other law, a contempt of court may be punished with simple imprisonment for a term which may extend to six months, or with fine which may extend to two thousand rupees, or with both:

Provided that the accused may be discharged or the punishment awarded may be remitted on apology being made to the satisfaction of the court.

Explanation. An apology shall not be rejected merely on the ground that it is qualified or conditional if the accused makes it *bona fide.*

(2) Notwithstanding anything contained in any law for the time being in force, no court shall impose a sentence in excess of that specified in sub-section (1) for any contempt either in respect of itself or of a court subordinate to it.

(3) Notwithstanding anything contained in this section, where a person is found guilty of a civil contempt, the court, if it considers that a fine will not meet the ends of justice and that a sentence of imprisonment is necessary shall, instead of sentencing him to simple imprisonment, direct that he be detained in a civil prison for such period not exceeding six months as it may think fit.

(4) Where the person found guilty of contempt of court in respect of any undertaking given to a court is a company, every person who, at the time the contempt was committed, was in charge of, and was responsible to, the company for the conduct of the business of the company, as well as the company, shall be deemed to be guilty of the contempt and the punishment may be enforced, with the leave of the court, by the detention in civil prison of each such person:

Provided that nothing contained in this sub-section shall render any such person liable to such punishment if he proves that the contempt was committed without his knowledge or that he exercised all due diligence to prevent its commission.

(5) Notwithstanding anything contained in sub-section (4), where the contempt of court referred to therein has been committed by a company and it is proved that the contempt

has been committed with the consent or connivance of, or is attributable to any neglect on the part of, any director, manager, secretary or other officer of the company, such director, manager, secretary or other officer shall also be deemed to be guilty of the contempt and the punishment may be enforced, with the leave of the court, by the detention in civil prison of such director, manager, secretary or other officer.

Explanation. For the purpose of sub-sections (4) and (5),—

(a) "company" means any body corporate and includes a firm or other association of individuals; and

(b) "director" in relation to a firm, means a partner in the firm.

13. Contempt not punishable in certain cases

Notwithstanding anything contained in any law for the time being in force, no court shall impose a sentence under this Act for a contempt of court unless it is satisfied that the contempt is of such a nature that it substantially interferes, or tends substantially to interfere with the due course of justice.

14. Procedure where contempt is in the face of the Supreme Court or a High Court

(1) When it is alleged, or appears to the Supreme Court or the High Court upon its own view, that a person has been guilty of contempt committed in its presence or hearing, the Court may cause such person to be detained in custody, and, at any time before the rising of the Court, on the same day, or as early as possible thereafter, shall:

(a) cause him to be informed in writing of the contempt with which he is charged;

(b) afford him an opportunity to make his defence to the charge;

(c) after taking such evidence as may be necessary or as may be offered by such person and after hearing him, proceed, either forthwith or after adjournment, to determine the matter of the charge; and

(d) make such order for the punishment or discharge of such person as may be just.

(2) Notwithstanding anything contained in sub-section (1), where a person charged with contempt under that sub-section

applies, whether orally or in writing, to have the charge against him tried by some Judge other than the Judge or Judges in whose presence or hearing the offence is alleged to have been committed, and the Court is of opinion that it is practicable to do so and that in the interest of proper administration of justice the application should be allowed, it shall cause the matter to be placed, together with a statement of the facts of the case, before the Chief Justice for such directions as he may think fit to issue as respects the trial thereof.

(3) Notwithstanding anything contained in any other law, in any trial of a person charged with contempt under sub-section (1) which is held, in pursuance of a direction given under sub-section (2), by a Judge other than the Judge or Judges in whose presence or hearing the offence is alleged to have been committed, it shall not be necessary for the Judge or Judges in whose presence or hearing the offence is alleged to have been committed to appear as a witness and the statement placed before the Chief Justice under sub-section (2) shall be treated as evidence in the case.

(4) Pending the determination of the charge, the Court may direct that a person charged with contempt under this section shall be detained in such custody as it may specify:

Provided that he shall be released on bail, if a bond for such sum of money as the Court thinks sufficient is executed with or without sureties conditioned that the person charged shall attend at the time and place mentioned in the bond and shall continue to so attend until otherwise directed by the Court:

Provided further that the Court may, if it thinks fit, instead of taking bail from such person, discharge him on his executing a bond without sureties for his attendance as aforesaid.

15. Cognizance of criminal contempt in other cases

(1) In the case of a criminal contempt, other than a contempt referred to in section 14, the Supreme Court or the High Court may take action on its own motion or on a motion made by:

(a) the Advocate-General, or

(b) any other person, with the consent in writing of the Advocate-General, [or

(c) in relation to the High Court for the Union territory of Delhi, such Law Officer as the Central Government may, by notification in the Official Gagette, specify in this behalf, or any other person, with the consent in writing of such Law Officer].*

(2) In the case of any criminal contempt of a subordinate court, the High Court may take action on a reference made to it by the subordinate court or on a motion made by the Advocate-General, or in relation to a Union territory, by such Law Officer as the Central Government may, by notification in the Official Gazette, specify in this behalf.

(3) Every motion or reference made under this section shall specify the contempt of which the person charged is alleged to be guilty.

Explanation. In this section, the expression "Advocate-General" means,—

(a) in relation to the Supreme Court, the Attorney-General or the Solicitor-General;

(b) in relation to the High Court, the Advocate-General of the State or any of the States for which the High Court has been established;

(c) in relation to the Court of Judicial Commissioner, such Law Officer as the Central Government may, by notification in the Official Gazette, specify in this behalf.

16. Contempt by judge, magistrate or other person acting judicially

(1) Subject to the provisions of any law for the time being in force, a judge, magistrate or other person acting judicially shall also be liable for contempt of his own court or of any other court in the same manner as any other individual is liable and the provisions of this Act shall, so far as may be, apply accordingly.

(2) Nothing in this section shall apply to any observations or remarks made by a judge, magistrate or other person acting judicially, regarding a subordinate court in an appeal or revision

---

* Inserted by Act 45 of 1976, section 2 (30-6-1976).

pending before such judge, magistrate or other person against the order or judgment of the subordinate court.

17. Procedure after cognizance

(1) Notice of every proceeding under section 15 shall be served personally on the person charged, unless the Court for reasons to be recorded directs otherwise.

(2) The notice shall be accompanied,—

(a) in the case of proceedings commenced on a motion, by a copy of the motion as also copies of the affidavits, if any, on which such motion is founded; and

(b) in the case of proceedings commenced on a reference by a subordinate court, by a copy of the reference.

(3) The Court may, if it is satisfied that a person charged under section 15 is likely to abscond or keep out of the way to avoid service of the notice, order the attachment of his property of such value or amount as it may deem reasonable.

(4) Every attachment under sub-section (3) shall be effected in the manner provided in the Code of Civil Procedure, 1908, for the attachment of property in execution of a decree for payment of money, and if, after such attachment, the person charged appears and shows to the satisfaction of the Court that he did not abscond or keep out of the way to avoid service of the notice, the Court shall order the release of his property from attachment upon such terms as to costs or otherwise as it may think fit.

(5) Any person charged with contempt under section 15 may file an affidavit in support of his defence, and the Court may determine the matter of the charge either on the affidavits filed or after taking such further evidence as may be necessary, and pass such order as the justice of the case requires.

18. Hearing of cases of criminal contempt to be by Benches

(1) Every case of criminal contempt under section 15 shall be heard and determined by a Bench of not less than two Judges.

(2) Sub-section (1) shall not apply to the Court of a Judicial Commissioner.

19. Appeals

(1) An appeal shall lie as of right from any order or decision of a High Court in the exercise of its jurisdiction to punish for contempt:

(a) where the order or decision is that of a single judge, to a Bench of not less than two Judges of the Court;

(b) where the order or decision is that of a Bench, to the Supreme Court:

Provided that where the order or decision is that of the Court of the Judicial Commissioner in any Union territory, such appeal shall lie to the Supreme Court.

(2) Pending any appeal, the appellate Court may order that:

(a) the execution of the punishment or order appealed against be suspended;

(b) if the appellant is in confinement, he be released on bail; and

(c) the appeal be heard notwithstanding that the appellant has not purged his contempt.

(3) Where any person aggrieved by any order against which an appeal may be filed satisfies the High Court that he intends to prefer an appeal, the High Court may also exercise all or any of the powers conferred by sub-section (2).

(4) An appeal under sub-section (1) shall be filed:

(a) in the case of an appeal to a Bench of the High Court, within thirty days;

(b) in the case of an appeal to the Supreme Court, within sixty days, from the date of the order appealed against.

20. Limitation for actions for contempt

No court shall initiate any proceedings for contempt either on its own motion or otherwise, after the expiry of a period of one year from the date on which the contempt is alleged to have been committed.

21. Act not to apply to Nyaya Panchayats or other village courts

Nothing contained in this Act shall apply in relation to contempt of *Nyaya Panchayats* or other village courts, by whatever name known, for the administration of justice, established under any law.

22. Act to be in addition to, and not in derogation of, other laws relating to contempt

The provisions of this Act shall be in addition to, and not in derogation of, the provisions of any other law relating to contempt of courts.

23. Power of Supreme Court and High Courts to make rules

The Supreme Court or, as the case may be, any High Court, may make rules, not inconsistent with the provisions of this Act, for any matter relating to its procedure.

24. Repeal

The Contempt of Courts Act, 1952, is hereby repealed.

Appendix 2

The Contempt of Court Act 1981 (1981 c 49)

ARRANGEMENT OF SECTIONS

THE CONTEMPT OF COURT ACT, 1981 (1981 C 49)

An Act to amend the laws relating to contempt of court and related matters. [27*th July* 1981]

Northern Ireland. This Act, except ss 15 and 17, and Schs 2 and 3, post, applies subject to the modifications made by s 18 and Sch 4, post; see s 21(5), post.

Strict liability

1. The strict liability rule. In this Act "the strict liability rule" means the rule of law whereby conduct may be treated as a contempt of court as tending to interfere with the course of justice in particular legal proceedings regardless of intent to do so.

2. Limitation of scope of strict liability. (1) The strict liability rule applies only in relation to publications, and for this purpose "publication" includes any speech, writing, broadcast or other communication in whatever form, which is addressed to the public at large or any section of the public.

(2) The strict liability rule applies only to a publication which creates a substantial risk that the course of justice in the proceedings in question will be seriously impeded or prejudiced.

(3) The strict liability rule applies to a publication only if the proceedings in question are active within the meaning of this section at the time of the publication.

(4) Schedule 1 applies for determining the times at which

proceedings are to be treated as active within the meaning of this section.

3. Defence of innocent publication or distribution. (1) A person is not guilty of contempt of court under the strict liability rule as the publisher of any matter to which that rule applies if at the time of publication (having taken all reasonable care) he does not know and has no reason to suspect that relevant proceedings are active.

(2) A person is not guilty of contempt of court under the strict liability rule as the distributor of a publication containing any such matter if at the time of distribution (having taken all reasonable care) he does not know that it contains such matter and has no reason to suspect that it is likely to do so.

(3) The burden of proof of any fact tending to establish a defence afforded by this section to any person lies upon that person.

(4) Section 11 of the Administration of Justice Act, 1960 is repealed.

4. Contemporary reports of proceedings. (1) Subject to this section a person is not guilty of contempt of court under the strict liability rule in respect of a fair and accurate report of legal proceedings held in public, published contemporaneously and in good faith.

(2) In any such proceedings the court may, where it appears to be necessary for avoiding a substantial risk of prejudice to the administration of justice in those proceedings, or in any other proceedings pending or imminent, order that the publication of any report of the proceedings, or any part of the proceedings, be postponed for such period as the court thinks necessary for that purpose.

(3) For the purposes of sub-section (1) of this section and of section 3 of the Law of Libel Amendment Act, 1888 (privilege) a report of proceedings shall be treated as published contemporaneously:

(a) in the case of a report of which publication is postponed pursuant to an order under sub-section (2) of this section, if published as soon as practicable after that order expires;

(b) in the case of a report of committal proceedings of which publication is permitted by virtue only of sub-section (3) of section 8 of the Magistrates' Courts Act, 1980, if published as soon as practicable after publication is so permitted.

(4) Sub-section (9) of the said section 8 is repealed.

5. Discussion of public affairs. A publication made as or as part of a discussion in good faith of public affairs or other matters of general public interest is not to be treated as a contempt of court under the strict liability rule if the risk of impediment or prejudice to particular legal proceedings is merely incidental to the discussion.

6. Savings. Nothing in the foregoing provisions of this Act:

(a) prejudices any defence available at common law to a charge of contempt of court under the strict liability rule;

(b) implies that any publication is punishable as contempt of court under that rule which would not be so punishable apart from those provisions;

(c) restricts liability for contempt of court in respect of conduct intended to impede or prejudice the administration of justice.

7. Consent required for institution of proceedings. Proceedings for a contempt of court under the strict liability rule (other than Scottish proceedings) shall not be instituted except by or with the consent of the Attorney General or on the motion of a court having jurisdiction to deal with it.

Other aspects of law and procedure

8. Confidentiality of jury's deliberations. (1) Subject to sub-section (2) below, it is a contempt of court to obtain, disclose or solicit any particulars of statements made, opinions expressed, arguments advanced or votes cast by members of a jury in the course of their deliberations in any legal proceedings.

(2) This section does not apply to any disclosure of any particulars:

(a) in the proceedings in question for the purpose of

enabling the jury to arrive at their verdict, or in connection with the delivery of that verdict, or

(b) in evidence in any subsequent proceedings for an offence alleged to have been committed in relation to the jury in the first mentioned proceedings.

or to the publication of any particulars so disclosed.

(3) Proceedings for a contempt of court under this section (other than Scottish proceedings) shall not be instituted except by or with the consent of the Attorney General or on the motion of a court having jurisdiction to deal with it.

9. Use of tape recorders. (1) Subject to sub-section (4) below, it is a contempt of court:

(a) to use in court, or bring into court for use, any tape recorder or other instrument for recording sound, except with the leave of the court;

(b) to publish a recording of legal proceedings made by means of any such instrument, or any recording derived directly or indirectly from it, by playing it in the hearing of the public or any section of the public, or to dispose of it or any recording so derived, with a view to such publication;

(c) to use any such recording in contravention of any conditions of leave granted under paragraph (a).

(2) Leave under paragraph (a) of sub-section (1) may be granted or refused at the discretion of the court, and if granted may be granted subject to such conditions as the court thinks proper with respect to the use of any recording made pursuant to the leave; and where leave has been granted the court may at the like discretion withdraw or amend it either generally or in relation to any particular part of the proceedings.

(3) Without prejudice to any other power to deal with an act of contempt under paragraph (a) of sub-section (1), the court may order the instrument, or any recording made with it, or both, to be forfeited; and any object so forfeited shall (unless the court otherwise determines on application by a person appearing to be the owner) be sold or otherwise disposed of in such manner as the court may direct.

(4) This section does not apply to the making or use of

sound recordings for purposes of official transcripts of proceedings.

10. Sources of information. No court may require a person to disclose, nor is any person guilty of contempt of court for refusing to disclose, the source of information contained in a publication for which he is responsible, unless it be established to the satisfaction of the court that disclosure is necessary in the interests of justice or national security or for the prevention of disorder or crime.

11. Publication of matters exempted from disclosure in court. In any case where a court (having power to do so) allows a name or other matter to be withheld from the public in proceedings before the court, the court may give such directions prohibiting the publication of that name or matter in connection with the proceedings as appear to the court to be necessary for the purpose for which it was so withheld.

12. Offences of contempt of magistrates' court. (1) A Magistrates' court has jurisdiction under this section to deal with any person who:

(a) wilfully insults the justice or justices, any witness before or officer of the court or any solicitor or counsel having business in the court, during his or their sitting or attendance in court or in going to or returning from the court; or

(b) wilfully interrupts the proceedings of the court or otherwise misbehaves in court.

(2) In any such case the court may order any officer of the court, or any constable, to take the offender into custody and detain him until the rising of the court; and the court may, if it thinks fit, commit the offender to custody for a specified period not exceeding one month or impose on him a fine not exceeding £500, or both.

(3) The court shall not deal with the offender by making an order under section 19 of the Criminal Justice Act, 1948 (an attendance centre order) if it appears to the court, after considering any available evidence, that he is under 17 years of age.

(4) A magistrates' court may at any time revoke an order

of committal made under sub-section (2) and, if the offender is in custody, order his discharge.

(5) The following provisions of the Magistrates' Courts Act, 1980 apply in relation to an order under this section as they apply in relation to a sentence on conviction or finding of guilty of an offence, namely: section 36 (restriction on fines in respect of young persons); sections 75 to 91 (enforcement); section 108 (appeal to Crown Court); section 136 (overnight detention in default of payment); and section 142(1) (power to rectify mistakes).

13. Legal aid. (1) in any case where a person is liable to be committed or fined:

(a) by a magistrates' court under section 12 of this Act;

(b) by a county court under section 30, 127 or 157 of the County Courts Act, 1959; or

(c) by any superior court for contempt in the face of that or any other court,

the court may order that he shall be given legal aid for the purposes of the proceedings.

(2) Where an order under sub-section (1) is made by any court, the court may order that the legal aid to be given shall consist of representation by counsel only or, in any court where solicitors have a right of audience, by a solicitor only; and the court may assign for the purpose any counsel or solicitor who is within the precincts of the court at the time when the order is made.

(3) Part II of the Legal Aid Act, 1974 shall have effect subject to the amendments set out in Part I of Schedule 2, being amendments consequential on the foregoing provisions of this section.

(4) Scotland.

(5) This section is without prejudice to any other enactment by virtue of which legal aid may be granted in or for purposes of civil or criminal proceedings.

Penalties for contempt and kindred offences

14. Proceeding in England and Wales. (1) In any case where a court has power to commit a person to prison for contempt of court and (apart from this provision) no limitation applies to the period of committal, the committal shall (without prejudice to the power of the court to order his earlier discharge) be for a fixed term, and that term shall not on any occasion exceed two years in the case of committal by a superior court, or one month in the case of committal by an inferior court.

(2) In any case where an inferior court has power to fine a person for contempt of court and (apart from this provision) no limit applies to the amount of the fine, the fine shall not on any occasion exceed £500.

(3) In relation to the exercise of jurisdiction to commit for contempt of court or any kindred offence, sub-section (1) of section 19 of the Powers of Criminal Courts Act, 1973 (prohibition of imprisonment of persons under seventeen years of age) shall apply to all courts having that jurisdiction as it applies to the Crown Court and magistrates' courts.

(4) Each of the superior courts shall have the like power to make a hospital order or guardianship order under section 60 of the Mental Health Act, 1959 in the case of a person suffering from mental illness or severe subnormality who could otherwise be committed to prison for contempt of court as the Crown Court has under that section in the case of a person convicted of an offence.

(5) The enactments specified in Part III of Schedule 2 shall have effect subject to the amendments set out in that Part, being amendments relating to the penalties and procedure in respect of certain offences of contempt in coroners' courts, county courts and magistrates' courts.

15. Scotland.

16. Enforcement of fines imposed by certain superior courts. (1) Payment of a fine for contempt of court imposed by a superior court, other than the Crown Court or one of the courts specified in sub-section (4) below, may be enforced upon the order of the court:

(a) in like manner as a judgment of the High Court for the payment of money; or

(b) in like manner as a fine imposed by the Crown Court.

(2) Where payment of a fine imposed by any court falls to be enforced as mentioned in paragraph (a) of sub-section (1):

(a) the court shall, if the fine is not paid in full forthwith or within such time as the court may allow, certify to Her Majesty's Remembrancer the sum payable;

(b) Her Majesty's Remembrancer shall thereupon proceed to enforce payment of that sum as if it were due to him as a judgment debt; and

(c) any payment received in respect of the fine shall be dealt with by him in the manner for the time being prescribed under section 28 of the Fines Act, 1833 for receipts within that section.

(3) Where payment of a fine imposed by any court falls to be enforced as mentioned in paragraph (b) of sub-section (1), the provisions of sections 31 and 32 of the Powers of Criminal Courts Act, 1973 shall apply as they apply to a fine imposed by the Crown Court.

(4) Sub-section (1) of this section does not apply to fines imposed by the criminal division of the Court of Appeal or by the House of Lords on appeal from that division.

(5) The Fines Act, 1833 shall not apply to a fine to which sub-section (1) of this section applies.

(6) Repeals.

17. Disobedience to certain orders of magistrates' courts. (1) The powers of a magistrates' court under sub-section (3) of section 63 of the Magistrates' Courts Act, 1980 (punishment by fine or committal for disobeying an order to do anything other than the payment of money or to abstain from doing anything) may be exercised either on the court's own motion or by order on complaint.

(2) In relation to the exercise of those powers the provisions of the Magistrates' Court Act, 1980 shall apply subject to the modifications set out in Schedule 3 to this Act.

Supplemental

18. Northern Ireland.

19. Interpretation. In this Act:

"court" includes any tribunal or body exercising the judicial power of the State, and "legal proceedings" shall be construed accordingly;

"publication" has the meaning assigned by sub-section (1) of section 2, and "publish" (except in section 9) shall be construed accordingly;

"Scottish proceedings" means proceedings before any court, including the Courts-Martial Appeal Court, the Restrictive Practices Court and the Employment Appeal Tribunal, sitting in Scotland, and includes proceedings before the House of Lords in the exercise of any appellate jurisdiction over proceedings in such a court;

"the strict liability rule" has the meaning assigned by section 1;

"superior court" means the Court of Appeal, the High Court, the Crown Court, the Courts-Martial Appeal Court, the Restrictive Practices Court, the Employment Appeal Tribunal and any other court exercising in relation to its proceedings powers equivalent to those of the High Court, and includes the House of Lords in the exercise of its appellate jurisdiction.

20. Tribunals of Inquiry.

SCHEDULES

not printed.

Table of Cases

A. Dharmarajan v. *Collector of Kamarajar District, Virudhunagar* 1994 Cri. L.J. (Madras High Court) 3585.

A. Haleem v. *M.S. Tajudeen* AIR 1995 S.C. 260.

A.K. Jain and another v. *State of Sikkim* AIR 1992 Sikkim 20.

A.K. Prakash, In re 1995 Cri. L.J. (Kerala High Court) 1663.

A.N. Jindel v. *P.L. Chhabra* AIR 1969 Del. 291.

Advocate General, Andhra Pradesh, Hyderabad v. *Abbaraju Ramarao* AIR 1968 A.P. 207.

Advocate General, Andhra Pradesh v. *Vankadaru Laxmi Narayan Tobacco Merchant Eluru W. Godawari* AIR 1968 Andh. Pra. 370.

Advocate General, Andhra Pradesh v. *Ashok Kumar, Inspector of Police* 1994 Cri. L.J. (Andhra Pradesh High Court) 1333.

Advocate General, Kerala v. *Abraham George* 1976 Cri. L.J. (Kerala High Court) 158.

Advocate General, Orissa v. *Baradakanta Misra* 1974 Cri. L.J. (Orissa High Court) 70.

Advocate General, Madras v. *S. Sundaram Ex Sub-Inspector of Police Illuppur, Tiruchirappalli Dist.* AIR 1965 Mad. 336.

Advocate General of Sikkim v. *Ashok Kumar Subba* 1994 Cri. L.J. (Sikkim High Court) 3555.

Alarakha Hasan Hamirkha v. *Keshavlal Dhaneshwar Dwivedi and others* AIR 1956 Saurashtra 102.

Afzal v. *State of Haryana* AIR 1996 Supreme Court, 2326.

Amalgamated Electricity Co. (Belgium) Ltd. v. *Municipal Committee Ajmer* AIR 1969 S.C. 227.

Amarnath v. *Municipal Corporation of Delhi* 1981 Cri. L.J. (Delhi High Court) 1880.

Amarnath Sawan Mal v. *Joginder Singh and others* AIR 1961 Punj. 18.

Amar Bahadur Singh, S/o Girija Singh Kushwaha v. *P.D.Wasnik* 1994 Cri. L.J. (Bombay High Court) 1359.

Ananta Lal Singh and others v. *Alfred Henry Watson and others* AIR 1931 Cal. 257.

Andre Paul Terence Ambard v. *The Attorney General of Trinidad and Tobago* AIR 1936 P.C. 141.

Arts and Commerce College, Pen, District Raigad v. *State of Maharashtra* 1994 Cri. L.J. (Bombay High Court) 172.

Arun Kshetrapal v. *Registrar High Court, Orissa* AIR 1976 S.C. 1967.

Asgharali v. *Motilal Dave and others* 1966 Cri. L.J. (Madhya Pradesh High Court) 214.

Asharam M. Jain v. *A.T. Gupta and others* AIR 1983 S.C. 1151.

Ashok Baherwani v. *Ishwar Prakash Chopra* 1988 Cri. L.J. (Bombay High Court at Nagpur) 1530.

Ashok Kumar Singh v. *State of Bihar* AIR 1992 S.C. 407.

Asoka Kumar Sarkar v. *Radhakanto Pandey* AIR 1967 Cal. 178.

Aswini Kumar Rath and others v. *P.C. Mukherjee and others* AIR 1965 Cal. 484.

Attorney General v. *Times News Papers Ltd.*, (1973) 3 All. E.R. 54.

Attorney General v. *Times News Papers Ltd.*, (1973) 3 All. E.R. 1136.

Attorney General v. *Times News Papers Ltd.*, (1972) 1 All. E.R. 815.

Awadh Narain Singh v. *Jwala Prasad Singh and others* AIR 1956 Pat. 321.

B. Himmat Sinka v. *M/s. Kuldip Industrial Corporation* 1981 Cri. L.J. (Himachal Pradesh High Court) 1414.

B.A. Rather v. *H.K. Dua* 1994 Cri. L.J. (Jammu and Kashmir High Court) 3414.

B.K. Kar v. *Hon'ble Chief Justice and his companion justices of the Orissa High Court* AIR 1961 S.C. 1367.

B.M. Bhattacharjee v. *Russel Estate Corporation* AIR 1993 S.C. 1632.

B.V. Nagvekar v. *Municipal Commissioner Mangalore City Municipality, Mangalore* Vol. XIV. The Madras Law Journal Reports (Criminal) 139.

Babulal Shukla v. *Shivpratap Singh* AIR 1957 Madhya Pradesh 152.

Babu Ram Gupta v. *Sudhir Bhasin* AIR 1979 S.C. 1528.

Badrilal v. *Prahlad Datta,* AIR 1955 NOC Madhya Pradesh 3758.

Bahri v. *Emperor* AIR 1926 All. 263.

Bajranglal Gangadhar Khemka v. *Kapurchand Ltd.* AIR 1950 Bombay 336.

Baker v. *Queen* 1975 A.C. 774.

Bala Chandra Gangadhar Ghate v. *Pralhad Saduji Raghute and others* 1977 Cri. L.J. (Bombay High Court) 1490.

Bankin Chandra Paira v. *Ananda Bazar Patrika* AIR 1950 Calcutta 129.

Balaram Singh v. *Bhikam Chand Jain* AIR 1985 S.C. 1726.

Bapusaheb Bala Saheb Patil and others v. *The State of Maharashtra and others* AIR 1975 Bombay 143.

Baradakanta Mishra v. *Registrar Orissa High Court,* AIR 1974 S.C. 710.

Baradakanta Mishra v. *Chief Justice Orissa High Court,* AIR 1974 Orissa 1.

Baros v. *Bethal* (1982) 1 All. E.R. 106.

Bathina Ramakrishna Reddy v. *State of Madras* (1952)1 M.L.J. 736.

Bhramerbar Sar Sanmatra v. *State of Orissa,* AIR 1970 Orissa 141.

Brahma Prakash Sharma and others v. *State of U.P.* XVI Supreme Court Journal 1953 S.C. 521.

Brig. E.T. Sen (Retd.) Petitioner v. *Edatata Narayanan and others* AIR 1969 Del. 201.

Bukhtiarpur-Bihar Light Rly. Co. Ltd. v. *State of Bihar and others* AIR (38) 1951 Pat. 231.

Bunna Prasad v. *The State of U.P.* AIR 1963 S.C. 1348.

C. Hariprasad v. *G. Vasantha Pai* AIR 1966 Madras 136.

C.N. Presannan, Judl. Second Class Magistrate, Cochin v. *K.A. Mohammed Ali, Adv. Cochin* 1991 Cri. L.J. (Kerala High Court) 2194.

Captain Dushyant Somal v. *Smt. Sushama Somal* 1981 Cri. L.J. (Supreme Court) 719.

Captain Virender Kumar v. *Union of India* AIR 1994 S.C. 1711.

Chhaganbhai Norsinbhai v. *Soni Chandubhai Gordhan Bhai* AIR 1976 S.C. 1909.

Chintamani Palai v. *State* AIR 1952 Ori. 167.

Chunnilal Ken v. *Shyamlal Sukhram and other* AIR 1959 Madhya Pradesh 50.

Commissioner, Agra v. *Rohtas Singh* AIR 1998 Supreme Court 685.

Court on its own motion v. *H.L. Seghal* 1997 Cr. L.J. (Delhi High Court) 1472.

Court on its own motion v. *Kasthurilal and another* AIR 1980 P. and H. 72.

Court on its own motion v. *N.S. Kanwar* 1995 Cri. L.J. (Punjab and Haryana High Court) 1261.

Court on its own motion v. *Sukhvinder Singh* AIR 1981 P. and H. 361.

Court on its own motion v. *Bansilal and others* 1979 Cri. L.J. NOC 165.

Crown v. *Amin-ud-Din-Sahrait* AIR 1949 Lah. 266.

D. Jones Shield v. *N. Ramesan and others* 1955 Cri. L.J. (Andhra Pradesh High Court) 1028.

Dalpatraj Bhandari v. *The President of India* AIR 1993 Raj. 1.

Dayaram v. *Goverdhan* ILR 28 Bom. 458.

Debabrata Bandopadhyay v. *State of West Bengal* AIR 1969 Supreme Court 189.

Deben Adhicary v. *State of West Bengal and others* AIR 1972 Cal. 84.

Debi Prasad Sharma and others v. *Emperor* AIR 1936 P.C. 141.

Dibakar Satpathy v. *Hon'ble the Chief Justice and his companion justices of the Orissa High Court* AIR 1961 S.C. 1315.

Dinesh A. Parikh v. *Kripalu Co-operative Housing Society, Nagarvel Ahmedabad* AIR 1980 Gujarat 194.

District Magistrate, Bidar v. *R. Madhava Rao* AIR 1961 Mys. 12.

Diwan Durga Das v. *B.R. Kishore and others* AIR 1959 All. 211.

Dr. Dhukan Ram and another v. *State of Bihar and others* AIR 1972 Pat. 465.

Dr. Laxmi Narain v. *Jia Lal Jain* AIR 1975 All. 213.

Dr. Rohit Gupta v. *The Principal, S.N. Medical College, Agra* AIR 1995 All. 152.

Dr. (Mrs.) Roshan Sam Joyce v. *S.R. Cotton Mills Ltd.* AIR 1990 S.C. 1881.

Dr. Subhash Chandra Pratihar v. *Mrs. Leena Chakraborty* 1995 Cri. L.J. (Calcutta High Court) 707.

Dulal Chandra Bhar v. *Sukumar Banerjee* AIR 1958 Cal. 474.

Dwarka Prasad Agarwal v. *Krishna Chandra and others* AIR 1953 All. 600.

Delhi Water Supply and Sewage Disposal Undertaking v. *State of Haryana* AIR 1996 Supreme Court 2992.

Devi Lal v. *Mohan Prasad* (1996) 5 Supreme Court Cases 378.

Delhi Development Authority v. *Skipper Construction Co. (P) Ltd.* AIR 1996 (Supreme Court) 2005.

E. v. *Balakrishna Govinda Kulkarni* AIR 1922 Bombay 52.

E.M. Sankaran Namboodiripad v. *T. Narayanan Nambiar* AIR 1970 S.C. 2015.

E.V. Ramaswami, Leader Dravida Kazhagam v. *Jawaharlal Nehru* AIR 1958 Mad. 558.

Emperor v. *Mahashe Khushal Chand and another* AIR (32) 1945 Lah. 206.

Emperor v. *Murli Manohar Prasad and others* AIR 1929 Pat. 72.

Ex parte Langley; Ex parte Smith, In re Bishop (1879) Ch. D. Vol. XIII, p. 110.

Express News Papers Ltd. New Delhi v. *M/s. Raisina Publications Private Ltd.* AIR 1964 Punjab 428.

Fatima Begum v. *The Commissioner of the Hyderabad Municipal Corporation* AIR 1958 A.P. 170.

First National Bank Ltd. (in liquidation) through official liquidator v. *Dr. Kali Charan* AIR 1959 Punjab 627.

G.G. Suryakant v. *M/s. Leema Resorts Pvt. Ltd.* 1994 Cri. L.J. (Madras High Court) 724.

G.N. Verma v. *Hargovind Dayal and others* AIR 1975 All. 52.

Giani Ram v. *Ramnath Dutt* AIR 1955 Raj. 123.

Gokulananda Roy v. *Tarapada Mukherjee and others* AIR 1973 Cal. 233.

Gouri Shankar Jain v. *State of Bihar and another* 1973 Cri. L.J. (Patna High Court) 137.

Gour Gopal Dutt v. *Smt. Shantilata Mitra* AIR 1976 Cal. 475.

Government Pleader v. *Mathai Manjooran and another* AIR 1959 Ker. 266.

Govind Sahai v. *State of U.P.* AIR 1968 S.C. 1513.

Gurbachand Singh Lachhman Singh v. *Ch. Hoshiar Singh and another* AIR 1959 Punjab 205.

Gurbakhsh Singh v. *S. Pratap Singh and another* AIR 1959 Punjab 182.

Guru Charan Das Chadha v. *State of Rajasthan* AIR 1966 S.C. 1418.

Gyan Chand v. *Ramesh Chand* 1985 Cri. L.J. (Allahabad High Court)1907.

H.P. Singh v. *Thakur Prasad Tewari and another* AIR 1953 S.C. 436.

Habib son of Sadullah Khan, In the matter of AIR 1926 Lah. 1.

Hans Raj Dhir v. *State of Himachal Pradesh* 1985 Cri. L.J. (Himachal Pradesh High Court) 1030.

Hare Krishna Mahatab v. *Balakrishna Kar and another* AIR 1954 Orissa 57.

Hargovind Dayal Srivastava v. *G.N. Verma* 1977 Cri. L.J. (Supreme Court) 1003.

Hari Shankar Bhandari v. *Secretary Public Health and Family Welfare Dept.* 1994 Cri. L.J. (Madhya Pradesh High Court) 3518.

Har Kishun Singh and others v. *Chhotan Mahtan and others* AIR (38) 1951 Pat. 494.

High Court of Kerala v. *Fazulludin* 1994 Cri. L.J. (Kerala High Court) 2982.

Hoshiar Singh and another v. *Gurbachan Singh and others* 1962 (2) Cri. L.J. (Supreme Court) 236.

Hoshie Shavaksha Dolikuka v. *Thirty Hoshie Dolikuka* 1982 Cri. L.J. (Supreme Court) 1937.

I. Manilal Singh v. *Dr. H. Borobabu Singh* AIR 1994 S.C. 505.

Indrani Dutta v. *Baldeo Sharma* 1994 Cri. L.J. (Madhya Pradesh High Court) 1958.

In re Abdool and Mehtaf (1867) 8 W.R. (Cr.) 32.

In Re Anand Dhar Diwan Contemner 1982 Cri. L.J. (Madhya Pradesh High Court) 1744.

In re Hadi Hussain v. *Nassiruddin Haider* AIR 1926 All. 623.

In re Mohandas Karam Chand Gandhi AIR 1920 Bombay 175.

In re K.E. Johnson, Commissioner of Income Tax, Assam, Tripura and Manipur AIR 1964 Assam and N.L. 92.

In re P.C. Sen, Appellant AIR 1970 S.C. 1821.

In Re S. Mulgaokar AIR 1978 S.C. 727.

In Re Sham Lal AIR 1978 S.C. 489.

In re Subramanyan, Editor, Tribune and others AIR 1943 Lah. 329.

In re Vinay Chandra Mishra (1995) 2 S.C.C. 584.

In Re Vinod Maheshwari and others contemners AIR 1967 Madhya Pradesh 104.

In re : *Chandigarh News Line* (Indian Express Group) AIR 1999 Supreme Court 144.

In re : *Harijai Singh* 1997 Cri. L.J. (Supreme Court) 58.

In re : *Sanjiv Datta* 1995 Cri. L.J. (Supreme Court) 2910.

In re : *Ajay Kumar Pandey* 1997 Cri. L.J. (Supreme Court) 231.

In re : *V.L. Das* AIR 1999 (Supreme Court) 99.

In re : *Tapan Roy*, 1997 Cri. L.J. (Calcutta High Court) 2166.

In re : *Dr. D.C. Saxena* AIR 1996 (Supreme Court) 2481.

In the matter of Banks and Fenwick AIR 1918 Cal. 752.

In the matter of Basanta Chandra Ghosh, Advocate Patna and others AIR 1960 Pat. 430.

In the matter of Bhola Nath Chaudhary, Contemner AIR 1961 Pat. 1.

In the matter of D.B. Vohra etc. 1974 Cri. L.J. (Delhi High Court) 899.

In the matter of Hiren Bose, Contemner AIR 1969 Cal. 1.

In the matter of Muslim outlook, Lahore AIR 1927 Lah. 610.

In the matter of Sudhir Chandra Ray Choudhuri, an Attorney AIR (39) 1952 Cal. 258.

In the matter of Tushar Kanti Ghosh, Editor Amrit Bazar Patrika and another AIR 1935 Cal. 419.

In the matter of K. Venkat Rao 12 I.C. 293.

In the matter of William Taylor AIR 1918 Cal. 713.

J.C. Medhi, Registrar, Assam High Court v. *Frank Moraes, Resident Editor, The Times of India and others* AIR 1954 Assam 201.

Jabhiulla v. *The Chief Engineer Karnataka Electricity Board* 1995 Cri. L.J. (Karnataka High Court) 718.

Jahurul Islam v. *Abdul Kalam* AIR 1994 S.C. 1403.

Jaipur Development Authority v. *Hari Nath Sharma* 1994 Cri. L.J. (Rajasthan High Court) 1290.

J. Vasudevan v. *T.R. Dhananjaya* AIR 1996 (Supreme Court) 137.

J.S. Parihar v. *Ganpat Duggar* (1996) 6 Supreme Court cases 291.

Jai Prakash Beni Pershad and others v. *Ram Sarup and others* AIR 1958 Punj. 471.

Jang Bahadur Singh v. *Baij Nath Tiwari* AIR 1969 S.C. 30.

Jawand Singh Hukam Singh v. *Om Prakash Aggarwal, Sub-Judge 1st Class, Jagadhri* AIR 1959 Punj. 632.

Jeswant Singh v. *Virendra Singh* AIR 1995 S.C. 520.

Jitan Chowdhary v. *State of Bihar* 1979 Cri. L.J. Noc. 85 (Pat.).

Jyoti Narayan v. *Brij Nandan Sinha* AIR 1954 Pat. 289.

Jyotirmoy Bhattacharjee v. *Chief Secretary to Government of West Bengal* AIR 1952 Cal. 562.

K. Ramadas Shenoy v. *The Chief Officer, Town Municipal Council Udipi and others* AIR 1976 S.C. 994.

K.A. Mohammed Ali v. *C.N. Prasannan,* AIR 1995 S.C. 454.

K.M. Nanawati v. *State of Bombay* AIR 1961 S.C. 112.

K.P. Isaac and Sons Private Limited v. *K. Prathyodhanan* 1992 Cri. L.J. (Kerala High Court) 2587.

K.P. Noordeen Mohammed v. *A.K. Gopalan and others* AIR 1968 Ker. 301.

K.T. Chandy v. *Mansa Ramzade* AIR 1974 S.C. 642.

Ku. Meena v. *S.D. Chacharkar* 1994 Cri. L.J. (Bombay High Court) 2647.

K.V. Venkatesh v. *Taluka Executive Magistrate, Magadi Taluk, Magadi* AIR 1990 Karn. 86.

K.S. Jhunjhunwala v. *Tayebhai Mohammedbhai Bagasapwalla* 1997 Cri. L.J. (Bombay High Court) 1953.

Kashinath Kher v. *Dinesh Kumar Bhagat* 1998 Cri. L.J. (Supreme Court) 666.

Kamta Prasad v. *Ram Agyan and another* AIR 1952 All. 674.

Kedar Prasad Sinha and another v. *State of Bihar and others* AIR 1969 Pat. 140.

King v. *Almon* 97 E.R. 94.

Kuldip Rastogi v. *Vishvanath Khanna* AIR 1979 Del. 202.

L.D. Jaikwal v. *State of U.P.* AIR 1984 S.C. 1374.

L.S. Shukla v. *Ishwar Chandra Jain* AIR 1955 M.B. 183.

Lakhan Singh S/o Sri Sadhu Singh v. *Ram Bahadur Srivastava* 1994 Cri. L.J. (Allahabad High Court) 2997.

Lakhan Singh v. *Balbir Singh and another* AIR 1953 All. 342.

Lakshmi Naryana Dutta v. *Smt. Mira Rani* 1984 Cri. L.J. (Calcutta High Court) 1033.

Lala Baijnath Prasad v. *Lala Shyan Sunder* 1961 (2) Cri. L.J. (Calcutta High Court) 222.

Legal Remembrancer, Bihar v. *Bibhuti Bhusan Das Gupta and others* AIR 1954 Pat. 203.

Legal Remembrancer v. *Motilal Ghose* 1913 ILR Cal. 173.

Leo Roy Frey v. *R. Prasad and others* AIR 1958 Punjab 377.

M. Kalyana Sundaram and another v. *Karunanidhi* AIR 1981 S.C. 1416.

M.C. Joseph v. *The State of Kerala* AIR 1973 Ker. 216.

M.K. Prakash v. *A.P. Parukutty Moopilamma* AIR 1971 Ker. 248.

M.K. Sachdev v. *Union of India* AIR 1991 S.C. 311.

M.R. Parashar v. *Dr. Farooq Abdullah* AIR 1984 S.C. 615.

Maharashtra State Road Transport Corporation Ltd. v. *Balwant Regular Motor Service, Amravati and others* AIR 1969 S.C. 329.

Manik Chand Gupta and another v. *Virendra Kumar and others* 1977 Cri. L.J. (Allahabad High Court) 412.

Maniyeri Madhavan v. *Inspector of Police Cannanore* AIR 1993 S.C. 356.

Manza Ram Zade v. *M/s. Hindusthan Steel Ltd.* 1971 Cri. L.J. (Calcutta High Court) 699.

Martin v. *Lawrence*, I.L.R. 4 Cal. 655.

Mc Leod v. *St. Abyn* 1899 AC 549.

Messers Bhatnagars and Co. Ltd. v. *Union of India* AIR 1957 S.C. 478.

Mira Bose v. *Santhosh Kumar Bose* AIR 1973 Cal. 483.

Miss Baljeet Oberaia v. *The State and others* AIR 1985 J. and K. 16.

Miss. Sumedha Kalia v. *State of Haryana* AIR 1990 P. and H. 239.

Mohd. Aslan alias Bhure v. *Union of India and Acchan Rizvi* v. *State of Uttar Pradesh* AIR 1995 S.C. 548.

Mohd. Iqbal Khanday v. *Abdul Majid Rather* AIR 1994 S.C. 2252.

Mohd. Osman Shaheed v. *Mohd. Baqur Hussain Shaa and others* 1980 Cri. L.J. (Andh. Prad. High Court) 845.

Mohd. Ikram Hussain v. *State of U.P. and others* AIR 1964 S.C. 1625.

Mohammed Ibrahim v. *Bhopal Singh* AIR 1948 Ludhiana 131.

Mohammed Vamin and others v. *Om Prakash Bansal* 1982 Cri. L.J. (Rajasthan High Court) 322.

Mohammed Idris and another v. *Rustam Jehangir Bapuji and others* AIR 1984 S.C. 1826.

Mohammed Ibrahim v. *Bhopal Singh and another* AIR (35) 1948 Oudh. 131.

Monoharlal v. *Sri Prem Shankar Tandon and others.* AIR 1960 All. 231.

Motilal Ghose and others In re XLV I.L.R. (1917) Cal. 169.

Mottur Hajee Abdul Rahman and Co. v. *Deputy Commercial Tax Officer, Vaniyambadi North Arcot District* AIR 1969 Mad. 232.

M/s. Indokeniyan Industrial Enterprises v. *M/s Metal Forgings (P) Ltd.* 1986 Cri. L.J. (Delhi High Court) 1592.

M/s Jyoti Ltd. v. *Smt. Kanwalji Kaur* 1987 Cri. L.J. (Delhi High Court) 1281.

M/s. Kalloo Mal Visheshwar Prasad v. *Secretary to Government of U.P. Lucknow* 1974 Cri. L.J. (Allahabad High Court) 529.

Mrs. Damayanti G. Chandiramani v. *S. Vaney Registrar City Civil Court* AIR 1966 Bombay 19.

Mrs. V.G. Peterson v. *O.V. Forbes* AIR 1963 S.C. 692.

N. Venkataramanappa v. *D.K. Naicker* AIR 1978 Karn. 57.

Naba Kumar Saha v. *S. Banerjee and another* AIR 1953 Cal. 96.

Nalin Chandra Pal v. *Bejoy Ranjan Ganguly and another* AIR 1953 Cal. 53.

Nalla Senapathi Sarkarai Manradiar Palayamkottai, Dharapuram Taluk v. *Sri Ambal Mills (P) Ltd.* AIR 1966 Mad. 53.

Nand Gopal v. *Karter Singh* 1984 Cri. L.J. (Delhi High Court) 213.

Nand Kishore Chala Mal v. *Commissioner of the Municipal Corporation of Delhi and others* AIR 1969 Del. 137.

Narain Singh v. *S. Hardayal Singh Harika Executive Officer Municipal Committee Patiala* AIR 1958 Punj. 180.

Narayanan Nambiar v. *E.M.S. Namboodiripad* 1968 KLT 306.

Naraindas v. *Government of Madhya Pradesh* 1974 Cri. L.J. (Supreme Court) 924.

National Textile Workers Union v. *P.R. Ramakrishnan* AIR 1983 (Supreme Court) 759.

National Enterprises Ltd. vs. *Racal Communications Ltd.* (1975) Ch. 397.

N.C. Das v. *M.A. Mohsin* 1997 Cri. L.J. (Supreme Court) 4410.

Nawal Kishore Prasad Sinha v. *State of Bihar* AIR 1983 Pat. 8.

Niaz Mohammed v. *State of Haryana* AIR 1995 S.C. 308.

Nitin Chakravarti v. *V.S.C. Banarjee* AIR 1970 Cal. 477.

Omesh Saigal v. *R.K. Dalma* AIR 1969 Del. 214.

P.K. Kripalani v. *Mahabir Ram* AIR 1952 Cal. 452.

P.N. Duda v. *P. Shiv Shankar* AIR 1988 S.C. 1208.

P.S. Tulajarama Rao v. *Sir James Taylor, Governor of Reserve Bank of India, Central Office, Calcutta and two others* (1939) II Madras Law Journal Reports, Madras High Court 843.

P.V. Jagannath Rao and others v. *State of Orissa and others* AIR 1969 S.C. 215.

Panchanand Jha v. *Surendra Misra and others* AIR 1955 Pat. 141.

Panna Lal v. *R.K. Sinha* 1967 Cri. L.J. (Allahabad High Court) 980.

Parkash Chand v. *S.S. Grewal* 1975 Cri. L.J. (Punjab and Haryana High Court) 679.

Perspective Publications (P) Ltd. and another v. *State of Maharashtra* AIR 1971 S.C. 221.

Peter Munda v. *State* AIR 1958 Ori. 69.

Pitrus Lahra v. *R.V. Dalal and others* AIR 1953 Nag. 179.

Prabhakar Laxman Mokashi v. *Sadanand Trimbak Yardi and others* 1975 Cri. L.J. (Bombay High Court) 531.

Prahlad Prasad Mahrotra v. *Chandra Bhusan* AIR 1958 Pat. 144.

Prakash Chandra Agarwal v. *Amar Singh* 1982 Cri. L.J. (Rajasthan High Court) 40.

Pratap Singh v. *Gurbakhsh Singh* AIR 1962 S.C. 1172.

President, Municipal Board v. *Raghubir Sahai Kaithwar* AIR 1958 All. 436.

Principal Ranji Parekh Arts K.B. Commerce and B.C.J. Science College v. *Mahendra Ambalal Shah* AIR 1986 S.C. 1074.

Purushotam Dass Goel v. *Hon'ble Mr. Justice B.S. Dhillon and others* AIR 1978 S.C. 1014.

R v. *Odham Press Ltd.* (1956) 3 QBD 494.

R v. *Parke* (1900-3), All E.R. 721.

R v. *Tibbits and another* (1900-3) All E.R. Rep. 896-90.

R.K. Garg v. *State of Himachal Pradesh* AIR 1981 S.C. 1382.

R.M. Ramaul v. *The State of Himachal Pradesh* AIR 1991 S.C. 1171.

Rachapudi Subba Rao v. *The Advocate General Andhra Pradesh* AIR 1981 S.C. 755.

Rahmat Ali v. *Beni Madho Baijpal and another* AIR 1957 All. 457.

Rajendra Kumar Garg v. *Shafiq Ahmad Azad and another* AIR 1957 All. 37.

Rajiv K. Garg v. *Shanti Bhushan, Senior Advocate* AIR 1995 S.C. 573.

Rajiv Choudhary v. *Jagadish Narain Khanna* (1996) I Supreme Court Cases 508.

Ramachandra Mahapatra v. *State of Orissa* AIR 1983 S.C. 508.

Ram Charan v. *Debi Dayal* 1955 Cri. L.J. (Allahabad High Court) 1223.

Ramadas Shenoy v. *The Chief Officer, Town Municipal Council Udipi and others* AIR 1976 S.C. 994.

Rama Dayal Markarha v. *State of M.P.* AIR 1978 S.C. 921.

Ram Narain Mathur v. *Chief Justice and Judges of the High Court Chandigarh* AIR 1958 Punjab 445.

Ram Pratap Sharma and others v. *Daya Nand and others* AIR 1977 S.C. 809.

Rameshwar Singh v. *A.N. Choubey and another* AIR 1954 Pat. 554.

Ram Roop Yadav v. *State of Bihar and others* AIR 1969 Pat. 151.

Ram Parikchan Pandey v. *M.S.M. Sharma and another* AIR 1961 Pat. 217.

Ram Saran Tewari v. *Raj Bahadur Varma and others* AIR 1962 All. 315.

Rao Har Narain Singh Sheoji Singh v. *Gumani Ram Arya* AIR 1958 Punjab 273.

Ratan Narain Mulla v. *The Chief Secretary Govt. of U.P.* 1975 Cri. L.J. (Allahabad High Court) 1283.

Ratnakar Jha v. *Krishna Sewak Agarwal and others* AIR 1954 Nag. 99.

Red light on the cars of the Hon'ble Judges of the High Court v. *State of U.P.* AIR 1993 All. 211.

Reg. v. *Grey* (1900) 2 Q.B. 36.

Registrar Assam High Court v. *Frank Morasse Resident Editor, Times of India,* AIR 1954 Ass. 201.

Registrar High Court A.S. Bombay v. *S.K. Irani, Advocate and others* AIR 1963 Bombay 254.

Registrar of the Orissa High Court v. *Baradakanta Misra and another* AIR 1973 Ori. 244.

Re Read and Hugginson (St. James Evening Post Case) (1742) 2 Atk. 469.

Rev. Father Sebastian Onamkulam v. *K. Karunakaran and another* AIR 1967 Ker. 177.

Rex v. *Mohd. Etizad Rasulkhan* AIR 1953 All. 266.

Rita Markanday v. *Surjit Singh Arora* AIR 1997 Supreme Court 2174.

Rizwan-ul-Hasan v. *State of Uttar Pradesh AIR* 1953 S.C. 185.

Roop Chand Sharma v. *Avtar Singh* AIR 1961 Punj. 101.

Roshanlal Thakur v. *Kishanlal Kapoor* 1977 Cri. L.J. (Notes) 23.

Rudraiah v. *State of Karnataka and others* AIR 1982 Karn. 182.

S. Gyan Singh Vohra v. *Ram Bheja Lal Malik* AIR 1959 Punjab 319.

S. Teja Singh v. *Ram Lal and others* 1978 Cri. L.J. (Allahabad High Court) 612.

S.C. Tyagi v. *N.C. Gupta and another* 1974 Cri. L.J. (Allahabad High Court) 428.

S.K. Samsudin v. *Ravikant* 1997 Cri. L.J. (Calcutta High Court) 1603.

S.K. Sarkar Member Board of Revenue v. *Vinay Chandra Misra* AIR 1981 S.C. 723.

S.N. Chakraborty v. *Bimalendu Mazumdar* AIR 1972 Cal. 352.

S.P. Agarwal v. *R.R. Upadhya* 1978 Cri. L.J. (Allahabad High Court) 789.

S.P. Sawhney v. *Life Insurance Corporation of India* AIR 1991 S.C. 661.

S.S. Roy v. *Damodar Valley Corporation* AIR 1974 Cal. 69.

S.S. Roy v. *State of Orissa and others* AIR 1960 S.C. 190.

S. Venkataraman v. *P.V. Singri and another* 1997 Cri. L.J. (Karnatak H.C.) 1840.

Sadanand M. Dhond v. *State* 1977 Cri. L.J. (NOC) 103 (Goa, Daman and Diu).

Sadhu Venkeyya v. *Colla Meenakshamma* AIR 1952 Mad. 180.

Sadhvi Ritumbhara v. *Digvijay Singh* 1997Cri. L.J. (Supreme Court) 1905.

Saibal Kumar Gupta and others v. *B.K. Sen and another* AIR 1961 S.C. 633.

Saleemuddin v. *Sharfuddin* AIR 1980 Del. 39.

Samar Ghosh and others v. *Somnath Chakraborthy* 1989 Cri. L.J. (Calcutta High Court) 1638.

Sambu Nath Jha v. *Kedar Prasad Sinha and others* AIR 1972 S.C. 1515.

Saṇkara Narayana Panicker v. *Unni Omana and others* AIR 1962 Ker. 52.

Santosh Kumar Saman v. *Raja Sri Birachandra Jadumani Deo* AIR 1955 Orissa 222.

Sarat Chandra Biswal and another v. *Surendra Mohanty, Editor 'Kalinga' and others* AIR 1969 Ori. 177.

Sardarilal v. *Ram Rakha* 1984 Cri. L.J. (Delhi High Court) 1098.

Satyendra Nath Mitra v. *Superintendant of Police 24 Parganas and others* AIR 1963 Cal. 336.

Satyabrata Biswas v. *Kalyan Kumar Kisku* AIR 1994 S.C. 1837.

Sebastian M. Hongray v. *Union of India* AIR 1984 S.C. 1026.

Shankar Lal Sharma v. *M.S. Bisht* AIR 1956 All. 160.

Shamim Rehmaney v. *Zinat Kausar Dehalvi and others* 1971 Cri. L.J. (Allahabad High Court) 1588.

Shamsher Singh Bedi v. *High Court of Punjab and Haryana* AIR 1995 Supreme Court 1974.

Sheoraj v. *A.P. Batra and another* 1955 Cri. L.J. (Allahabad High Court) 1451.

Shri Wasudeoraoji Sheorey v. *Shri A.D. Mani, Managing Editor 'Hitavada'* 52 Cri. L.J. 1951 (Nagpur High Court) 452.

Shri C.K. Daphtary, Sr. Advocate and others v. *Shri O.P. Gupta and others* AIR 1971 S.C. 1132.

Shri Amrit Nahata v. *Union of India* AIR 1986 S.C. 791.

Shri Baradakanta Mishra v. *Shri Bhimsen Dixit* AIR 1972 S.C. 2466.

Sita Ram Sahu v. *Smt. Lalpari Devi* AIR 1991 S.C. 1054.

Sm. Lajuklata v. *Nrishingha Prosad* AIR 1952 Cal. 669.

Smt. Indu Tewari v. *Ram Bahadur Chandhari* AIR 1981 All. 309.

Smt. Pushpa Ben v. *Narandas* v. *Bandari* AIR 1979 S.C. 1536.

Smt. Padmawati Devi Bhargava v. *R.K. Karanjia and others* AIR 1963 Madhya Pradesh 61.

Smt. Prabha Dutt v. *Union of India and others* (1982) 1 S.C.C. 1.

Smt. Ram Pyari v. *Jagadish* AIR 1992 S.C. 1537.

Sri Harish Chandra Mishra v. *The Hon'ble Mr. Justice Ali Ahmed* AIR 1986 Pat. 65.

State v. *Sankar Charan Sahu and another* AIR 1952 Ori. 215.

State v. *Bhawani Prasad and others* AIR 1954 Nag. 36.

State v. *D. Rudra, A.D.M. and another* AIR 1969 Cal. 602.

State v. *Radhagobinda Das and others* AIR 1954 Ori. 1.

State v. *Kawas Manekshaw Nanawati* AIR 1960 Bom. 502.

State v. *Kamla Ram Nautiyal and others* 1970 Cri. L.J. (Allahabad High Court) 1283.

State v. *Faquir Chand and another* AIR 1957 All. 657.

State v. *Brahma Prakash and others* AIR 1950 All. 556.

State v. *Harihar Shukla* 1976 Cri. L.J. (Allahabad High Court) 507.

State v. *R.N. Patra* 1976 Cri. L.J. (Orissa High Court) 440.

State of Bihar v. *Kraipalu Sankaer* AIR 1987 S.C. 1554.

State of Haryana and others v. *Ch. Bhajan Lal and another* v. *Shri S.A. Khan* 1993 Cri. L.J. (Supreme Court) 1042.

State of J. and K. v. *Mohd. Yaqoob Khan* (1992) 4 S.C.C. 167.

State of Himachal Pradesh v. *Sri Raghunandan Lal Gupta* AIR 1954 H.P. 70.

State of Rajasthan v. *Shyam Narain Moriva* 1973 Cri. L.J. (Rajasthan High Court) 1340.

State of Rajasthan v. *M.R. Mitruka* 1978 Cri. L.J. (Rajasthan High Court) 1440.

State of Kutch v. *Saiffudin Kharawala* AIR 1956 Kutch 7.

State of U.P. v. *D.K. Dass Vidhi* 1973 Cri. L.J. (Allahabad High Court) 1271.

State of U.P. v. *Narendra Pal Singh and another* 1990 Cri. L.J. (Allahabad High Court) 1637.

State of Rajasthan v. *Prakash Chand* 1998 Cri. L.J. (Supreme Court) 2012.

State of Maharashtra v. *Mahboob S. Allibhoy* AIR 1996 Supreme Court 2131.

State of Uttar Pradesh v. *Ashok Kumar Saxena* AIR 1998 Supreme Court 925.

Suresh v. *Imran Khan* 1995 Cri. L.J. (Supreme Court) 3652.

State of Uttar Pradesh v. *Shyam Sundar Lal Jain* AIR 1954 All. 308.

Subhash Chand v. *S.M. Aggarwal and another* 1984 Cri. L.J. (Delhi High Court) 481.

Subodh Gopal Bose v. *State of Bihar* AIR 1969 Pat. 72.

Sudhakar Mahadeorao Kawale v. *State of Maharashtra* 1994 Cri. L.J. (Bombay High Court) 735.

Sukhdeo Baiswar v. *Brij Bhushan Misra and others* AIR 1951 All. 667.

Sukh Raj v. *Hem Raj and others* AIR 1967 Raj. 152.

Sukumar Mukhopadhyay v. *T.D. Karam Chandani* 1995 Cri. L.J. (Calcutta High Court) 1610.

Sukumar Mitra v. *Tarasankar Ghosh* AIR 1952 Cal. 591.

Sunnulal Badhavallabha v. *Yeshwant Singh and others* 1952 Cri. L.J. 1951 (Madhya Bharat) 532.

Surendra Nath Chatterjee v. *Surendra Nath Basu* AIR (38) 1951 Pat. 451.

Surendranath Banerjee v. *The Chief Justice and Judges of the High Court at Fort William in Bengal* YLR 10 Cal. 109.

Suretennessa Bibi v. *Chintaharan Das* 1955 Cri. L.J. (Calcutta High Court) 654.

Swami Prasad Pradhan v. *Hargovind Sahai Mathur and others* AIR 1970 All. 251.

Swarnamayi Panigrahi v. *B. Nayak and others* AIR 1959 Ori. 89.

Syed Azimudin v. *Syed Mazharuddin and another* 1977 M.L.J. Reports 464.

T.A. Rajendran v. *Vayalar Ravi* AIR 1983 Ker. 105.

Tapan Kumar Mukherjee v. *Sri Heromoni Mondal* AIR 1991 S.C. 281.

Tarafatulah Mandal and others v. *S.N. Maitra and others* AIR 1952 Cal. 919.

Taradas Dutt and another v. *Administrative Officer of the Corporation of Calcutta and another* AIR 1951 Cal. 397.

Thakurlal and others v. *Mahabir Prasad Sharma and another* 1955 Cri. L.J. (Allahabad High Court) 1023.

The Advocate General (A.P.) v. *Rachapudi Subba Rao* 1976 Cri. L.J. (Andhra Pradesh High Court) 746.

The Bukhtiarpur—Bihar Light Rly. Co. v. *The District Board Patna and another* AIR 1952 Pat. 23.

The King v. *Clements* 106 E.R. 918.

The Legal Remembrancer Bihar v. *Atul Chandra Ghose and another* AIR 1955 Pat. 135.

The State v. *Maqbool Ahmad and another* AIR 1958 All. 728.

The State v. *Krishna Madho and others* AIR 1952 All. 86.

The State v. *Padma Kant Malviya and another* 1955 Cri. L.J. (Allahabad High Court) 904.

The State v. *S. Gurdial Singh* AIR 1953 Pepsu 79.

The State v. *Nur-ud-Din Sufi* AIR 1955 J. and K. 30.

The State v. *Debi Neogi and others* AIR 1955 NUC (Calcutta) 2868.

The State v. *Pt. Ram Chander Sharma* AIR 1959 Punjab 41.

The State v. *Ram Briksh Benipuri and another* AIR 1953 Pat. 364.

The State v. *Editors, Printers and Publishers of the News Papers Matrubhumi and Krushak and others* AIR 1954 Orissa 149.

The State v. *The Editors and Publishers of Eastern Times and Prajatantra* AIR 1952 Ori. 318.

The State v. *Bhawani Singh and others* AIR 1968 Del. 208.

The State of U.P. v. *M.V. Siddiqui* AIR 1980 S.C. 2052.

The State of Bihar v. *Rani Sonabati Kumari* AIR 1961 S.C. 221.

The State of Karnataka v. *Shivadeva* 1975 Cri. L.J. (Karnataka High Court) 1958.

The State of Maharashtra v. *Chandrakant Tripathi and others* 1983 Cri. L.J. (Bombay High Court) 1841.

The Sunday Times v. *United Kingdom* (1979) 2 EHHR 245.

The Aligarh Municipal Board v. *Ekka Tonga Mazdoor Union and others* AIR 1970 S.C. 1767.

Tharain Joseph v. *K.P. Viswanathan, Minister of Forests, Government of Kerala* 1994 Cri. L.J. (Kerala High Court) 82.

T.M.A. Pai Foundation v. *State of Karnataka* AIR 1995 (Supreme Court) 1938.

Tukaram G. Gaokar v. *R.N. Shukla and others* AIR 1968 S.C. 1050.

Tukaram S/o Khanduji Gaikwad v. *Santhosh Mahadeo Sayam* 1995 Cri. L.J. (Bombay High Court) 577.

The Crown v. *Amin-Ud-Din Sahrahi and another* AIR (36) 1949 Lah. 266.

Trikamlal Manilal Shah v. *Musamiya Isam Haider Bux Razvi* AIR 1992 Guj. 155.

Union of India and others v. *Mario Cabral e sa* AIR 1982 S.C. 691.

Union of India v. *Satish Chandra Sharma* AIR 1980 S.C. 600.

Union of India v. *M/s. Oswal Woollen Mills Ltd.* AIR 1984 S.C. 1264.

U.P. Sales Tax Service Association v. *Taxation Bar Association, Agra,* AIR 1996 Supreme Court 98.

V.G. Nigam v. *Kedaranath Gupta* AIR 1992 S.C. 2153.

V.M. Kanade v. *Madhav Gadkari and others* 1990 Cri. L.J. (Bombay High Court) 190.

Venubhai Savleram v. *Gajanan Savleram* 1992 Cri. L.J. (Bombay High Court) 1160.

Vidya Charan Shukla v. *Tamil Nadu Olympic Association* AIR 1991 Mad. 323.

Vineeth Kumar Mathur v. *Union of India* (1996) 7 Supreme Court cases 714.

Video Movies by Propr. Haji Rasheed Mohammed v. *Ramanujam, Madras* AIR 1986 Mad. 119.

Vijai Pratap Singh v. *Ajit Prasad* AIR 1968 All. 308.

Vincent Panikulangara v. *Gopala Kurup* 1982 Cri. L.J. (Kerala High Court) 2094.

Vine Products Ltd. v. *Meckenzie and Co.* (1965) 3 A11. E.R. 58.

Viswa Dev Sharma v. *State of Rajasthan* 1994 Cri. L.J. (Supreme Court) 1223.

Vishwas Narayan Limaye v. *Sharad Pawar* Vol. LXXVIII The Bom. Law Reporter 616.

Virochan v. *Ram Charan Das* 1982 Cri. L.J. (Punjab and Haryana High Court) 1219.

Wasudeorao G. Sheorey v. *Gopal Dattatraya Karkare* 52 Cri. L.J. 1951 (Nagpur High Court) 663.

Y.V. Hanumantha Rao v. *K.R. Pattabhiraman and another* AIR 1975 A.P. 30.

Bibliography

(a) Articles

Alan Ward, 'A substantial change in the Law of Contempt' 46, *Mod. L.R.* 85 (1983).

Arthur E. Hughes, 'Contempt of Court and the Press' 16, *L.Q.R.* 292 (1900).

Arthur L. Goodhart, 'News Paper and Contempt of Court in English Law' 48, *Harv. L.R.* 885 (1935).

Bakshi P.M., 'The Press and the Courts' 33, *J.I.L.I.* 113, (1991).

Bailey, 'Legislation—The Contempt of Court Act 1981' *Mod. L.R.* 301 (1982).

Charles P. Curtis Jr. and Richard C. Curtis, 'The story of a Notion in the Law of Criminal Contempt' 21, *Harv. L.R.* 51 (1908).

'Contempt-Right to Jury Trial' 87, *Harv. L.R.*, 865 (1974).

Desai V.R., 'Can a judge commit contempt of his own court', *AIR* 1963 (Jnl.) 33.

Eliahu Harnon, 'Civil and Criminal Contempt of Court' 25, *Mod. L.R.* 179 (1962).

Felix Frankfurter and James M. Landis, 'Power of Congress over procedure in Criminal Contempts in Inferior Federal Courts—A study in separation of powers' 37, *Harv. L.R.* 1010 (1924).

Gupta D.N., 'The Quality of Justice' *AIR* 1984 (Jnl.) 65.

Graham Zellick, 'Criminal trial and the Disruptive Defendant 43, *Mod. L.R. Part-I-121, Part-II-284* (1980).

Harold J. Laski, 'Procedure for constructive contempt in England' 41, *Harv. L.R.* 1031 (1928).

Ishar I.S., 'Contempt by Scandalising the Court' *Delhi Law Review* 69 (1977-78).

Joseph H. Beale Jr., 'Contempt of Court Criminal and Civil' 21, *Harv. L.R.* 161 (1908).

'Disqualifications of Judge in Contempt proceedings' 85, *Harv. L.R.* 293.

John Charles Fox, 'Criminal Contempt' 30, *L.Q.R.* 56.

John Charles Fox, 'Eccentricities of the law of Contempt of Court' 36, *L.Q.R.* 394.

John Charles Fox, 'The King v. *Almon*-I' 24, *L.Q.R.* 184 (1908).

John Charles Fox, '*The King* v. *Almon*-II' 24, *L.Q.R.* 266 (1908).

John Charles Fox, 'The Summary Process to Punish Contempt-I' 25, *L.Q.R.* 238 (1909).

John Charles Fox, 'The Summary Process to Punish Contempt-II' 25, *L.Q.R.* 354, (1909).

John Charles Fox, 'The Nature of Contempt of Court' 37, *L.Q.R.* 191 (1921).

John Charles Fox, 'The Writ of Attachment' 40, *L.Q.R.* 43 (1924).

John Paul, 'The Dismissal proceedings of Munsiff Vedanayagam Pillai, An investigation into Indian Legal History' 12, *Indian Bar Review* 207 (1985).

Sir Jack Jacob, 'Sequestration for Contempt of Court' 39, *Current Legal Problems* 219.

John T.J., 'Side Lights on Contempt' 1984 *KLT* (Jnl.) 71.

Kamalakar, S., 'Justice must appear to be done in the law of contempt' 85, *The Bombay Law Reporter* (Jnl.) 33.

Louis L. Jaffe, 'The Judicial enforcement of Administrative Orders' 76, *Harv. L.R.* 885.

Lowe N.V., 'Wardship, Contempt and Freedom of Speech' 93, *L.Q.R.* 180 (1977).

Lowe N.V. and Rawlings, H.F., 'Tribunals and the Laws protecting the Administration of Justice' 1982 *P.L.* 418.

Karwande S.D., 'Cognizance of Contempt of the Subordinate Courts' *AIR* 1981 (Jnl.) 81.

Madon D.P., 'Judicial activism—An essential part of the Judicial function' 11, *Indian Bar Review* 246 (1984).

Mann F.A., 'Contempt of court in the House of Lords and European Court of Human Rights' 95, *L.Q.R.* 348 (1979).

Mani V.S., 'Contempt of Court and Democratic Criticism The Khadilkar Contempt case' 36, *The Cuttack Law Times* (Jnl.) 53 (1970).

Margaret Brazier, 'Judicial immunity and the independence of judiciary', *P.L.* 397 (1976).

Mathew M., 'Contempt of Court against Jinnah' 1984, *KLT* (Jnl.) 90.

Noorani A.G., 'Public Discussion and Contempt of Court' (1984) 19, *EPW* 2070.

Parthasarathi, 'Concept of Criminal Contempt—How far it can be extended?' 13-5 *Lawyer* 82 (1981).

Ramachandran, V.G., '*Comments on cases E.M.S. Namboodiripad* v. *T.N. Nambiar*' (1970) 2, *S.C.C.* 325.

Richard C. Donnelly Ronald Goldfarb, 'Contempt by Publication in the United States' 24, *Mod. L.R.* 239 (1961).

Rajeev Dhavan, 'Contempt of Court and the Phillimore Committee Report' 5, *Anglo American Law Review* 186, (1976).

Sathyavan Nair V.K., 'Sensational Journalism—A Challenge to due course of Justice' (1984), *KLT* (Jnl.) 61.

Seervai H.M., 'Supreme Court and Contempt of Court' 73 (1971) *The Bombay Law Reporter* (Jnl.) 5.

Sharma B.R., 'Public Confidence in the judiciary; Some Perspective' 12, *Cochin University Law Review* 204 (1988).

Singhi S.R., 'Corruption in the Administration of Justice and Accountability of the Profession' *AIR* 1981 (Jnl.) 158.

Soli J. Sorabjee, 'Truth and the Law of Contempt' 1985, *S.C.W.R.*-II (Jnl.) 17.

Thomas Paul, 'Jurisdiction of the High Court to punish for contempt. *A critique of D.N. Taneja* v. *Bhajanlal*' 30, *J.I.L.I.* 345 (1988).

Upendra Baxi, 'On How not to Judge the Judges: Notes towards Evaluation of the judicial Role' 25, *J.I.L.I.* 211 (1983).

Upendra Baxi, 'On the Shame of not being an activist: Thoughts on judicial activism' 11, *Indian Bar Review* 259 (1984).

Varma S.K., 'Amend the Law of Contempt' 1983, *Allahabad Law Journal* 45.

William T. Mayton, 'Seditious libel and the lost guarantee of a Freedom of Expression' 84, *Columbia Law Review* 91 (1984).

'Act done in defiance of Court order' Editorial 89, *Calcutta Weekly Notes* 161 (1985).

'Commission of Inquiry and Contempt of Court' 88, *Calcutta Weekly Notes* 146.

'Contempt of Court and Pending Proceedings' Editorial 68, *Calcutta Weekly Notes* 6 (1973).

'Contempt of Court by Lawful Action' Editorial 68, *Calcutta Weekly Notes* 21 (1964).

'Contempt of Court' Editorial 78, *Calcutta Weekly Notes* 29 (1973).

'Contempt of Court and pending proceedings' Editorial 77, *Calcutta Weekly Notes* 133 (1973).

'Contempt of Court, Pending Proceedings and Freedom of Press' Editorial 87, *Calcutta Weekly Notes* 13 (1982).

'Contempt of Court and Pending Proceedings' Editorial 78, *Calcutta Weekly Notes* 133 (1974).

'Contempt of Court — Muggeridge's Article' Editorial 87, *Calcutta Weekly Notes* 25 (1983).

'Contempt of Board of Revenue' Editorial 74, *Calcutta Weekly Notes* 125 (1970).

'Contempt of Court and Official Secrets' Editorial 84, *Calcutta Weekly Notes* 41 (1980).

'Contempt of Court and Laughing Gas' Editorial 79, *Calcutta Weekly Notes* 123.

'Discussion of pending case and Contempt of Court' 70, *Calcutta Weekly Notes* 42.

'Freedom of the Press and Contempt of Court' Editorial 82, *Calcutta Weekly Notes* cli (1978).

'Law of Contempt' Editorial 70, *Calcutta Weekly Notes* 46 (1966).

'Law of Contempt' Editorial, 68, *Calcutta Weekly Notes* xi (1963).

'Marx and Engels and Contempt of Court' Editorial, 84, *Calcutta Weekly Notes* 141 (1970).

'Pending Proceedings and Contempt' Editorial, 78, *Calcutta Weekly Notes* XXV, (1973).

'Thalidomide Children and Contempt of Court' Editorial, 77, *Calcutta Weekly Notes* 5 (1972).

(b) Books

Aiyar K.J., *Law of Contempt of Court Legislatures and Public Servants* (6th Edn. 1983 Law Book Agency, Allahabad).

Allen Wm.H. and Co., *The Law Relating to India and the East India Company* (Fourth Edn. 1842: Leadenhall Street, London).

American Jurisprudence 17 Am. Jur. 2d.

Anthony Alridge David Ealy, *The Law of Contempt* (1982, Sweet and Maxwell).

Avirah A.K. and Moothath Parameswaran P., *Law of Contempt of Court* (1973).

Benjamin Nathan Cardozo, *The Nature of Judicial Process* (1957 New Haven: Yale University Press).

Borrie Gordan and Lowe Nigil, *Law of Contempt* (1973).

Dias R.W.M., *Jurisprudence* (Fourth Edn., 1976 Butterworths London).

Dicey A.V., *An Introduction to the Study of the Law of the Constitution* (10th Edn. 1994 Universal Book Traders, Delhi).

Durga Das Basu, *Shorter Constitution of India* (Sixth Edition 1970 R.C. Sarkar and Sons Private Ltd., Calcutta).

Fitzgerald P.J. *Salmond on Jurisprudence* (1966 Sweet and Maxwel, London).

Gopal K.N., *Administrative Tribunals Act* (1985 Eastern Book Co).

Gower L.C.B., *The Principles of Modern Company Law* (3rd Edn., 1969 Stevens and Sons, London).

Halsbury's Laws of England, Vol. 8 (3rd Edn.).

Hart H.L.A., *The Concept of Law* (1979 English Language Book Society and Oxford University Press).

Hidayathullah M., *Judges Miscellany* (1984 N.M. Tripathi Private Ltd., Bombay).

Jain M.P., Outlines of Indian Legal History (Third Edn. 1972, N.M. Tripathi Pvt. Ltd., Bombay).

James M. Neal and Suzanne S. Brown, *News Writing and Reporting* (1976, The Lowa State University Press/Amer.)

John Agresto, *The Supreme Court and Constitutional Democracy* (1986 Pentice Hall of India Pvt. Ltd., New Delhi).

John Charles Fox, *The History of Contempt of Court* (1927 Edn.).

Joseph Minattur, *Freedom of the Press in India Constitutional Provisions and their Applications* (1961 Edn.).

Julius Stone, *Social Dimensions of Law and Justice* (1966).

Julius Stone, *Legal System and Lawyer's Reasoning* (1968, Maitland Publications Private Ltd., Sydney).

Julius Stone, *Precedent and Law* (1984, Butterworths).

Kenny, *Outlines of Criminal Law* (9th Edn. 1968, Cambridge University Press).

Krishna Iyer V.R., *Judicial Justice—A New Focus Towards Social Justice* (1985, N.M. Tripathi Pvt. Ltd., Bombay).

Lakshmi Nath, *Precedent in the Indian Legal System* (1990, Eastern Book Company).

Lord Denning, *The Due Process of Law* (1980, Butterworths).

Lord Denning, *The Closing Chapter* (1983, Butterworths).

Lord Denning, *Land Marks in the Law* (1984, Butterworths).

Mathew K.K. Justice, *Three Lectures* (1982, Eastern Book Co., Lucknow).

Miller C.J., *Contempt of Court* (1976 Paul Elek, London).

Nandan Lal, *Code of Civil Procedure* (Second Edn. Law Publishers, Allahabad).

Netherin G., Chisholm R., *Understanding Law* (1974, Butterworths).

Oswald J.F., *Oswald on Contempt of Court* (1910 Edn.).

Rajeev Dhavan, *Contempt of Court and the Press* (1982, Indian Law Institute).

Rajeev Dhavan, *Only the Good News* (1987, Indian Law Institute).

Ramachandran V.G. and Gopalan V.R., *Contempt of Court under the Constitution* (Fifth Edn., 1983).

Ramachandran V.G., *Law of Contempt of Court* (1951).

Ramasubramanian, *The Commissions of Inquiry Act*, 1952 (1980).

Ronald L. Goldfard, *The Contempt Power* (1963 Columbia University Press, New York and London).

Rupert Cross, *Precedent in English Law* (1991, Clarendon Press, Oxford).

Sarkar R.C.S., *The Press in India* (1984).

Seervai, *Constitutional Law of India* Vol. I and II (3rd Edn., N.M. Tripathi, Bombay).

Steward Repalje, *A Treatise on Contempt Civil and Criminal Contempts* (1987).

Subba Rao G.C.V., *Commentary on Contempt of Court Act, 1971* (1974).

Tek Chand and Sarin H.C., *A Treatise on the Law of Contempt of Court* (1938).

Tek Chand and Sarin H.C., *The Law of Contempt of Court and Legislature* (1949 The University Book Agency, Allahabad).

Varma B.R., *The Law of Contempt of Court* (1986, N.M. Tripathi, Bombay).

William Holds Worth, *History of English Law* (1969).

(c) Reports and Documents

Constituent Assembly Debates Vol. VIII.

Indian Record Series—Vestiges of Old Madras 1640 to 1800 by Henry Davison Love, Published by Government of India (1913) 3 Volumes.

Report of Committee on Contempt of Court (1954) Vol. I.

Report of Justice (1959).

Report of Committee on Contempt of Court (1974).

Report of the Inter Departmental Committee on the Law of Contempt as it affects Tribunals of Inquiry (1969).

Report of the Committee on Contempt of Courts (1963).

Shawcross Committee Report (1959).

(d) Statutes

Administration of Justice Act, 1960 (England).

An Act for establishing High Courts of Judicature in India (1861).

Charter granted by the Governor and Company of Merchants Trading into East Indies to the Mayor Alderman and Burgeses of Madras (1687).

Charter granted to the United Company of Merchants of England, Trading to the East Indies (1727).

Charters Relating to the East India Company from 1600 to 1761.

The Contempt of Courts Act, 1926.

The Contempt of Courts Act, 1952.

The Contempt of Courts Act, 1971.

The Contempt of Court Act, 1981 (England).

The Commissions of Inquiry Act, 1952.

The Code of Civil Procedure, 1908.

The Code of Criminal Procedure, 1973.

The Copyright Act, 1957.

The Indian Telegraph Act, 1885.

The Indian Post Office Act, 1898.

The Indian Penal Code 1862.

The Press Council Act, 1978.

The Press and Registration of Books Act, 1867.

The Working Journalists and other Newspaper Employees (Conditions of Service and Miscellaneous Provisions) Act, 1955.

Index